D0948801

AMBUSH AT RUBY RIDGE

AMBUSH AT RUBY RIDGE

How Government Agents
Set Randy Weaver Up and
Took His Family Down

by Alan W. Bock
Foreword by Dean Koontz

Dickens Press
Irvine, California

All information in this book is given without guarantees on the part of the author or publisher, and the author and publisher disclaim all liability in connection with the implementation of this information. Every effort has been made to make this book as authentic and accurate as possible. With regard to all documents and letters, most spelling and punctuation has been retained closest to the original version. Some minor editing has been done to improve readability.

The author and publisher greatly acknowledge the following publishing houses who have granted permission to reproduce portions of their books:

Excerpts from *The Politics of Righteousness: Idaho Christian Patriotism* and *This Thing of Darkness: A Sociology of the Enemy* reprinted by permission from University of Washington Press.

Excerpts from *The Arrogance of Power* reprinted by permission from Random House.

Library of Congress Cataloging-in-Publication Data

Bock, Alan W., 1943–
    Ambush at Ruby Ridge : how government agents set Randy Weaver up and took his family down / by Alan W. Bock : foreword by Dean Koontz.
        p.   cm.
    Includes index.
    ISBN 1-880741-48-2
    1. Criminal justice. Administration of—United States. 2. Weaver, Randy, 1948– .   3. Political persecution—United States. 4. Political correctness—United States.   I. Title.
HV8141.B63 1995
979.6 ' 98—dc20   95-21471
                                                CIP

Distributed to the trade by National Book Network, Inc.
ISBN: 1-880741-48-2
Printed in the United States of America on acid-free paper
10 9 8 7 6 5 4 3 2 1
First printing 1995

Interior and cover design © 1995 Michele Lanci-Altomare

To Jennifer
Who understands

TABLE OF CONTENTS

I DO NOT HAVE MUCH IN COMMON WITH RANDY WEAVER. I'M SURE THAT we would disagree on most issues; and certainly one of the biggest differences between us would be his apparent belief that the races should live separately and my faith in America as a great equalizer and an agent of understanding. No doubt each of us would find the other to be stubborn, opinionated, and frustrating. It would never occur to me, however, that I should shoot Mr. Weaver *solely because of what he believes*. In spite of our differences, we are both, after all, Americans; therefore, we share a history and a bond that is, if not sacred, at least profound. In a sane and democratic society, one neighbor doesn't shoot another over political disagreements.

Judging by all the available evidence, the government of the United States dealt with Mr. Weaver and his family neither in a sane nor democratic fashion. Repeated attempts were made to entrap him in criminal activity; apparently, trickery was used to ensure that he would be unaware of the correct date of a court appearance and would therefore be cited for failure to appear; his fourteen-year-old son was shot in the back and killed; and, while holding a baby, Weaver's unarmed wife was shot in the head and killed. To those familiar with the case, no credible evidence has yet been presented to counter the alarming impression that the Weavers were targeted largely—and perhaps solely—because the government (or elements within it) found their beliefs to be politically incorrect and wished to make examples of them.

The United States of America has become the brightest beacon for freedom in history expressly because it tolerates diverse opinion to an extent unequaled elsewhere. During the past decade, however, many institutions that traditionally supported the never-ending struggle to maintain freedom of speech have come down squarely on the side of repression and thought control. Numerous universities have instituted speech codes that forbid the use of long lists of words deemed to be offensive for one reason or another, and students have been expelled for violations. Many newspapers have developed codes of their own, even restricting the use of such honorable words as "indian" in favor of "Native Americans." Toni Morrison, Nobel laureate in literature, has said that hurtful speech is the same as a hurtful act, equating hateful words with violence—without ever apparently realizing that this position puts her in the camp of the Iranian ayatollahs who have sentenced Salman Rushdie to death for what he wrote about Islam.

We should be terrified of the notion—now endorsed in circles that were once staunchly supportive of all civil rights—that some beliefs and opinions are beyond the pale and should be silenced in the pursuit of compassion and a just society. Though the beliefs we are demonizing and repressing are antithetical to our own, we should realize that even well-meaning repression like this opens the door to forces far more destructive than those in Pandora's box. When the political tide turns, as it always does eventually, those with whom we disagree will use the laws and enforcement mechanisms that we created to repress *us*, and we can blame only ourselves for establishing the precedent that ensures our inevitable misery as we take our turn on the rack.

For example, our society includes various black religious groups whose members are separatists or supremacists and who have disdain—and no trust—for whites. Those who excuse—or remain undisturbed by—the government's assault on the Weaver family would either have to admit to hypocrisy or enthusiastically endorse raids on those black churches equal to the assault on the Weavers or on the Branch Davidians in Waco, Texas. And what of the Amish? They live apart from the rest of society, reclusive and strange by some standards. Although they are pacifists, they consider their beliefs and customs superior to those of people who aren't Amish. It may seem far-fetched to suppose that a government policy against political incorrectness would eventually target a group as peaceable as the Amish; however, when a government routinely resorts to violence to repress unapproved beliefs, it loses its legitimacy—and comes to fear those groups who, by their quiet exhibition of moral conscience, expose the hollowness and rot at the core of corrupted authority. No group in pre-war Germany was as respectful of the law and as nonviolent as the Jews, who were rounded up not merely because Hitler was virulently anti-Semitic but because he needed to delegitimatize the voices of those who might, by both their speech and their example, provide arguments against his regime.

When I was researching my recent novel, *Dark Rivers of the Heart*, which concerns an out-of-control government agency, I built a large file of clippings about assaults against citizens similar to those on the Weavers and the Branch Davidians, although none in which the injustice was so egregious as in Idaho. In the final chapters of *Ambush at Ruby Ridge*, Alan Bock makes reference to several of the more well-known cases. The number of such incidents seems to argue that the Department of Justice, as currently constituted, is either blind to the need for visible justice for *all* citizens regardless of the unpleasantness of their beliefs or is so preoccupied with avoiding the political fallout that comes with the admission of mistakes that it risks creating the widespread impression of bias and conspiracy.

Personally, I have little patience with conspiracy theories and talk of secret webs of elitists bent on one-world government. I tend to distrust most politicians, regardless of which end of the spectrum they occupy, not because I think they're all totalitarians, which I don't, but because I think they are generally incompetent, or in pursuit of petty advantages for themselves, or both.

Unfortunately, when the Attorney General, as the highest law enforcement official in the country, does not vigorously pursue justice in cases where the government clearly employed improper force, a cancerous suspicion metastasizes in the body of society with potentially devastating effects. Not least of all, it encourages dangerous extremists like those in the Oklahoma City bombing.

Over a sufficient length of time and after a critical mass of cases that feed this suspicion, various elements in society sink into a grudge fight with the government. No thinking American could want to see this country descend into the endless animosity of Northern Ireland or of Lebanon during the 1980s, which is why it is incumbent upon the Attorney General to establish bipartisan commissions to investigate all controversial cases, seek justice even when the political fallout will be detrimental to the party in power, and institute new rules of procedure for all federal law enforcement agencies to ensure that the likelihood of similar outrages is drastically diminished.

I am an ardent believer in America, so I am confident that the particular federal police agencies that have generated distrust in some quarters in recent years will become more responsive to public concerns and more responsible in their procedures. This will happen, unfortunately, not because politicians and their appointees will suddenly develop guilty consciences or even common sense, but because investigative reporting combined with public opinion will build irresistible pressure for change. Until recently, much of the press has been shamefully indifferent to the Weaver case and others like it, but these days one sees more and more references to the events on Ruby Ridge and to other similar violations of civil liberties. Likewise, for the better part of two years, one could have read the major newspapers without ever discovering that David Koresh, leader of the Branch Davidian cult in Waco, left his compound virtually every day and might have been arrested peacefully, without any need of the SWAT team raid and the subsequent tragedy in which so many innocent children died; but recently the *Los Angeles Times*, which for so long seemed to do little more than repeat government press releases on that incident, produced a long in-depth piece raising serious questions about the conduct of that operation.

In this book, journalist Alan Bock serves his country admirably by presenting the well-researched facts of the Weaver case in a highly readable and balanced account. Mr. Bock shows Randy Weaver with all his warts and avoids glossing over any aspects of his character that we might find troublesome. Likewise, he does not portray the federal agents as monsters. Page by page, a curious sadness comes upon us like a wave, as we see how the politicization of law enforcement and but a few wrong decisions on both sides of an emotionally charged situation can lead inevitably to a tragedy that should never occur in a democracy.

Democracy works. Human beings make mistakes, and from time to time human beings commit evil acts, but in the long run, the institutions of a true democracy rise above human failure. In the long run, the institutions of a democracy reject evil and correct mistakes. In July 1993, after Mr. Weaver was put on trial by the federal government subsequent to the events on Ruby Ridge, a jury found him innocent of the murder of a U.S. marshal (who died in the incident), innocent of conspiracy to provoke a confrontation with the government, and innocent of aiding and abetting murder. The jury was especially offended by the government's attempt to demonize the Weavers as neo-Nazis, when it was clear that they held no such beliefs. Make no mistake, the result of this trial should encourage us to believe that democracy always prevails in the long run, and it should be a convincing argument against extremists who would meet any violence with violence.

Of course, for Mr. Weaver, who lost his wife and son, it is understandable that seeing justice done in the long run will offer little consolation. One's heart goes out to him and to the law enforcement officers and their families as well—because the *real* villains in these situations are the politicians and their appointees who politicize law enforcement and divert the energies of the police from the pursuit of serious criminals to the suppression of opinions that are deemed incorrect. Until a citizen makes the mistake of trying to support his beliefs with violence, no mere opinion can be deemed punishable in a democracy.

—*Dean Koontz*
June 1995

A<small>T A CERTAIN POINT AS YOU DRIVE FROM SOUTHERN</small> I<small>DAHO TO NORTHERN</small> Idaho along U.S. Highway 95, it becomes almost impossible not to pay attention to Chief Joseph and the tragic, extended battle he and a band of Nez Perce Indians fought with the U.S. Cavalry over several months in 1877. At White Bird, just north of the forbidding but spectacular Hell's Canyon national recreation area is a battlefield, where drivers are invited to read historical markers and imagine the battle fought there so many years ago. From there to Lewiston, some eighty miles to the northwest, it seems there are markers every few miles, noting places where skirmishes, firefights, ambushes, and other events took place.

I was intrigued by the bits and pieces of the story I learned on the way to visit and try to make sense of a more recent site of confrontation: between the U.S. government and a white separatist named Randy Weaver. I stopped at the Nez Perce National Park Museum along the banks of a branch of the Snake River. Amid the exhibits of Nez Perce native dress and artifacts, I began to absorb some of the customs and history of this Native American tribe that had greeted Lewis and Clark on their monumental journey of exploration to the Oregon coast from 1804 to 1806, and had generally lived in peace with the European–descended explorers. I bought a booklet that outlined Chief Joseph's saga.

Nez Perce is the French name (meaning pierced nose, although the wearing of nose pendants, which inspired the name, doesn't appear to have been all that common) for a tribe of Sahaptin–speaking peoples. It was one of the most populous and powerful tribes of the Pacific Northwest. Before 1800, they lived mostly in small villages on streams. Salmon was the staple of life, along with game, berries, and roots. Their dwellings were communal A-frame lodges covered in mats. In the early 1800s, some Nez Perce groups acquired horses, and became more adventurous and warlike, participating in bison hunts, and building up one of the largest horse herds in the continent. They learned about and practiced selective breeding of horses, and some Nez Perce groups adopted the tipi more characteristic of Plains Indians. They became a dominant tribe in the region.

The arrival of European traders and settlers led to important changes in their lives. Fur traders and trappers began to penetrate their tribal lands beginning shortly after Lewis and Clark came through in 1805. By the 1840s, settlers were moving to the West Coast along the Oregon Trail in a fairly steady stream. This led to some clashes and hostile feelings as European settlers began to settle in what had traditionally been Nez Perce land.

In 1855 some tribal representatives at the Walla Walla Council sponsored by the U.S. government signed a treaty that created a large Nez Perce reservation encompassing most of the tribe's traditional land. Chief Joseph, born in 1840, was part of a group within the tribe that never really accepted the terms of that treaty. Believing they hadn't been properly represented at the negotiations, they called it the "thief treaty." However, most Nez Perce grudgingly accepted the treaty's terms and lived on the reservation.

In 1860, however, gold was discovered along the Salmon and Clearwater Rivers in Nez Perce territory. Miners and gold-thirsty adventurers began to intrude on the Nez Perce lands. More settlers kept arriving as well. In 1863, U.S. commissioners forced the renegotiation of the 1855 treaty, and fraudulently reduced the size of the reservation by three-fourths, taking almost all the gold-producing areas. Subsequent invasions by squatters and other settlers effectively reduced the size of the tribal lands even more.

Chief Joseph was born in the Wallowa valley in Oregon, a place marked by the graves of his ancestors for generations. His father, also named Joseph, had converted to Christianity in 1839, and he saw to it that his tall, thoughtful, impressive son was educated in mission schools. He also imbued in him the importance of keeping the peoples' ancestral lands. He died in 1871. The 1863 treaty took away the Nez Perce lands in Oregon where Chief Joseph had been born, forcing the tribe to move to the Lapwai Reservation in Idaho.

The U.S. government had found cooperative tribe members to sign the treaties of 1855 and 1863, but many Nez Perce, probably a majority, had never accepted the validity of either agreement. Chief Joseph—not the undisputed leader but one of the most respected chiefs—tried to negotiate with U.S. government officials to allow the Nez Perce to stay in the valley with the graves of their ancestors. But the government was adamant. Finally, in 1877, all nontreaty Nez Perce were given an ultimatum to move to Lapwai within thirty days. Chief Joseph, although bitterly disappointed at being forced to leave his family's homeland, was one of the peacemakers within the tribe, working to control violence, and to persuade more hot-headed warriors that a confrontation with the U.S. Cavalry would only lead to too many tragic deaths. He reluctantly agreed to lead the journey to the Idaho reservation.

As preparations were being made for the journey, however— herds of animals being rounded up, belongings packed, scattered tribe members gathered into a group ready to travel—a confrontation ensued between three volatile warriors and a group of squatters. The young warriors went on a violent spree, killing sixteen or seventeen of the gold seekers encamped along a river. Chief Joseph later said he wanted to report the incident to the government's Indian agency and try to avoid further bloodshed or hostility, but he doubted that his innocence would be believed. He was convinced that the only viable course was to flee. Thus began, on June 13 to 15, what is known as the Nez Perce War of 1877.

Many Nez Perce who had had nothing to do with the violence and in fact disapproved of it feared that the innocent would be punished along with the guilty. So many—eventually as many as eight hundred—joined the flight.

After a few skirmishes along the way, the Nez Perce first took refuge at White Bird Creek. There Chief Joseph joined them and took charge. Although he would eventually achieve a reputation in some Eastern newspapers as something of a military genius, Joseph was not primarily a war chief. Other leaders led most of the battles that would eventually capture the imagination of readers in other parts of the country.

While the Nez Perce were encamped at White Bird Creek, friendly indians apparently convinced them that if they surrendered those responsible for the massacre, the rest would eventually be allowed to go free. But when a Nez Perce group under a white flag approached an army group to begin discussing the possibility, civilians with the army opened fire on them. After the battle that followed, thirty-four whites, mostly settlers, were dead, and four wounded. The Nez Perce suffered two wounded.

Both sides now believed the other side couldn't be trusted. The Nez Perce began a retreat and the U.S. Army brought four hundred men into the field, led by General Oliver Howard. As the Nez Perce paused for awhile at Cottonwood Creek, they were joined by others, and eventually could count some three hundred fighting men, along with some five hundred women and children. On July 3, 1877, at Cottonwood Creek, a scouting party of ten troopers was surprised and wiped out. The Nez Perce moved east to Clearwater, where a pitched battle was fought on July 11 and 12. The army lost fifteen soldiers and twenty-five were wounded, while the Nez Perce suffered four casualties and had six wounded.

The Nez Perce then crossed the rugged Bitterroot Mountains into Montana. After an arduous retreat over very difficult terrain, they made a camp at Big Hole, near what is now the Idaho-Montana border. There the army caught them by surprise. In the battle that followed, the army lost twenty-nine men, while Nez Perce deaths amounted to eighty-nine, many of them women and children. But the Nez Perce were not defeated. Although seriously diminished in numbers and morale, they kept up the retreat eastward. On August 13, they raided an army camp at Camas Meadows in eastern Idaho, near the Montana border, running off 150 mules and taking some provisions. They crossed into Wyoming, into Yellowstone Park, where they frightened and scattered tourists, killing two.

As the Nez Perce retreat continued, frustrating the U.S. Army, stories of the war began to be printed in newspapers around the country. Many Americans cheered for the army, but many sympathized with or admired the Nez Perce. The tribe gained a reputation for humane treatment of prisoners, and Chief Joseph, while fighting the retreat, struggling to find provisions, and wondering where to go next, showed great concern for the women and children under his care. As he moved northward through Montana, he sometimes raided settlers for provisions, but whenever possible he traded stock instead of stealing to supply his tribe's needs. Chief Joseph became something of a folk hero in certain circles back east. Many people were quietly or openly cheering him, hoping he would make it to Canada before being forced to capitulate.

As the Nez Perce continued their trek north by horseback and on foot, the army was able to use the railroads and telegraph to marshal its resources. On September 13, the army caught up with the fleeing tribe at Canyon Creek in the southern part of central Montana. But after a skirmish, the Nez Perce again escaped, and with a forced march moved well ahead of the army. Crossing the Missouri River on September 25, they raided an army depot at Cow Island for supplies. They pressed northward to Bear Paw Mountain, knowing they had left General Howard's army far behind.

By this time, they had retreated some 1,500 miles, much of it over difficult terrain, outmaneuvering the U.S. Army several times but suffering casualties and hunger. They had been constantly on the move for four months, sometimes fighting, sometimes raiding or trading, but always in peril. The Canadian border was about forty miles north of Bear Paw Mountain. If they made it, the U.S. Army would be constrained to give up the chase. It wouldn't be home, but it would be safe. Chief Joseph ordered a pause, to rest for the final leg of the journey, treat some of the wounded, and hunt buffalo.

He didn't know, however, that while General Howard's army was indeed far behind, another troop led by then Colonel Nelson A. Miles, after a two-hundred-mile forced march, was nearby.

Colonel Nelson's troop surprised the exhausted Nez Perce on September 30. After a five-day battle, Chief Joseph finally surrendered on October 5. Some 418 Nez Perce of the original band of 800 were captured—87 men, 184 women, and 147 children. The U.S. Army had suffered 127 killed and 147 wounded. In addition, about 50 civilians were dead.

When he surrendered, Chief Joseph delivered what has become perhaps the most famous statement in the history of white-Indian relations:

> *I am tired of fighting. Our chiefs are killed . . . the old men are all killed . . . it is cold and we have no blankets. The little children are freezing to death. My people, some of them, have run away to the hills and have no blankets, no food; no one knows where they are, perhaps freezing to death. I want time to look for my children and see how many of them I can find. Maybe I shall find them among the dead. Hear me, my chiefs, I am tired; my heart is sick and sad. From where the sun now stands, I will fight no more forever.*

Although Chief Joseph had been promised that the Nez Perce would be resettled at the Lapwai Reservation, the captured tribe was shipped to a completely unfamiliar, barren area in what was called Indian Territory and is now Oklahoma. There, in malarial conditions, many sickened and died. The remnant of the tribe was finally allowed to return to the northwest in 1885. But while most of them went to Lapwai, Chief Joseph had to go to the unfamiliar Colville Reservation in northeastern Washington State. He died there in 1904, but he never gave up trying to convince the federal government to allow him and other Nez Perce to return to their home in the valley "where most of my relatives and friends are sleeping their last sleep." He made two trips to Washington, D.C., for this purpose, on one occasion being presented to President Theodore Roosevelt.

Chief Joseph became an enduring symbol of Native American resistance to being forcibly resettled by the U.S. government, but also a symbol of acquiescing to defeat while retaining dignity, never quite accepting his fate, continuing to protest and trying to persuade, with dignity and persistence, even after armed resistance had been defeated. There was little reason for him to hope that the federal government would relent and allow the Nez Perce to return to the ancestral lands that had been stolen from them. But he never gave up. He made his pleas with reserved passion. He was true to his pledge to "fight no more forever," but he continued his campaign. Although he was not successful, he managed to achieve an aura of moral force, laying much of the groundwork that led many Americans to reassess the Indian wars, and to develop the belief that Native American tribes had been treated with disrespect and inhumanity during the settling of the West.

Many observers, from 1877 to this day, see the pursuit of Chief Joseph and his bedraggled band as unnecessary excess. The pursuit cost the military, in addition to the lives lost and the dignity sacrificed, some $931,329, at a time when a million dollars was a lot of money. After the first few skirmishes, when the Nez Perce were decimated and obviously seeking to escape, it could have done little real harm to the safety of settlers in Montana and Idaho to have either given up the pursuit or allowed Chief Joseph to make it across the Canadian border. Instead, however, Colonel (later General) Miles spurred his troops to extraordinary efforts to ensure that the Nez Perce were not able to make good their escape to Canada, where the government had already made it known that the Nez Perce would be allowed to find a place to live in relative peace.

Why put forward such an extraordinary—heroic or foolish, depending on your perspective—effort to capture and humiliate a weary and hungry band that posed no threat to national security?

Perhaps embarrassment played a role. Chief Joseph had frustrated the U.S. Army, which at first had assumed that controlling his flight would be a simple matter. There was the matter of both civilian and army personnel who had been killed by the Nez Perce. You might make a case that those deaths needed to be avenged—even though the Nez Perce had suffered a comparable number of casualties during the course of the campaign. And perhaps some military and political authorities reasoned that if the Nez Perce were allowed to escape after embarrassing the army and inflicting casualties, other Native American tribes would be inspired to attempt revolts of a more deadly character. The unquestioned authority of the federal government had to be established. Indeed, whether they were inspired or discouraged by the Nez Perce experience, several hundred Cheyenne escaped from Indian Territory in 1878 and led the army on a grueling chase before being caught.

Why make such an extraordinary effort to capture and punish Chief Joseph? The late senator J. William Fulbright, in his 1966 book *The Arrogance of Power*, wrote:

> *The more I puzzle over the great wars of history, the more I am inclined to the view that the causes attributed to them—territory, markets, resources, the defense or perpetuation of great principles— were not the root causes at all, but rather explanations or excuses for certain unfathomable drives of human nature. For lack of a clear and precise understanding of exactly what these motives are, I refer to them as the "arrogance of power"—as a psychological need that nations seem to have in order to prove that they are bigger, better, or stronger than other nations.*

Donald Kagan, a historian at Yale University, has for many years taught a celebrated course on the origins of war. In his recent book, *On the Origins of War and the Preservation of Peace*, he claims that "we have not done as well as the ancient Greeks" in understanding how and why peoples go to war or engage in hostile or warlike behavior. The Greek historian Thucydides said people fight wars out of "honor, fear, and interest," with the Greek word for honor covering a whole range of concepts, like "deference, esteem, just due, regard, respect, or prestige."

In the four wars Kagan's book examines in detail, "the reader may be surprised by how small a role . . . considerations of practical utility and material gain, and even ambition for power itself, play in bringing on wars and how often some aspect of honor is decisive."

Honor is usually viewed in a favorable light, but every virtue can be twisted or taken to extremes and become a vice or a fault. So a certain understanding of the sense of honor might require a cavalry commander to go to extraordinary lengths to make sure a weary band of Native Americans, who have already been cheated out of their ancestral homeland, does not escape to a place where the U.S. government no longer can claim authority over them. From a strictly practical standpoint, and perhaps from a humanitarian standpoint, little harm would have ensued had Chief Joseph and his band of Nez Perce been able to leave U.S. jurisdiction. But a type of honor—or prestige, or wounded pride, or determination not to allow authority to be challenged—led to a final battle that, from a historical standpoint, doesn't look honorable at all.

The U.S. government, of course, is far from the only institution or organization to have been led into foolish, excessive, or dishonorable activities out of a skewed sense of honor. But as the story of Chief Joseph reminds us, it has been led to such actions, not just in this century but in the distant past as well. Perhaps that doesn't make the government evil or sinister, but simply human, sharing the imperfection and occasional egregious excess that marks every human institution or endeavor.

Other stories could be told, from our own century, stories of Watergate or Waco, of Iran–Contra, or Donald Scott. But Chief Joseph's story forms an especially poignant background for the story of Ruby Ridge, and only in part because it occurred in the same part of the country. Chief Joseph was not eager for a fight or confrontation, yet through a series of unfortunate coincidences and accidents, he became the focus of the government's attention. A case could have been made for simply letting him go. But he had embarrassed the army, undermining its own conception of its authority. So the army engaged in what a later generation might have called overkill. Honor—or its less attractive cousin, pride—was at stake.

—Alan W. Bock
Lake Elsinore, California
June 1995

A C K N O W L E D G M E N T S

THIS BOOK HAS BEEN BOTH FULFILLING AND FRUSTRATING TO WRITE. I HAVE tried to tell the story of what happened between Randy Weaver and his family and agents from various federal and state police agencies in August, 1992 as objectively, conscientiously, and completely as possible, with enough background and context to make the incident comprehensible. But it is never possible to know everything about such a complex occurrence, especially about the motivations of some of those involved. And the search for the truth has been complicated by the fact that for various understandable reasons, the principal players have been reluctant to talk to writers: Randy Weaver and Kevin Harris are involved in pending litigation which also involves most of the federal agents who were at Ruby Ridge or had command responsibilities. Aside from issuing some reports, portions of which have been leaked to or acquired by some media outlets, the federal government has had little to say about Ruby Ridge.

Fortunately, however, the original incident and the subsequent trial were covered thoroughly and competently by numerous news media outlets, and many of the reporters involved have been more than generous in sharing their clippings, recollections, and reflections with an "outsider" trying to make sense of this incident without having lived through it. Special thanks go to Dean Miller and Jess Walter of the Spokane newspaper, the *Spokesman-Review*, Dan Popkey and Melanie Threlkeld of the *Idaho Statesman*, and Mike McLean of the Northern Idaho News Network. *Jubilee*, a monthly newspaper, has a decided point of view, but its reports on the Weaver incident, especially by Chris Temple and Paul Hall, were factual and informative, and both have been generous with their time. Jerry White of Las Vegas provided a running chronicle of the trial for the American Patriot Fax Network, which provided useful details. Kirby Ferris, who wrote *A Mountain of Lies* before the trial, has spent hours on the phone with me.

Many people who kept vigil at Ruby Creek or attended the trial have shared their experiences and thoughts with me, notably Jackie Brown—who guided me around the Weaver cabin and property in July 1993, and along with her husband Tony has been generous beyond the call of duty since then—Bill Rich, Don Stewart, George and Catherine Dennis, Eva Vail, John, Dave, Carolyn and Randy Trochmann, and numerous residents and businesspeople in the Naples–Bonners Ferry area, and other people who for various reasons must go unnamed. Mike McNulty has been a constant source of encouragement, Jim Bovard has offered concrete information and intangible moral support, and Durk and Sandy's enthusiasm is always infectious.

Jacob Sullum and Virginia Postrel of *Reason* magazine commissioned the article that became the basis for this book and guided me gently through its completion. Diane Fallon has been as supportive and helpful a publisher as a writer could want.

My thanks to Stephen, who has usually understood why Dad can't play baseball right now, and to Jennifer, who has reluctantly understood that the process of writing isn't always tapping on a keyboard: sometimes it's reading, sometimes it's staring into space in an apparent daze, sometimes it's walking around the house distractedly, and sometimes it bears a suspicious resemblance to goofing off. Their forbearance and patience has been noted and appreciated, if not always at the time it was shown.

Finally, a word of thanks to Antonio Vivaldi, Wolfgang Mozart, Ludwig van Beethoven, Dmitri Shostakovich, Gustav Mahler, Nicolai Rimsky-Korsakov, George F. Handel, Johann Sebastian Bach, Antonin Dvořák, Verdi, and numerous other composers, along with the artists and orchestras who have recorded their works over the years–along with performers like Miles Davis, Wynton Marsalis, Randell Young, Benny Goodman,

Ahmad Jamal, Dave Brubeck, Joe Henderson, and others. I am one of those odd people who likes to write with music blasting—or gently flowing—and it is hard to imagine completing this book without the unknowing spiritual assistance of these and other great musicians.

While I freely acknowledge the help and encouragement of these and others, the responsibility for any errors of fact or interpretation is mine alone.

CAST OF CHARACTERS

IN THE WEAVER CABIN

Randy Weaver, 44
Vicki Weaver, 43
Sara Weaver, 16
Samuel Weaver, 14
Rachel Weaver, 10
Elisheba Weaver, 10 months
Kevin Harris, 25

U.S. MARSHALS ON GROUNDS
AUGUST 21–AUGUST 22, 1992

Larry Cooper
William F. Degan
Arthur Roderick
David Hunt
Larry Thomas
Frank Norris
All members, Special Operations Group

OTHER U.S. MARSHALS

Ron Evans, chief deputy marshal for Idaho
Ron Mays, deputy marshal
Jack Cluff, deputy marshal
Warren Mays, surveillance team
William Hufnagle, electronic specialist
Mark Jurgensen, surveillance team
Ron Libby, surveillance team emergency medical technician
Antonio Perez, chief of enforcement, U.S. Marshals Service
Henry Hudson, director, U.S. Marshals Service
John Roche, deputy director, U.S. Marshals Service
G. Wayne "Duke" Smith, associate director, U.S. Marshals Service
Joyce McDonald, press spokesperson, Washington, D.C.
Mike Johnson, press spokesperson, Washington, D.C.

FEDERAL BUREAU OF INVESTIGATION

Richard Rogers, head, Hostage Rescue Team
Larry Potts, assistant director, criminal division
Danny O. Coulson, deputy assistant director, criminal division
Eugene Glenn, special agent–in–charge, Salt Lake City office and
field commander at Ruby Ridge
Dave Tubbs, assistant to Gene Glenn
Greg Rampton, special agent, debriefed marshals
George Calley, special agent, debriefed marshals
Frank Costanza, special agent
Mark Thundercloud, special agent, gathered evidence
Larry Wages, special agent, gathered evidence
Wayne Manis, special agent

Lon Horiuchi, Hostage Rescue Team sniper
Joe Venkus, special agent, gathered evidence
Gregory Sexton, Denver SWAT Team leader
Fred Lanceley, hostage negotiator

BUREAU OF ALCOHOL, TOBACCO AND FIREARMS

Kenneth Fadeley/Gus Magisono, undercover operative
Herb Byerly, special agent, Fadeley's "control"

OTHER LAW ENFORCEMENT PERSONNEL

David Neal, captain, Idaho State Police Crisis Response Team

NEIGHBORS, FRIENDS, SUPPORTERS

Wayne and Ruth Rau, Weaver neighbors who cooperated
with federal agencies
Jackie and Tony Brown, Weaver friends
Judy and Bill Grider, Weaver acquaintances, active protesters
Alan Jeppeson, Weaver neighbor
Sean Maguire, Naples resident
Rodney Willey, Naples resident, Weaver friend

George Torrence, Weaver neighbor

Bill Rich, Portland resident

Don Stewart, Portland resident, former government
undercover operative

Eva Vail, Hayden Lake resident

John and Carolyn Trochmann, Montana residents,
later formed Militia of Montana

Chris Temple, Montana financial consultant, writer for *Jubilee*

James G. "Bo" Gritz, former Special Forces lieutenant colonel,
POW hunter, 1992 Populist Party presidential candidate

Jack McLamb, former Phoenix police officer, patriot activist

Brian and Barbara Pierce, Kevin Harris's stepfather and mother

IN COURT

U.S. District Court, Judge Edward J. Lodge, presiding

Maurice Ellsworth, U.S. attorney for Idaho

Ron Howen, assistant U.S. attorney in Idaho, lead prosecutor

Kim Lindquist, assistant U.S. attorney in Idaho, co-prosecutor

Gerry Spence, Randy Weaver's lead defense attorney

Kent Spence, Gerry's son, co-counsel

Chuck Peterson, Boise defense attorney, Weaver co-counsel

Garry Gilman, Boise defense attorney, Weaver co-counsel

David Nevin, Boise defense attorney, Kevin Harris's
lead defense attorney

Ellison Matthews, Boise defense attorney, Harris co-counsel

Dr. Martin Fackler, ballistics expert witness

Lucien Haag, ballistics expert witness

SELECTED JURORS

Cyril Hatfield, first jury foreman
Anita Brewer, alternate who joined in mid-deliberation
John Harris Weaver, second jury foreman
Mary Flenor, recording secretary
Dorothy Mitchell, spoke at sentencing hearing
Dorothy Hoffman, spoke at sentencing hearing

AMBUSH AT RUBY RIDGE

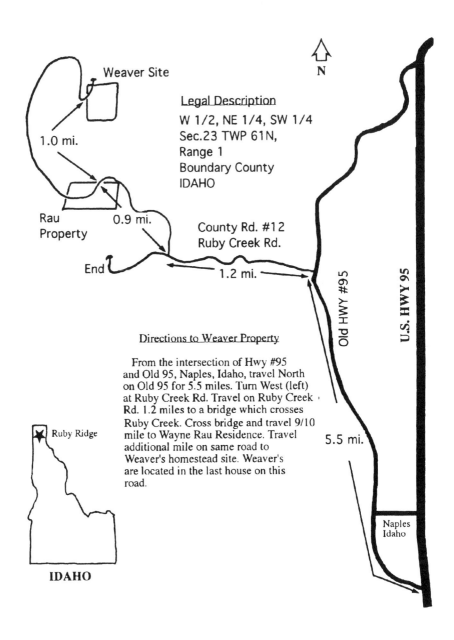

Weaver Site

1.0 mi.

Rau
Property

0.9 mi.

End

N

Legal Description
W 1/2, NE 1/4, SW 1/4
Sec.23 TWP 61N,
Range 1
Boundary County
IDAHO

County Rd. #12
Ruby Creek Rd.

1.2 mi.

Old HWY #95

U.S. HWY 95

Directions to Weaver Property

From the intersection of Hwy #95
and Old 95, Naples, Idaho, travel North
on Old 95 for 5.5 miles. Turn West (left)
at Ruby Creek Rd. Travel on Ruby Creek
Rd. 1.2 miles to a bridge which crosses
Ruby Creek. Cross bridge and travel 9/10
mile to Wayne Rau Residence. Travel
additional mile on same road to
Weaver's homestead site. Weaver's
are located in the last house on this
road.

Ruby Ridge

5.5 mi.

Naples
Idaho

IDAHO

Redrawing of Government Exhibit D

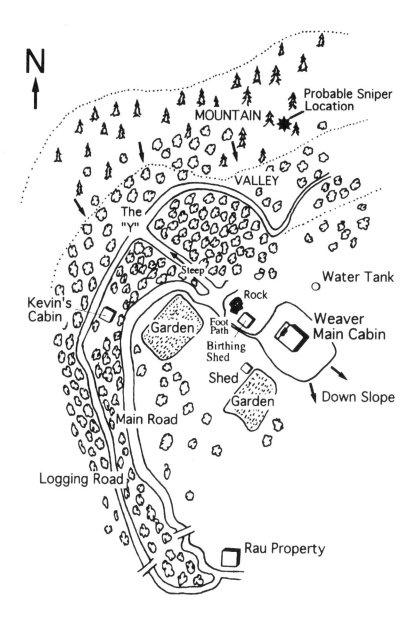

N

Probable Sniper Location

MOUNTAIN

VALLEY

The "Y"

Steep

Water Tank

Rock

Kevin's Cabin

Garden

Foot Path

Birthing Shed

Weaver Main Cabin

Shed

Garden

Down Slope

Main Road

Logging Road

Rau Property

Author's Rendition of Weaver Property

August 21–August 22, 1992:
The Siege

I T WAS EARLY, JUST BEFORE DAWN, ON A SUMMER MORNING IN THE northern panhandle of Idaho. Birds were beginning their morning songs among the pine, alder, larch, and maple trees as six U.S. deputy marshals, part of a highly trained SWAT-like team called the Special Operations Group (SOG), moved onto the steep, mountainous, heavily wooded property of Randall Weaver, a federal fugitive living in a remote, mountainous area near the small town of Naples. They were on what was later termed a reconnaissance mission, that is, a nonaggressive mission simply to check out the terrain and its inhabitants for possible future action. But the previous day they had gone to a shooting range and spent several hours "sighting-in" their weapons. They were armed with automatic rifles (Colt Commando 9 millimeter submachine guns, some with silencers), dressed in full camouflage regalia, including black ski masks, and wearing body armor. A medical team was on alert at the bottom of the hill that ended Weaver's property.

The six marshals spent several hours tramping over Randall Weaver's twenty acres—all except the area immediately surrounding Weaver's plywood cabin—and some of the rugged terrain surrounding the property, which was about a mile in steep, rough countryside from the nearest neighbor's house. Some of them had been there before, but a couple were seeing the area for the first time, having been flown in from the East Coast. They avoided the small cleared area around the cabin. But aside from that small patch, set on a little higher ground than most of the surrounding terrain, the land lent itself to concealment. It was necessary to walk carefully to avoid noise, but the woods were so thick that an experienced, trained woodsman could probably avoid having a less experienced person see him for hours.

After some time spent getting the lay of the land and sizing up the territory and the logistical problems and opportunities it presented, the marshals split into two teams.

Deputy marshals William Degan, Larry Cooper, and Art Roderick were one team, and Dave Hunt, Larry Thomas, Frank Norris, an emergency medical technician (EMT), were the other. The Degan–Cooper–Roderick team was the "forward" group. They would precipitate and participate in the tragic action of the day. The Hunt–Thomas–Norris team stayed at a back–up location about a mile away, down the hill from the Weaver property.

The area around Naples is not quite the remotest region in the Idaho backwoods, but it's hardly a bustling metropolis. Some thirty–five miles south of the Canadian border, Naples is about fifteen miles north of Sandpoint (population 5,200), a lovely resort community on the shore of the big, beautiful Lake Pend Oreille, which ranges south and east for miles. About five miles north is Bonners Ferry (population 2,000), founded in 1863 as a trapper's outpost, with an economy based on lumber, farming, mining, and recreation.

Fewer than two thousand people live in the Naples zip code. The zip code on a map is about ten miles square, but because heavily wooded mountains rise on either side of the valley through which Highway 95 runs north and south, only an area about two miles east and west by eight miles north and south is inhabited. A general store and a small sawmill are the only signs of commercial activity in the town. The area first "boomed" in the 1930s, and in the 1970s managed to tolerate an influx of hippies getting back to nature. Many of the residents are retirees. Others are attracted by the beautiful mountains, the low cost of living, the friendly, small-town atmosphere, the four seasons, and, as Earl at the general store put it, "the freedom." Some people live in the area part of the year and work at some job in a larger city for months at a time to make a living.

Randy Weaver's cabin is on a dirt road that takes off to the left (or west) from a two-lane paved road that roughly parallels the state highway, about five and one-half miles north of the center of town. County road number 12, or Ruby Creek Road, is a reasonably smooth dirt road that ventures into the woods and steep mountainous country to the left, over a bridge that spans Deep Creek, a small stream. A driver on the dirt road is almost immediately into heavily wooded, mountainous country, with ridges rising on either side of a little valley. The map on the federal search warrant (see page xxxvi) shows 1.2 miles before a little bridge where one turns right, but it's more like three miles. Shortly past the bridge is the home of Wayne and Ruth Rau, a neat, pleasant house with a basketball hoop on the front of the garage.

Just past the Raus' house, the road gets a lot steeper, curvier, and more rutted. A four-wheel-drive vehicle might not be absolutely necessary to negotiate it, but few people would feel comfortable without one. The road twists and turns and climbs and rocks the bones for about a mile before ending in a wide spot or circle, where the Weaver family parked their vehicles. There's a small storage shed by a huge rock, some ten feet high. The trail to the actual cabin leads up and around that rock.

Randy Weaver's cabin is a wood-frame structure, twenty-four by thirty-two feet, covered with plywood. It's two stories high (the second level functioning as a sleeping deck), with a sheet-metal roof. The cabin is built on a small outcropping that overlooks the Ruby Creek valley to the south and drops off steeply on three sides. There's a small, reasonably level yard that ends at the big rock that serves as, for lack of a better word, the cabin's entranceway. A small shed was right next to the rock, thirty to fifty feet from the main cabin. It was called a "birthing shed" by the Weavers because their religious beliefs called for a woman to be separated from others while giving birth; indeed, Randy's youngest child had been born there ten months before. In the center of the porch is a door which leads into the kitchen. The ground slopes radically enough that, while there's a porch and a door at ground level, the cabin is actually built on a stilt-like framework, leaving an open storage area under the living area.

The Weaver family owned twenty acres, very little of it level. West of the porch are extensive gardens and a tool and garden shed. Another garden, with little sheds for tools, is just beyond and below the first garden, approximately northwesterly from the porch. But it's not easy to see from the cabin because the ground slopes down and the whole area is so heavily wooded. A trail runs next to this garden, leading down through thick woods until it hits an old logging road about half a mile from the cabin (which breaks off the main dirt road near the Raus' house and runs up past the Weaver property, almost encircling it before meandering off into the woods to the north and east). Along the main dirt road that leads to the cabin is a small meadow-like area with the beginning of a smaller cabin that the Weavers' friend, Kevin Harris, had been building.

The view from the outcropping on which the cabin is built is simply spectacular. To the north, the mountains rise high above the cabin, rugged and covered with trees. To the south and east is a valley that the property overlooks, with mountains rising on the other side, perhaps a couple of miles away.

The cabin had been built mostly from scrap lumber—two-by-fours and plywood, with no insulation. It was sturdy enough, but rudimentary, and it must have been cold during the long northern Idaho winters.

Living in the cabin on August 21, 1992, were Randy Weaver, forty-four, a slight, slender former Green Beret, and his wife Vicki, forty-three, a dark-haired, attractive woman, and their children, Sara, sixteen, Samuel (Sammy), fourteen, Rachel, ten, and Elisheba, ten months. Also living at the cabin was Kevin Harris, twenty-five, a close friend of the family who had lived off and on with them for almost ten years at the cabin on what was called Ruby Ridge— actually, the ridge originally called Ruby Ridge is on the other side of the draw through which Ruby Creek runs, but the place where Randy Weaver lived is now and probably always will be called Ruby Ridge by most people. The family also had three dogs, including a young yellow Labrador named Striker, who was Sammy's special pet.

By August 1992, Randy Weaver had been at his property for about eighteen months, hardly venturing out of the cabin during much of that time, although Kevin and the rest of the family went out to work the gardens, hunt, or set traps. For Randy was a federal fugitive, wanted by the Bureau of Alcohol, Tobacco and Firearms on a weapons charge for selling sawed-off shotguns. The U.S. Marshals Service had been keeping an eye on him. On August 21, whether by plan or by inadvertence, they were finally to make direct contact.

By late morning, Randy, Sammy, and Kevin were in the yard by the cabin's kitchen door. All were carrying firearms. The adults and the older children almost always carried weapons when they were outside the cabin. This is not universally done by residents of the Idaho backwoods, but it's not uncommon among people who live in similarly remote circumstances in that part of the country. You never knew when you might see a deer or some other game, and bears roamed the area as well. In addition, the family was aware that federal agents had them under surveillance, although they might not have been aware of just how extensive the surveillance operation was. When the ambush at Ruby Ridge finally ended, officials found fourteen weapons in the cabin, mostly older, used weapons of marginal quality. To many objective listeners that might seem like an arsenal, but in the rural Northwest, it wasn't all that unusual.

Deputy marshals Degan, Cooper, and Roderick, after scouting in and around the property for awhile, took up a position crouched behind the huge rock that marks the edge of the yardlike area where the cabin was built. That put them some ten feet below the level of the cabin's yard area. They started to throw pebbles up over the rock and into the yard "to see if they could get the dog's attention," as Marshal Roderick later put it in court testimony.

Striker noticed. He started barking and running back and forth, sniffing in the vicinity of the giant boulder that marks the entranceway to the Weaver property. Randy, Kevin, and Sammy ran out toward the rock with their weapons: Randy with a double-barrel 12-gauge shotgun, Kevin with a .30-06 bolt-action rifle, and Sammy with a .223 mini-14.

The marshals ran into the woods in a northeasterly direction, to the right if one were standing on the cabin's kitchen porch, to the old logging road that encircled the property.

By the time the Weaver entourage got to the rock, Striker was down at the little storage shed near the bottom of the rock, barking at something in the woods. Then the dog started to chase the marshals. They fled to where the logging road met the road next to the Weaver garden that came down more directly—a place called "the Y" though it could also be described as a T. At that intersection is a thick stand of woods off the trails where it is possible to hide and still have a view of who is coming from all three directions. Whether the marshals had scouted this location in advance or dived into it because Striker was about to catch up to them is subject to some dispute. Perhaps nobody but the marshals will ever know. But they took cover in a thick stand of trees at that spot.

The hiding place was useful more because it gave the marshals a view of whoever might approach rather than because it was necessarily the thickest stand of trees around. The relatively direct trail from the cabin is not very wide, and the trees on either side overhang it with a thick canopy of branches. The trail is also on a fairly steep incline.

After Striker had begun to chase the marshals, Kevin, Sammy, and Randy gave chase also. Randy later wrote in an account of the day's incident, "I didn't have any idea what we were chasing, but I hoped it was a deer." The family was almost out of meat. Kevin and Sammy followed the dog along the logging road. Randy went down the trail that went past the garden and met the road. It is fairly common hunting practice, if the hunting party consists of more than one person, to surround and trap a deer or to have one set of hunters chase and drive a deer into the waiting sights of the other.

What happened next is still a little unclear. Randy was coming down the trail, toward the Y, armed with his shotgun. Kevin and Sammy were headed around toward the Y on the old logging trail, armed with their rifles. The three marshals were hidden in the stand of trees, or, at the beginning of the encounter they may have been on the road at the intersection, where Randy at least could see them.

Randy later wrote, "When I reached the first fork in the logging road, a very well-camouflaged person yelled 'Freeze, Randy!' I immediately said 'Fuck you,' and retreated eighty to one hundred feet toward home. I realized immediately that we had run smack into a ZOG [Zionist Occupational Government]/New World Order ambush. I stopped to see if I was being followed."

Art Roderick also said later that the marshals encountered Randy before they could hide themselves, which they felt they needed to do because they feared being shot in the back if Kevin or Sammy saw them.

Within moments, Striker, followed by Sammy, with Kevin a little behind, came to the Y area. They apparently didn't see anybody or anything, but might well have heard Randy yelling something about an ambush and that they should return to the cabin. The dog turned up the trail toward the cabin, followed by Sammy. A brief from the Weaver attorneys claims the federal agents planned in advance to shoot the dog, in the belief that this would bring the adults into the open, where they could be shot and/or brought into custody. Whether that was the plan or not, after the dog had gone up the trail toward the cabin, Marshal Roderick fired at the dog. The bullet shattered Striker's spine, and the dog let out a yelp. According to testimony before the grand jury, the dog almost certainly cried out in great pain, pulling itself about on its front legs for some time before it died, all in plain sight of Sammy Weaver and Kevin Harris. Stories differ as to whether Sammy and

Kevin saw a man in full camouflage, standing or kneeling on the road, shoot Striker, or whether they merely noted that a bullet seemed to have come from a stand of trees.

When Sammy saw that his dog had been shot, he yelled, "You shot Striker, you sonofabitch!" and fired his gun in the direction from which the shots had come. There has been no allegation or contention backed by any evidence that he hit anything. He then turned and ran toward the cabin.

Randy Weaver, waiting a small distance up the trail, heard the shots, heard Striker yelp and then go quiet. He couldn't see what was happening, but he guessed that Striker had been killed. He yelled for Sammy and Kevin to return home, saying the feds had killed Striker. He fired his shotgun into the air, hoping to draw attention away from the boys. He tried to reload, but jammed his shotgun. So he pulled the 9 millimeter pistol he had out of his holster and fired a few more shots into the air.

Back at the Y, Sammy was running up the trail when another shot came from the concealed position, hitting him in the arm. He yelled in pain and fell, then got back up and started running again. He heard his father yelling for him to come home. He shouted, "I'm coming Dad!" Those were the last words he ever spoke.

Another burst came from the concealed shooters, and fourteen-year-old Sammy Weaver fell dead, shot in the back as he was trying to run home to get away from shooters who had never identified themselves to him or to Kevin Harris, never said they were federal agents, and did not have a warrant in their possession.

Seeing Sammy fall, Harris opened fire in the direction of the bushes from which the shots had come that had killed Sammy. He believed that he had shot the person who had killed Sammy. He ran up the trail, stopped to examine Sammy's body, confirmed that the boy was dead, and kept running. When he got to the cabin, he informed Randy and Vicki Weaver that their son was dead.

Whether Harris shot him or not, William Degan, one of the most highly decorated officers in the U.S. Marshals Service, was dead in the stand of woods where the officers had concealed themselves. The government at first put out the story that Marshal

Degan had been killed when Harris fired first without warning, but seven cartridges from his gun were found in the little stand of trees. The defense at the trial also put forward the possibility, backed by some circumstantial evidence, that one of the other marshals had shot Degan during the wild flurry of gunshots.

Marshal Roderick ran for help to marshals Dave Hunt, Frank Norris, and Larry Thomas, who had been down the road. Whatever he told his superiors, they got—or at least gave to others—the impression that a fierce two-way gun battle was raging in the woods around Ruby Ridge or that agents were pinned down by gunfire from the cabin, a virtual impossibility given the terrain. In fact, during the days-long standoff that followed, not a single shot was fired from the cabin.

In a statement prepared later in the cabin during the siege, Randy Weaver told what happened next, according to the occupants of the cabin:

> When Kevin got home and told us Sam was dead, Kevin and I (Randy) and Vicki walked back down to get Sam's body. We brought him home and laid him in the guest shed. We cleaned his body and wrapped him in a sheet. We also brought Sam's rifle home and that is the weapon I (R) am using now. We left NO WEAPON with Sam's body, as was reported on the local news. From that point on we have never left the knoll, and prepared to defend ourselves here.

This statement suggests that while the cabin had no electricity, the Weavers did have a radio or television on which they were able to discover how the siege was being reported, and that they felt a need to correct what they believed were false reports, insofar as they were able to do so.

Within minutes of the shootout, which took place between 11:30 A.M. and noon, federal officials began to evacuate residents from the entire area, from the bridge that leads over Deep Creek next to the paved road almost five miles from the Weaver property to the end of all the dirt roads that take off from it. That amounted to thirty people. In a small town like Naples, it's an unusual situation, noticed rather quickly, when thirty people are forced from their homes and a roadblock is set up at a bridge. A few people—some neighbors, some curiosity seekers, a few friends of the Weavers—assembled at the roadblocked bridge. Most were in a mood to taunt the federal officials and to marvel at the speed with which military and paramilitary equipment began moving into the area.

The practical result of the roadblock was that federal authorities had complete tactical control of the Weaver property and a wide area surrounding it. This meant that the news media had to rely entirely on statements from federal officials. Only one reporter had actually been to the cabin to do an interview in May 1992.

There are only two places where anybody could come under fire from the Weaver cabin. One is the yard and upper garden area, directly behind the cabin, which is, according to the account Randy and Kevin dictated later, the area from which Kevin, Randy, and Sammy left when Striker started chasing something. The other is a distant slope above the cabin, some 150 or 200 yards away. Aside from those two spots, there is no place in the area, given the ruggedness of the terrain and the heavy woods, where a bullet could travel in a straight line and hit anything or anyone on purpose.

If the marshals were under relentless fire, did they fire back? What did the marshals report to their command center? Surely they weren't under a regime of radio silence, and they all carried walkie-talkies. What did they say? Were these transmissions, if any, tape-recorded?

After the smoke had cleared, and the marshals had done a preliminary assessment of the situation, Marshal Hunt got down to the house of the Weavers' closest neighbors, the Raus, who had been cooperating with federal officials during the surveillance that had preceded this day. Hunt called the local sheriff's office, and made several other calls, including one to the U.S. Marshals Service headquarters in Washington, D.C. He told Mrs. Rau that the marshals had been ambushed, that the marshals had been fired upon, and that the marshals had not fired back. What he told his head office is unknown. But the process of clearing out the neighbors, setting up a roadblock, and building up a large force of agents and police armed with military equipment began almost immediately.

After the U.S. Marshals Service office in Washington was notified about the incident, it called in the Federal Bureau of Investigation (FBI). The marshals apparently conveyed very much the same story to the FBI that spokespeople on the scene were conveying to the press—that the marshals had been ambushed, that they were currently pinned down by gunfire, that they were, in essence, under siege. The FBI mobilized its crack Hostage Rescue Team, headed by Richard Rogers. It called in agents from around the country, especially from nearby offices in Spokane, Washington, and Salt Lake City, Utah. The National Guard was called up to offer support. Before the close of business Friday, August 21, Idaho governor Cecil Andrus had declared a state of emergency, authorizing the National Guard and the organized militia to be pressed into the service of the state. Dozens of federal agents, along with some local law enforcement officers arrived before the end of the day Friday. On Saturday, literally hundreds of specially trained agents began to arrive, along with military equipment, including a helicopter, "humvees," that were so much a part of the Iraqi Desert Storm war, armored transport vehicles, armored personnel carriers, radio and TV equipment, and weapons of all kinds. The Red Cross was called in to set up facilities to feed the officers and men, who soon totaled at least four hundred.

On the airplane on the way to Idaho from Washington, D.C., Richard Rogers had sat down to write the rules of engagement for the encounter. He seemed to have been convinced that a continuing firefight was being waged in those remote mountains, although he at that point had never been there himself and had yet to talk to anybody who was actually at the Weavers' cabin or on the Weaver property.

As a 542-page Department of Justice task force report explains:[1]

When FBI tactical teams, such as HRT [Hostage Rescue Team] or SWAT, are deployed and confrontations are a possibility, Rules of Engagement are commonly established. Rules of Engagement are described as instructions to deployed units or individuals that clearly indicate what action should be taken when confronted, threatened, or fired upon by someone. They are intended to provide a context within which decisions about the use of deadly force are to be made. They serve two purposes: to restrict the application of the standard FBI deadly force policy or to heighten the awareness of tactical personnel regarding the threat level of individual situations. Formulation and approval of the Rules of Engagement are the responsibility of the on-scene commander.

The need for special Rules of Engagement for the Ruby Ridge crisis was discussed and agreed upon at an early point. While en route to northern Idaho, Richard Rogers, commander of the HRT, and assistant director Larry Potts had a series of conversations in which Potts advised Rogers of intelligence received.

Rogers explained [to the task force, later] his initial thoughts about the Rules of Engagement:

"In this particular situation, after hearing the description of what had taken place, specifically the firefight, the loss of a marshal, it was clear to me that there was a shooting situation taking place at this location. It appeared to me that it would have been irresponsible for me to send my agents into the situation without at least giving them a set of rules

1. Only excerpts of this task force report have been made available to the general public through selective release to news media outlets. This portion is quoted in the Legal Times of Washington, D.C.

within the greater framework of the standard FBI rules, that would allow them to defend themselves. With that in mind, I proposed that the rules be that if any adult is seen with a weapon in the vicinity of where this firefight took place, of the Weaver cabin, that this individual could be the subject of deadly force."

Specifically, as the task force report relates a few paragraphs later:

Rogers acknowledged that the Rules of Engagement he proposed specified that any adult with a weapon observed in the vicinity of the Weaver cabin or in the firefight area "could and should be the subject of deadly force." According to Rogers, he discussed this rule with FBI assistant director Larry Potts, who concurred fully.

The report notes that Mr. Potts, who also consulted with the FBI's deputy assistant director Danny O. Coulson, considered this crisis the most dangerous situation into which the Hostage Rescue Team had ever been called. Potts did not discuss the rules of engagement with the FBI legal counsel. He explained later that legal review is not usually solicited because rules of engagement are generally written to fall within the bounds of the FBI's standard deadly force policy, which normally authorizes agents to use deadly force only when they or others are in imminent danger of death or serious bodily harm. These rules were different, however.

The report notes:

At approximately 2:40 P.M. (PDT) on August 22 [the day after the initial shootings] an operations plan, which includes the Rules of Engagement, was sent by facsimile to FBI headquarters and the U.S. Marshals Service for review. The Rules in the operations plan as submitted to the Bureau for review stated:

If any adult in the compound is observed with a weapon after the surrender announcement is made, deadly force can and should be used to neutralize this individual. If any adult male is observed with a weapon prior to the announcement, deadly force can and should be employed, if the shot can be taken without endangering any children.

FBI deputy assistant director Coulson received the operations plan at the FBI headquarters' Strategic Information and Operations Center; he did not approve the draft plan because it lacked a negotiations option. Coulson stopped reviewing the plan once he realized a negotiations option was absent. Thus, he never saw or reviewed the Rules of Engagement in the plan which appeared after the section in which a negotiations strategy should have appeared. . . .

Once it was pointed out that a negotiation plan was not included in the operations plan, a negotiation plan was drafted in the Salt Lake City office, headed by Agent Eugene Glenn, who was the senior agent and commander at Ruby Ridge. The task force report notes:

Eugene Glenn, in a signed sworn statement given to the FBI team that reviewed the shooting incident following the resolution of the crisis, stated that "[o]n August 22, 1992, at 12:30 P.M. (PDT), FBI headquarters approved the operations plan which included . . . Rules of Engagement." Glenn is the only person who has stated that an operations plan was ever approved.

In a statement given during this inquiry, Glenn recalled that, although FBI headquarters did not approve the proposed operations plan, Potts told him that the Rules of Engagement had been approved as formulated and could be put into effect. Glenn told Rogers about this approval. . . .

It is still not clear whether Richard Rogers knew about the hours and hours of surveillance videotape that had already been taken in and around the Weaver home. It showed that all the adults in the household carried weapons whenever they came out of the cabin, and the older children carried weapons most of the time when outside as well.

A great deal—but not everything—is now known about the circumstances surrounding the writing of the rules of engagement, about who in the FBI hierarchy knew about these highly unusual rules and who approved them. The task force report states:

> It is our conclusion that Rogers justifiably believed that the Rules of Engagement provided to the HRT and [U.S. Marshals Service Special Operations Group] personnel were fully authorized. On the trip to Idaho, Rogers had received oral authorization for the use of the special Rules from Potts and Coulson. Finally, before the snipers were briefed on the Rules and deployed, Rogers secured Glenn's acknowledgment that FBI headquarters had approved the final version of the rules. . . .

> However, since there is no written record of specifically what version of the Rules that FBI headquarters approved, we cannot confidently say that the word "should" was approved by FBI headquarters at any time. Nevertheless, since those Rules, which contained "should" remained in force at the crisis scene for days . . . it is inconceivable to us that FBI headquarters remained ignorant of the Rules of Engagement during that entire period.

What is not known is Richard Rogers's state of mind and just how much he knew at the time he wrote the special rules. Were they written, as Weaver attorneys were later to suggest, to eliminate witnesses to law enforcement misdeeds? Or were they written by a man under the impression that a fierce firefight with desperate and well-armed, violence-prone extremists who had already murdered one officer was under way even as he flew westward, a man who believed he faced a uniquely dangerous and perhaps unprecedented situation?

A lot of people knew before August 21 that the Weaver family routinely carried weapons when outside the house. Did Richard Rogers know? Did he know he was signing a death warrant for people for doing what they did normally and had done for months without hurting or directly threatening people—at least until Friday, August 21?

Whatever the answers to these questions, those rules of engagement proved fateful. They dictated the character of the events that were to follow.

In the aftermath of the death of Marshal Degan and Sammy Weaver, law enforcement officials were blockading the dirt road to Ruby Ridge, evacuating people who lived in the area, building up a formidable force of people and weapons, getting the Red Cross mobilized to provide food for the base camp being put together on a meadow across the road from the Raus' house, perhaps a mile down a winding road from the Weaver cabin. Inside the cabin, the Weavers were assessing their own situation. Kevin Harris told Randy and Vicki that he had checked Sammy's pulse and there was no question the young boy was dead. The family wept together for awhile, then decided something would have to be done for Sammy.

Toward nightfall, Randy, Vicki, and Kevin went down the path toward the Y and found Sammy's body. They brought it up to the birthing shed. They stripped Sammy's clothes off, cleaned the body as best they could, wrapped it in a clean sheet, and left it in the shed for the time being. They would worry about burial later. Right now, so far as they knew, they were under siege from a force of federal officers of unknown size. They didn't know when or if they would leave the cabin again. Their options appeared to be limited.

At her home in Naples, Jackie Brown, Vicki Weaver's best friend, received a telephone call about noon. Brown lives with her husband Tony in a house back in another canyon—not quite as remote as the one in which the Weaver cabin is situated. Brown's father, who lives in Bonners Ferry, likes to listen to a police scanner radio, and he had heard activity in which the Weaver name was mentioned. "I think they're going after the Weavers," he told his daughter over the phone. Brown jumped in her car and headed for the Weaver home. When she got to the bridge that crosses Deep Creek, she found a Bonners Ferry police car blocking it, and the Bonners Ferry police chief telling her nobody was permitted to go past the bridge.

"I thought that was unusual for two reasons," Brown later said. "The Bonners Ferry police don't usually come that far out of town, and this was the chief, not a patrolman." Brown pulled her car to the side of the road near the bridge, got out, and watched. A trickle of residents started to come out of the area. They were being evacuated, all of them except the Rau family, Randy Weaver's closest neighbors—a relative term in this terrain—who had been cooperating with the U.S. Marshals Service for some time. Before long, traffic started to move in the other direction—police cars, vans, trucks filled with law enforcement officers, and by late afternoon a few military style vehicles.

Soon a small crowd had gathered. The police set up a roadblock with yellow crime-scene tape, and some of the residents who had been evacuated hung around the bridge, curious about what was going on. As the afternoon wore on, some local curiosity seekers joined them. They watched, amazed, as vehicle after vehicle, some clearly military in nature, some police cars, and some unmarked vehicles were admitted through the roadblock to the staging area opposite the Raus' home. Little reliable information was available to them, although it soon became known that some sort of confrontation between Randy Weaver, who was known at least by name to many locals, and federal officials had taken place.

Some of those gathered shouted at those inside the vehicles allowed through, demanding information. The law enforcement officials maintained silence as they crossed the bridge. Some of the official vehicles gathered at the Deep Creek Inn, across the road and about a quarter-mile from the roadblock. By late afternoon, Brown, who had regularly visited the Weavers, bringing food and supplies during the time Randy had been a fugitive, stood weeping next to an ambulance at the Deep Creek Inn.

At the federal staging area, Eugene Glenn, head of the Salt Lake City FBI office and on-site commander, and Richard Rogers, head of the FBI Hostage Rescue Team, deployed their forces. Scouts in camouflage, with silenced weapons, were sent to the area surrounding the Weaver cabin—to take note of and block possible escape routes, to set up hidden observation posts, to scout out good sniper positions. The communication with FBI headquarters took place amid an atmosphere of continuing activity, a certain amount of confusion, some squabbling over who had primary jurisdiction and should be in overall charge of the situation, and a great deal of tension. Rogers, after arriving on the scene, still believed this was potentially the most dangerous situation into which his team had been called. The federal officers knew Weaver was a trained Green Beret, and had almost certainly discovered from his service records that he was a crack marksman. They believed he had many weapons and plenty of ammunition and that he was desperate enough for almost anything to happen.

Down at the roadblock, people started arriving again early the morning of August 22, and the mood quickly became angry. Each new truck or vehicle that arrived to go to the federal staging area was now met with boos and curses rather than pleas for information. Word of Marshal Degan's death had been in the morning newspapers, and rumors were flying that one of the Weaver children had been killed. Other rumors—the whole family had been killed, the feds were planning to burn them out—circulated, as they will when a crowd has no reliable information and most of its members don't believe the few things the authorities do tell them. The few representatives from local newspapers in the local towns of Bonners Ferry, Sandpoint, and Coeur d'Alene were soon supplemented by reporters from the Spokane and Boise newspapers and the wire services. By the end of the day, the first TV trucks and vans, bristling with satellite antennas, were on the scene at the roadblock. Handmade signs—Feds Go Home, Baby Killers, Leave the Weavers Alone—started to appear among the crowd, which numbered about thirty by Saturday evening.

In the cabin, the mood was altogether more somber. One of the Weavers' children was dead, and the adults were convinced that the woods were probably full of armed federal agents. Nobody had come to the cabin to demand surrender or to begin negotiations for a surrender. The Weavers had spent years gradually convincing themselves that the federal government is the agent of evil, perhaps the very embodiment of the Antichrist, a ruthless and heartless adversary that wishes people like them no good. They wondered if the whole family would be killed before it was all over. They were convinced that the gun exchange in which Sammy had been killed was an ambush, that the marshals (or whoever the people were who had not identified themselves, except one shouted reference to "federal agents") had intended to kill Randy and perhaps other members of the family as well.

As the morning wore on, however, and as nothing seemed to be happening, they began to hope that it might be safe to go outside. Randy wanted to visit with his son's body and pray with it one more time before they had to decide what to do about burial. Nothing seemed to be stirring in the woods outside, although they had little doubt they were being watched. But, as Randy said later, he figured they would shout a warning or demand surrender before shooting.

On the hillside to the north of the cabin, on the mountain that towered over the bluff on which the cabin was built, the Sierra 4 sniper team, consisting of West Point graduate Lon Horiuchi, the Hostage Rescue Team's top sniper, and Dale Monroe, his "spotter," was dug in behind a rock near a tree. Horiuchi was armed (as were other snipers scattered in the vicinity) with a Remington 700 single-shot target rifle, equipped with a ten-power scope, especially designed for precision shooting at great distances, up to one thousand yards. The Horiuchi–Monroe team was about two hundred yards from the cabin.

The enhanced rules of engagement called for a warning or ultimatum to be given. But that's not how the next incident happened.

Toward the middle of an afternoon of tension and uncertainty, the Weavers finally decided to take a chance on going to the birthing shed to visit Sammy's body. About 6:00 P.M., Randy Weaver, Kevin Harris, and the Weavers' sixteen-year-old daughter Sara ventured out of the cabin. Randy and Kevin carried rifles, but Sara did not have a weapon. They walked toward the shed where Sammy's body lay.

As Randy Weaver lifted his arm to unhitch the latch on the door of the shed, with his back toward the hill where the snipers were hidden, a shot rang out and a bullet ripped through the soft flesh under his arm. All three ran toward the cabin. "I ran up to my dad and tried to shield him and pushed him toward the house," Sara later told *Spokesman-Review* reporter Jess Walter. "If they were going to shoot someone, I was going to make them shoot a kid."

Vicki Weaver, in the cabin, had heard the shot. Holding her baby Elisheba, she ran to the kitchen door, which had a window set into it, holding the door open to make it easier for the other three to get back into the cabin. "She was yelling, 'You bastards,' " said Sara. "And she was holding the baby."

Sara, Randy, and Kevin tumbled through the door Vicki was holding open. Then a bullet hit Vicki Weaver in the temple, went through her mouth and tongue, through the jawbone, and severed her carotid artery. She screamed—very briefly. Baby Elisheba screamed longer. Vicki Weaver fell to the floor on her knees. Blood pumped out of her severed artery. On the other side of the room, Kevin Harris, who was apparently hit by the same bullet that hit Vicki, and had suffered massive wounds in his arm and his chest cavity, was moaning. Within minutes, Vicki Weaver bled to death, kneeling on the floor and still holding her baby in her arms.

The most shocking and horrifying aspects of the siege of Ruby Ridge had occurred. But this horrific event was not to end for another nine days.

The Weavers' Road
to Ruby Ridge

How did a couple of patriotic, God–fearing, humble farm kids from Iowa, devoted to family and, according to old friends, quick to help others, end up in a deadly confrontation with U.S. government agents in a remote section of Idaho? It started as a conventional love story, but moved through a strange terrain of unusual beliefs, bizarre events, and strange turning points. Is this an emblematic American tale or a uniquely personal set of circumstances?

Randall Claude Weaver was born in the little town of Villisca, Iowa, on January 3, 1948, the only boy among four children born to Clarence and Wilma Weaver, a farming couple. In 1962, the Weavers moved to a two-story, gabled house on a road lined with elm trees in the heart of Jefferson, Iowa. Life there was much as it is in many small Midwestern towns. The Weavers were farmers, and the children were expected to help with the constant chores and projects typical on a family farm. When Randy got to high school, there were football games on Friday nights, parades from time to time, some time for play and recreation, and the constant chores typical of small farm life.

Randy was a small kid. He got decent grades in school, played Little League baseball, and loved cars. Everyone called him Pete.

Even as a young boy, Randy was unusually serious, especially about church. The Weavers were devout, perhaps even fervent, Christians. But Clarence Weaver always had trouble finding a church strong enough to match his own strong beliefs. By the time Randy was in high school, the family had attended evangelical, Baptist, and Presbyterian churches.

Some fifty miles to the north, Vicki Jordison, a year younger, was growing up in Fort Dodge and experiencing similar strong but sometimes conflicting feelings about church. Her mother, Jeane, was raised as a Congregationalist, while her father, David, was a member of the Reformed Church of Latter Day Saints, a Mormon branch. As it still does now, the Mormon church urged members to stockpile food, and many members then believed that with the cold war so ingrained in the fabric of our lives that they must be prepared because these must be the latter days. At Mormon services, the elders would sometimes prophesy, weaving together passages from the Bible and the Book of Mormon with current events. After services, David Jordison would sometimes sit in the living room with a Bible and a newspaper, taking his own stab at trying to foretell or make sense of today's events in the light of ancient prophecies.

Vicki Jordison was smart and pretty, with long, black hair and strong, piercing eyes. Her relationship with her father was especially strong. In high school, she was vice president of the Future Business Leaders of America and a member of the Pleasant Valley Pixies 4-H group. "She could make anything with her hands," said her younger sister, Julie Brown. "Vicki was the kind of person everyone liked and envied."

In 1966, Randy Weaver graduated from Jefferson High School and enrolled in Iowa Central Community College. As a part-time job to help out with college expenses, he drove a bus for the Fort Dodge School District. It was while Vicki Jordison was a senior in high school that she first noticed a bus driver she considered cute.

Randy had enrolled at Iowa Central Community College along with a friend from high school, David Luther. Fort Dodge is not a bustling metropolis, but like many college kids, Randy and

David managed to fill their time with activities beyond attending classes. They would tool around town in Randy's 1965 red Mustang. They went to parties and dances.

Vicki Jordison graduated from high school in 1967 and enrolled in Iowa Central Community College. Randy saw her at a dance and thought she was pretty. He asked friends about her, and learned her name, then asked her to dance. Soon she and Randy began dating.

But 1967 was a time in the history of the United States when it was difficult simply to attend college without being caught up in larger events. The war in Vietnam had been escalating for several years, and protests on college campuses were escalating, too. The year 1967 marked the "summer of love" festivities in San Francisco and student (and nonstudent) activism around the country. Young people were searching for meaning in all the controversy. Some harkened to the call to "tune in, turn on, drop out." Some went to Canada to escape the draft. Some volunteered to fight in Vietnam. Many were drafted.

Randy Weaver was not one of those who protested. He believed the war was being fought for a righteous cause, the defense of a small nation against communism, and he told friends that Vietnam was where his generation would be asked to prove itself. In 1968 he dropped out of college to join the army. "He wanted to fight. He was ready to go over," said John Milligan, a high school friend who was drafted about the same time Randy went in. Randy Weaver enlisted on October 9, 1968.

Randy went through basic training at Fort Leonard Wood in Missouri. He finished in the upper one percent of trainees in firearms proficiency and was trained as a combat engineer. He qualified for paratroop training in Fort Benning, Georgia. Then he volunteered and qualified for Special Forces, the Green Berets. During that notoriously tough training he learned to survive in the field with little food or equipment, and became an expert in handling weapons like the M-14 and M-16 rifles. He was promoted to sergeant. He was trained as a warrior and ready to go to Vietnam and fight.

He was assigned to Fort Bragg in North Carolina. Many soldiers would have been quietly pleased, and perhaps offered a little prayer of thanksgiving at being assigned relatively low-stress stateside duty instead of being shipped into combat in Vietnam. Randy Weaver wasn't one of those. Friends testify, in fact, that he became somewhat bitter at not getting the opportunity to test and prove himself. It was at this point in his life that he first started to consider the possibility that the government he had sworn to serve, the government that was fighting the good fight against communist aggression in Vietnam, the government that had trained him, at great expense, to be a proficient warrior, simply didn't know what it was doing. Thousands of young American men who wanted nothing to do with Vietnam were being sent over to fight in a war they understood little if at all, while Randy Weaver (and others) who wanted to go and test their mettle in combat were kept at home on training bases.

A growing sense of disillusionment was fed by the time he participated in an army intelligence drug bust at Fort Bragg. Randy noticed that the head of the operation turned in only half the drugs that had been seized in the arrest. Randy went to a superior, figuring the army would want to clean up its act and discipline the man. Instead, he was advised that he would be better off to keep his mouth shut and mind his own business. Years later, he told the story several times to Jackie Brown, probably Vicki's closest friend in Idaho during the good times (and later on when things got rough as well). She told it to others who asked about Randy Weaver, emphasizing that this incident seemed to have made a strong impression on Randy, forcing him to consider that the government and the army sometimes operated in a way that smelled of hypocrisy.

While Randy Weaver was learning whatever lessons were to be learned from his experience at Fort Bragg, Vicki Jordison was finishing college and having a couple of relationships that didn't lead to anything permanent or deep. She finished her two-year degree in 1969, and went to work at United Way. When Randy Weaver came home on leave from Fort Bragg, confident after completing his Green Beret training, wondering what Vicki Jordison had been up to. Vicki was happy to go out with him again. A few weeks later she visited him in Fort Bragg, and came home with the news that they were engaged to be married.

Despite his mild disillusionment, Randy was a good soldier, earning the occasional commendation or extra privilege for good performance. His service record is clean, characterized by good performance reports and no problems beyond the minor unpleasantness over the drug bust, which didn't appear on any written record. He received an honorable discharge on October 8, 1971, after three years of duty. He and Vicki were married in November. They moved to a small apartment in Cedar Falls, two hours east of Fort Dodge. Randy Weaver enrolled at the University of Northern Iowa to take criminal justice classes. His intention was to become an FBI agent.

But after a few months, the two newlyweds decided that they couldn't afford the continuing cost of the school, so Randy dropped out. He and Vicki began selling Amway products—home products, including cleaning products, soap, shampoo, and other items— which are sold through one of the most successful multilevel sales plans this country has seen, the pattern for dozens of others. Amway requires diligent work and sales ability. Some Amway people make very good money, some just get by, and many never get very much beyond being a steady customer. In this endeavor the Weavers established a pattern that would characterize their relationship in other endeavors throughout their marriage.

Vicki became the expert on Amway—the plan, the products, how they were formulated to be friendly to the natural environment, how Amway had made many marketers independent. Perhaps she was a little obsessive about knowing all that was to be known about something she had decided to spend her time doing. Randy, meanwhile, was the salesman, sometimes relying on Vicki for details, but making the pitch to potential customers and closing the sales. The two made a good team.

The Weavers kept up with expenses by selling Amway for some time. In 1973, however, Randy got a good job at the John Deere and Co. tractor plant in Waterloo, an industrial town adjacent to the more residential Cedar Falls, and opted for the regular paycheck and benefits package. Vicki got a job as a secretary at Sears, and the two began saving money. It wasn't long before they could afford to buy a house, paying about $26,000 for a white, ranch-style cottage, set back sixty feet on a busy street.

The young couple settled into a moderately prosperous suburban existence. Randy had enough money after the bills were paid to indulge in his love of gadgets and cars, motorcycles and boats. Vicki bought clothes and craft materials—she had always loved doing crafts. She hunted rummage sales and went about fixing up and decorating the house. The two had what they had thought they wanted from life—a stable, loving marriage, a house they could afford, and money left over for some luxuries. Yet they were spiritually unsettled.

In 1973, the counterculture was all around them as other young people searched for meaning in their lives in all sorts of colorful and rebellious ways. But Vicki and Randy were not attracted to a hippie lifestyle—quite the contrary. Their lives were centered around church and their Christian beliefs. Like Weaver's father, however, they found it difficult to find a church that suited them for long. Most of the churches they attended didn't seem serious enough or as deeply concerned about the prophetic messages of the Bible as they would have liked. Randy and Vicki were doing quite a bit of reading—not only the Bible, but other Christian books that seemed to explain how events foretold in the Bible might be working themselves out in the modern world.

One book that made a big impact on the couple was Hal Lindsey's 1970 best-seller, *The Last Days of the Late, Great Planet Earth*. The book concentrates on the last chapter in the Bible, Revelation, in which the apostle John relates the experience of a vision or dream in which details about how the world as we know it will end with the triumph of Jesus Christ over Satan in the final battle sometimes called Armageddon or the Apocalypse. Incorporating Old Testament prophecies, mainly from the book of Daniel as well, Lindsey makes a case that events of the day, especially developments in the Middle East, seem to coincide with biblical prophecies and suggests that the "end–times" could well be imminent. The book includes the scenario that Israel could be invaded by an Arab–African alliance, which would set off a chain of events that would trigger a nuclear war between the Soviet Union and the United States, arguably (depending on how you interpret some rather difficult passages) fulfilling some biblical prophecies about the events that would trigger the return of Jesus Christ and the end of this phase of the world as we know it.

To many Americans, taking the prophecies, primarily the apocalyptic prophecies found mainly in the Old Testament books of Ezekiel and Daniel, and the New Testament prophecies found in the book of Revelation and in some chapters of Mark and Matthew, as a guide to future events in our world today seems strange and alien. But these books contain passages that seem to speak of a time when Jesus will return to rule the earth, establishing peace and justice for at least a thousand–year period, known as the Millennium. A 1983 Gallup poll found that 62 percent of Americans had "no doubts" that Jesus will return to earth again. In the 1988 Gallup poll, 80 percent of the respondents expressed the conviction that they will appear before God on Judgment Day.

As University of Wisconsin history professor Paul Boyer notes in his 1992 book, *When Time Shall Be No More*, "Because an individual avows such beliefs when asked by a polltaker does not mean that they necessarily impinge vitally on his or her daily life." For some people, such beliefs are part of the background of their lives, while for others they become quite central. The 1970s and 1980s saw a resurgence of religious belief in the United States, led by evangelistic denominations and groups that tend to view the Bible as the literal word of God, or at least divinely inspired, and to take the prophecies in the Bible very seriously. *The Last Days of the Late, Great Planet Earth* was far and away the nonfiction best–seller during the decade of the 1970s, with 9 million copies in print by 1978 and 28 million by 1990. Other books have sold in the hundreds of thousands.

Down through the centuries, Christian believers have disagreed about the significance of the apocalyptic sections of the

Bible. St. Augustine disagreed with those who expected an imminent second coming of Jesus and made a case for reading these sections more allegorically than literally. The poet John Milton (1608–1674) expected the final cataclysms foretold in Revelation to occur during his own lifetime or shortly thereafter. People have viewed many European wars, the downfall of the Turkish Ottoman Empire, the American Revolution, World War I, the establishment of the state of Israel, and the cold war as precursors of the last days. As Professor Boyer puts it, having noted that such eminent Americans as J. P. Morgan, John D. Rockefeller, and Cyrus McCormick signed an 1891 proclamation urging support for a Jewish state in Israel drafted by a strong prophecy believer: "Whatever else may be said of it, belief in an imminent Second Coming, in punishment of the wicked, and in a Millennium when the injustices of the present age will be set right, cannot be dismissed—in the Middle Ages, in the pre–World War I era, or in the late twentieth century—as merely the desperate creed of the disinherited."

As Hal Lindsey notes, however, many people will read scriptures or a book like *The Last Days of the Late Great Planet Earth* in an extreme or "aberrant" way. Lindsey doesn't counsel collecting weapons or taking to the hills; indeed, his central belief is that when the last times come (which he still expects to happen reasonably soon), Jesus himself will rescue believers in a powerful and supernatural way known as "the rapture." There's little or nothing, says Lindsey, that we can do to speed up or slow down the day of Jesus's Second Coming or to affect (beyond believing and repenting, which will affect how we as individuals are dealt with) how it will all unfold. But for many people, such counsel appears too passive.

In 1973, Egypt invaded Israel, beginning an Arab–Israeli war and an Arab oil embargo that noticeably increased tensions around the world (many Americans still remember the lines at gas stations, the occasional well-publicized fights, the rumors of oil tankers waiting off the Atlantic coast but not delivering oil). Vicki and Randy were convinced that these events were in line with biblical prophecies and couldn't understand why mainstream churches didn't show much sense of urgency. Shouldn't they be preparing their members more intensively for the possibility that the end of the world foretold by priests and prophets of old was imminent? If the churches weren't going to do the job, Randy and Vicki—along with millions of other Americans during that time—decided that they and their family—Sara, their first child, who was born in 1976—would be ready.

By the time Vicki and Randy attended a barbecue in 1978 hosted in Jefferson by a group of Randy's old high school friends, they had been thinking about such matters for quite some time. They had watched hours of religious television, especially programs hosted by Jerry Falwell and Jim and Tammy Faye Bakker. They studied the Bible together, interpreting it prophetically or discussing what certain passages might mean in light of today's events as Vicki had heard Mormon elders do when she was a child.

Baby Sara was two years old in 1978. Vicki had something in common with other high school friends and acquaintances who were starting families. The talk of mortgages and making ends meet was familiar to all. But Vicki and Randy Weaver had more dramatic news to tell. She had had a recurring dream or vision, and lately Randy had been having similar dreams as well. In the vision, which they perceived as occurring sometime in the future but they weren't sure exactly when, the Weavers were living in the mountains with Sara and two other children yet to be born, with the biblical names Samuel and Rachel. Below them, in the valleys, biblical prophecies of troubles and tribulations were being fulfilled; people were dying. The Weavers, in their mountaintop retreat, were for awhile safe from these tribulations. But soon some evil seemed to be chasing the family. The world was coming to an end around them, but the final outcome between the family and the forces seeking their destruction was still unknown.

David Luther, a high school and college friend of Randy's, listened politely. Later he told an interviewer: "Everyone had taken different paths then. I think my impression was just that they had found something to get into."

In July 1978, the Weavers had a second child. They named the baby boy Samuel.

Once the Weavers got into something, they tended to jump into it with both feet. They attended Cedarloo Baptist Church, on a hill above their house, and kept reading books and tracts, and watching religious television. There was a Sambo's restaurant a few blocks from the house, and when he wasn't working, Randy would sip coffee in the booths and hang around the bar, quietly but firmly warning customers to repent. Before long, a group of born-again Christians (those who accept Jesus Christ as their personal savior and are "born again" in Him) was meeting informally in the coffee shop, and studying the Bible with an emphasis on prophecies about the end-times. Then they formed a regular Bible study group of about ten people that would meet in peoples' basements.

Mike Roethler, former police chief of Cedar Falls, got to know Randy Weaver at Sambo's. He was especially impressed when he brought a homeless man there one day and asked the group of Christians meeting there if they couldn't do something to help the man. While the others hesitated, Randy pulled out a twenty-dollar bill and gave it to the man. From that point, Mike Roethler became more friendly with Randy.

The incident with the homeless man was not an isolated incident of impulsive generosity. Randy seemed to attract people who needed help. He was always bringing people around to the house—"strays" as Vicki came to call them—for a meal, some clothing, even a place to live for awhile. Even after one of the strays stole money from the family, Randy continued to bring others.

The Cedar Falls Bible study group evolved into a group mostly made up of what are called legalists—people who believe that present-day believers of European descent (or in some cases, Americans of diverse backgrounds) are the descendants of the lost tribes of Israel, and that present-day believers in the "New Israel," which is America, are called upon to follow the detailed laws laid down for the children of Israel in the Old Testament book of Leviticus, the much more detailed follow-up to the Ten Commandments, which most Orthodox Jews endeavor to follow today. The Weavers continued in the pattern they had followed when they had earlier sold Amway; Vicki was the reader, the student of religious tapes and biblical passages, and Randy was more the salesman, the preacher. They became the acknowledged leaders of the group and began sharing some of the visions they had been having with others. They became increasingly convinced that almost all organized religions had strayed far away from the truth of the Bible, and became especially convinced that Roman Catholics and Jews had strayed so far away as to become enemies of God—or Yahweh, as they were coming to refer to Him in the Old Testament fashion.

They claimed, however, not to harbor any racial animosity. Randy was friends with a black co-worker at John Deere who was also something of a car enthusiast. Vicki once warned a friend of the family, Carolee Flynn, not to trust neo-Nazis and other extremists.

During this time, in the late 1970s and early 1980s, Vicki Weaver said she was having visions from God about a cabin in the woods, a place where they would be safe from the apocalyptic and horrific events associated with prophecies about the end-times, which they were becoming increasingly convinced were imminent. Soon Randy was talking about visions of a cabin and outbuildings on a mountain bluff. Sometimes the visions included a confrontation between the Weaver family and some evil forces.

One day in 1980 Randy walked into Vaughn Trueman's gun shop in Cedar Falls, the Bullet Hole. He asked about what kinds of weapons a person would need to protect a cabin in the woods. He started telling Trueman about some of the reasons he was thinking about such a cabin, and soon convinced the proprietor to come to his Bible study sessions. "He led me to the Lord," Trueman would later tell a newspaper reporter. "He and I cried together many times . . . I saw healings and heard things you can't explain." Sometimes, during those intense study and prayer sessions, people would speak "in tongues," in unknown languages, as the Bible says in Acts some of the early apostles did. Speaking in tongues is considered a special gift of the Holy Spirit, especially among fundamentalist believers. In the late 1970s, however, groups of charismatic Christians, some of whom spoke in tongues or participated in other special "anointings" of the Holy Spirit, were coming forward and forming groups or study sessions in many mainline churches. Charismatic or spirit-centered groups could and can be found among Presbyterians, Episcopalians, Lutherans, Methodists, and Roman Catholics.

Sometime after the visions of a mountain cabin started coming to Vicki and Randy Weaver, the group was studying Matthew 24, in which Jesus speaks of the Apocalypse. According to the King James Version, Matthew 24: 3–22:

> And as he sat upon the mount of Olives, the disciples came to him privately, saying, Tell us, when shall these things be? and what shall be the sign of thy coming, and of the end of the world?
>
> And Jesus answered and said unto them, Take heed that no man deceive you.
>
> For many shall come in my name, saying, I am Christ, and shall deceive many.
>
> And ye shall hear of wars and rumours of wars: see that ye be not troubled: for all these things must come to pass, but the end is not yet.
>
> For nation shall rise against nation, and kingdom against kingdom: and there shall be famines, and pestilences, and earthquakes, in divers places.
>
> All these are the beginnings of sorrows.
>
> Then shall they deliver you up to be afflicted, and shall kill you: and ye shall be hated of all nations for my name's sake.
>
> And then shall many be offended, and shall betray one another, and shall hate one another.
>
> And many false prophets shall rise, and shall deceive many.
>
> And because iniquity shall abound, the love of many shall wax cold.
>
> But he that shall endure unto the end, the same shall be saved.
>
> And this gospel of the kingdom shall be preached in all the world for a witness unto all nations; and then shall the end come.
>
> When ye therefore shall see the abomination of desolation, spoken of by Daniel the prophet, stand in the holy place, (whoso readeth, let him understand:)

Then let them which be in Judaea flee into the mountains:

Let him which is on the housetop not come down to take any thing out of his house:

Neither let him which is in the field return back to take his clothes.

And woe unto them that are with child, and to them that give suck in those days.

But pray ye that your flight is not in the winter, neither on the sabbath day:

For then shall be great tribulation, such as was not since the beginning of the world to this time, no, nor ever shall be.

And except those days should be shortened, there should no flesh be saved: but for the elect's sake, those days shall be shortened.

But he that shall endure unto the end, the same shall be saved.

Then let them which be in Judaea flee into the mountains.

For then shall be great tribulation . . . But for the elect's sake, those days shall be shortened [emphasis added].

Those words resonated. It began to seem more and more clear to Vicki and Randy Weaver that those who would endure to the end should flee into the mountains. Perhaps that was the meaning of the visions . . . that God was telling them that they were called to move to the mountains, to be among the elect, those who would endure the time of tribulations and the abomination of desolations.

Since the early days of Christianity, some believers have been convinced that the end-times were near, that the tribulations would come upon the world in their own lifetimes and find most of the world napping, unaware, or scornful. Millennialist or apocalyptic-oriented Christians today have pointed to the nuclear standoff between the Soviet Union and the United States, the reestablishment of the state of Israel, Arab–Israeli wars, the Arab oil embargoes, and famines and pestilences in Africa or Asia as signs that the days foretold by the prophets must be near.

It is not necessarily inevitable that it should be so, but some fundamentalists with an apocalyptic bent are vulnerable to the preachers of anti-Semitism. Some Christians down through the ages have found reasons to hate or fear Jews, and anti-Semitism has at times been woven into genteel respectability in the United States and Europe. Some modern fundamentalists, on the other hand, noting the important role the reestablishment of Israel plays in some end-times prophecies, have become some of the closest allies of the state of Israel in the American political mosaic, being generally so pro-Israel as to be almost "philo-Semitic." Anti-Semitism is not solely a characteristic of the political right; indeed, it is possible that the most virulent anti-Semitism these days comes from what is usually identified as the political left, from black militant or Arab nationalist groups.

Nonetheless, it is almost impossible to delve into the literature of apocalyptic fundamentalism without encountering material that denigrates Jews—even though most modern fundamentalists specifically reject such expressions—ranging from expressions of regret that the Jews have given up their birthright and become corrupt, to theories that the Jews are the spawn of Satan and sworn enemies of God and His people.

Among the persuasions to be found in this mixture are a variety of beliefs commonly called the Christian Identity movement. Its modern roots can probably best be traced to Anglo-Israelism or British-Israelism, a doctrine developed into a movement in Great Britain in the nineteenth century, which held that the British Anglo-Saxons are the descendants of the ten lost tribes of Israel, and that these people are to be the legatees of the biblical promises to the chosen people. Anglo-Israelism was, if anything, a philo-Semitic belief, with its adherents viewing themselves as brethren, close kin, to modern Jews. W. Herbert Armstrong's Worldwide Church of God has its roots in British-Israelism and is free of anti-Semitism. As Syracuse University political scientist Michael Barkun explains in his recent book, *Religion and the Racist Right*, however, sometime after the doctrine made its way to the United States it became entangled with anti-Semitic and cult beliefs in the 1930s and emerged as a distinctive belief system with (usually) strong anti-Semitic overtones after World War II.

The essential Christian Identity belief is that the modern European races, not just the British, and those descended from them are the ten lost tribes of Israel, although the range of white European nationalities who are the real chosen people may vary. Those ten lost tribes of Israel disappear from biblical accounts of the history of Israel around the time the Israelites were defeated, enslaved, and taken into captivity in Babylon. Some versions of Christian Identity hold that the Israelites were corrupted by pagan beliefs or by Satan himself during the time in Babylon, and were fully corrupted when their descendants returned to Jerusalem. The religion practiced after the sojourn in Babylon, they say, was not the religion of the fathers who had been chosen by Yahweh, but a corruption of the true faith. That's why the Pharisees and others in Israel resisted Jesus's message. Others hold that those tribes led into captivity were already corrupted.

Christian Identity has no central church, no central doctrine. Its beliefs or variations of them can be found in scattered independent churches and organizations around the country. The few people who have tried to study it seriously place the number of believers in the United States at anywhere from 2,000 to 50,000. Some branches of Christian Identity view other races with hostility, while other branches say that Yahweh has a place for them and calls for them to be proud of what they are, but that the purity of the white race is to be maintained, that those white people who understand their true status as the children of Israel should separate themselves from unbelievers and from people of other races. Randy Weaver stresses that as a sympathizer of the Christian Identity movement he is not a white supremacist (one who believes whites are superior and that people from other races should be subjugated, in some cases killed) but a white separatist (one who wants to separate himself from people of other races, but doesn't necessarily wish any ill upon them).

Christian Identity churches tend to celebrate the Jewish Sabbath rather than Sunday, claiming that the use of Sunday as the day of worship is a corruption of the message or a mistake. Traditional Christian holidays like Christmas and Easter are often seen as adaptations of pagan celebrations and held on the wrong days anyway, and therefore a corruption of the true belief. Halloween celebrations are seen as a species of devil worship, and not to be participated in. Many Christian Identity followers believe that the Old Testament laws, including the dietary laws like not eating pork or shellfish or rare meat, are to be applied to them, as well. Some take the admonition against graven images in the Ten Commandments as prohibiting not just images that could be worshipped, but images like photographs, paintings, and even certain kinds of furniture. The Leviticus admonitions about what things are clean or unclean are taken as literally as Orthodox Jews take them today.

Christian Identity adherents make up a small proportion of fundamentalists and an even smaller portion of Christian believers taken altogether. The National Council of Churches, comprised mostly of mainstream Protestant churches (Methodist, Episcopal, Presbyterian, Lutheran, and others) has adopted a resolution to the effect that Christian Identity is not a valid expression of Christian beliefs. And most Christian Identity believers believe the National Council of Churches has strayed too far from biblical truth to be viewed as a valid exponent of true faith.

Christian Identity beliefs, like many minority persuasions of the right and left wings, are often accompanied by intense interest or belief in what are widely called conspiracy theories: any of a panoply of convictions revolving around the idea that a tight, generally malevolent, extremely influential, highly organized, and preternaturally effective group of conspirators or allies, operating behind the scenes, either off the periscope of conventional journalists (or in league with them), are plotting to rule the world, to influence or manipulate world events, to gather all effective power into their hands, and to generally make life miserable for poor or middle class people who are just trying to live their lives, raise their families, and strive for a little happiness. Dire events like the birth of communism, world wars, depressions, and other political cataclysms have been attributed to a coterie of international bankers (often with Jewish names like Rothschild), to the ancient sect called the Bavarian Illuminati founded by Adam Weishaupt, the Freemasons, the Catholics, the International Zionists, the Rockefellers, the Federal Reserve Board, the "insiders," the Council on Foreign Relations, the Trilateral Commission, the Skull and Bones club at Yale, and the Bilderberger Group. These mysterious, crafty, and almost infallible plotters are today often said to be planning for a New World Order under a malevolent and totalitarian United Nations or some new group that might emerge (or perhaps exists now, unseen and unknown to the poor, manipulated masses), to subvert the independence of the United States or to manipulate the money supply so as to enrich themselves and impoverish decent people.

Gradually, by reading books, holding Bible study sessions, listening to tapes, and living in an environment dominated by people with similar beliefs, the Weavers came to their own rather eclectic version of Christian Identity beliefs. Later, Randy would prefer the term Israelitish Identity.

Vicki and Randy Weaver weren't the kind of people to make their beliefs simply an intellectual game. Beliefs and ideals, if they were true, if they came from Yahweh, weren't simply to be discussed, but to be acted upon. The Weavers quit trusting Jerry Falwell and Jim Bakker, who seemed too noncommittal on certain issues, and sold their television. They stopped eating pork and shellfish and started following other Old Testament laws. When Sara's first-grade class had a dress-up party for Halloween, they viewed it as satanic and pulled her out of school. And, increasingly, they talked about leaving Iowa to move to some place in the mountains. Through Vaughn Trueman's gun shop, Randy collected the ten or so guns he thought he would need to protect himself in the mountain wilderness—handguns, shotguns, and mini-14 rifles—and thousands of rounds of ammunition. Vicki and Randy visited an Amish community to study self-sufficiency and learn about dehydrating fruits and vegetables, to see what supplies would be needed to make most of the family's clothes, toys, and other needs.

In 1982, Randy rented a ballroom at the Cedar Falls Holiday Inn for a talk from conspiracy buff and former "warlock" John Todd. Todd wore a pistol to the talk and kept glancing over his shoulder because, he said, he was sure somebody wanted to kill him. He said he knew the real story of John Kennedy's assassination. John Todd's visit and rumors that Weaver was collecting firearms brought Weaver to the attention of the police, but former chief Roethler, then Randy's friend, said there was no serious investigation. Still, the police interest somehow came to Weaver's attention, and he and several of his friends became almost persuaded their phones were being tapped, that they were being spied upon or set up. Like a lot of Americans in the early 1980s, the Weavers had become increasingly discontented with the government's public schools, and wanted to teach their children at home. But home-schooling was not legal in Iowa at the time.

One of Randy's "strays" also wanted to go to the mountains, a co-worker at John Deere named Shannon Brasher who had moved into the house. He had a friend in Idaho who told him it was a good place for people who believed as they did. When Brasher's girlfriend, however, described the kind of Bible studies that went on at the Weaver house to her parents, they became concerned that she was getting involved in a cult.

In 1982, a third child was born to Vicki and Randy Weaver, a girl they named Rachel.

In 1983, Weaver and his ideas came to enough prominence that the *Waterloo Courier* newspaper sent a reporter to talk to the Weavers and to Shannon Brasher. They told the reporter that the weapons they had collected were strictly for self-defense. But they made it clear that they were determined to carry out their plans of moving to the mountains. "We're servants," Vicki was quoted as saying, "and what the Lord tells us to do we will do. He has told us we have to pull up our roots and leave. I don't want to leave my home, but if we are obedient, then He will protect our children."

In spring 1983, after some sessions of praying alone in the church, Trueman concluded that the Lord was telling him that he shouldn't make the trip to the mountains. Brasher wasn't going either, at least not with the Weavers. Randy had come across him and his girlfriend sleeping together in the house and had thrown them out. But the Weavers still wanted to make the trip.

In August 1983, the Weavers sold their house for about $50,000. On a humid August night, they packed clothes, guns, and food around their plain furniture into the moving truck they had traded for their car. Next door, their neighbor and friend, Carolee Flynn, cried as she watched from her window. The Weaver children, serious seven-year-old Sara, five-year-old Sammy, who had broken his arm falling off a truck earlier in the week, and little baby Rachel, had been staying with her while their parents packed and prepared to leave. But now the children would be leaving with their parents—heading west, but neither the Weavers nor their friends and relatives in Iowa knew exactly where they were headed.

"Vicki said the Lord told her not to take any images with her," Flynn said. "She got rid of all her pictures and anything that had a flower or any image on it. I had to switch dishes with her because mine didn't have a pattern on them. She lost fifteen pounds getting everything ready to go. But there was no stopping her. The Lord had spoken. The night they left was like a death."

Randy and Vicki still weren't sure where they were going to go. They had ruled out Colorado, but Montana was under consideration. So was Idaho, in large part because the state allowed home-schooling. They drove west for two hours and stopped for a visit with Vicki's parents and her brother in Fort Dodge. Although Vicki's family had questioned what seemed to them like a harebrained scheme, this time they just said good-bye. Lanny Jordison hugged his sister and watched as she and Randy climbed into the moving truck's cab.

The Weavers drove west, through Colorado and through Montana. They looked for property in Montana, but considered most of what they looked at too expensive. They continued into Idaho, and on up into the northern panhandle country. Finally, after two weeks of searching, they found the piece of property they wanted, in the Selkirk Mountains, southwest of Bonners Ferry, near Naples. "When we drove up to see it," wrote Vicki in a letter to

Carolee Flynn, "Weaver couldn't believe it. It's just what the Lord showed him it would look like." That was the property on what came to be known as Ruby Ridge, overlooking Ruby Creek and the Kootenai valley. On a clear day, you can see parts of Idaho, Montana, and Washington, a view that, as *New York Times Magazine* writer Philip Weiss describes in a January 8, 1995, article, "could make you weep for the power of God's hand."

The Weavers started building a cabin almost immediately, mostly from scrap lumber they were able to salvage—a two-by-four frame with an uninsulated plywood shell. It took several years to complete the cabin and its outbuildings. They began living on the property early on, from the time the basic shell was completed around March 1984, but didn't stay there all the time. Sometimes, especially in winter, they would rent a house in Naples, down in the valley area. They taught their children at home, making sure they were well-schooled in evolving Christian Identity beliefs.

When the Weavers came to Idaho, other Identity Christians were moving there, too. "There are a lot of people here who say they're Christians and that the Lord sent them here," Vicki wrote in one letter back to Iowa. "They just smile and don't think we're crazy at all!" One separatist who befriended the Weavers says that at first the Weavers distanced themselves from the white supremacist or white separatist ideas many Identity Christians held. "They weren't radical at all, but they liked some of the ideas," he said. But Randy and Vicki always strove to be more knowledgeable and devout than those around them. Slowly, as they talked to other people in similar circumstances to them, they began to accept more white separatist ideas.

Vicki wrote newsy letters back to friends in Iowa. After an earthquake hit the Pacific Northwest in October 1983, she wrote that she believed the event was "the birth pangs of Matthew 24. You can expect more of them and more Grenadas." She believed the Russians were about to invade the United States.

As they became more intense in their beliefs, the Weavers also maintained some of the open ways they had shown in the Midwest. Randy continued to attract "strays." One was Kevin Harris, from Washington State, who at the age of seventeen was having trouble at home. He came to live with the Weavers in 1984, and lived with them off and on for long stretches of time over the next eight years.

In addition to the Identity Christians scattered throughout the hills, living apart and keeping to themselves, there were some concentrations of believers and/or activists nearby. In Hayden Lake, just outside Coeur d'Alene, some fifty miles south of Naples, was a forty-acre encampment of a group called the Aryan Nations, a, depending on which source you consult, white separatist or white supremacist group. The group has Christian Identity leanings and vague ambitions to transform the United States into an all-white country or to secede from the United States and form a white-dominated country in the Pacific Northwest, led by Richard Butler. Butler had attended, in Los Angeles, a church called the Anglo-Saxon Christian Congregation, founded by Wesley Swift, a one-time Ku Klux Klan organizer who had founded the church and a related Christian Defense League in the 1950s. When Swift died in 1970, Butler proclaimed the new church he then founded, Church of Jesus Christ Christian, to be the direct successor to Swift's church. During the 1970s, he moved the church to the property he had bought in Idaho, and called the result the Aryan Nations. The group holds a summer camp called the Aryan Nations World Congress each summer, at which a good deal of anti-Semitic, anti-black, and anti-homosexual literature is handed out, some weapons practice takes place, and courses on urban guerrilla warfare have been offered.

Beginning in 1979, the group began a program of recruiting prison inmates with warnings about how the white race was in danger of being exterminated or crippled by all the "alien" forces who ruled America. Richard Butler is seventy-five now and not in the best of health, but ten or fifteen years ago, quite a few of his activities alarmed many people. Some people in the Coeur d'Alene area thought the best approach was a live-and-let-live attitude. But some residents formed the Kootenai County Task Force on Human Relations in 1981, after a restaurant owned by a Jewish family was defaced with swastikas. There was conflict between these relatively liberal activists and Aryan Nations members and supporters—one task force leader's house was bombed as he sat in the living room. The task force publicized Aryan Nations beliefs and supported the prosecution of one Aryan Nations member, a Hitler devotee who issued various threats against a young white man whose mother had married a black man.

Whether the group called the Order, founded by Robert Matthews in 1983, grew directly from the Aryan Nations or simply had ties of sympathy is not entirely clear. Some say that insofar as Matthews had religious beliefs, they were supposedly based on Odinism, the pre–Christian religion of the Norse people. But some Aryan Nations members became involved in the Order. This self–proclaimed revolutionary group was involved in a series of violent crimes—bank robberies, bombings, some killings—in 1983 and 1984, including the brutal shooting of Alan Berg, a liberal, Jewish talk show host in Denver. Many members of that first group were prosecuted and sent to prison, with the FBI being especially prominent in the investigations that led to arrests. A second Order, with closer ties to the Aryan Nations, emerged in 1986, setting off some bombs in the Coeur d'Alene area and threatening further destruction. An interagency task force was involved in investigating and prosecuting this group, one that included the FBI, the Bureau of Alcohol, Tobacco and Firearms (BATF), the Secret Service, the sheriff's office, and the state police.

The Weaver family, on at least three occasions in the late 1980s, attended summer encampments at the Aryan Nations. There, under the larches and maples and alders, the children played while the adults, many decked out in neo–Nazi regalia, talked politics and attended classes and workshops. Butler sometimes gave out leaflets talking about "a nigger shoot." The Weavers had mixed feelings, being sympathetic to some of the causes espoused at these congresses. But they made a point of not joining Richard Butler's church. One of his neighbors, Gene Hopkins, says that Randy told him "that place was full of crooks and convicts."

James Aho, a sociologist at the University of Idaho at Pocatello, spent years attending meetings and interviewing believers for his 1990 book *The Politics of Righteousness: Idaho Christian Patriotism*. Most of the subjects he interviewed remained anonymous and he respected their preferences in the matter, especially where his major concern was with statistical results of questionnaires and polls. He remembered meeting Randy Weaver at a World Aryan Congress conference at the Aryan Nations in the summer of 1986. Randy Weaver was not one of the subjects about whom Jim Aho gathered very detailed information, but he did do an interview. He remembered that Randy had just moved from Iowa and was very enthusiastic about how well he and his wife were getting their lives together and crystallizing their beliefs. He was especially proud of how smart and pretty his wife was.

The Weavers became close to Tony and Jackie Brown, and soon Vicki and Jackie became best friends. "The Weavers were a curious blend of religious holy rollers and tactical soldiers of God, plus reactionaries," Tony Brown said in a recent interview with Philip Weiss of the *New York Times Magazine*. "Weaver believes the Bible tells people of the knowledge and that they should expound that knowledge to their brothers and sisters. Form a body of true believers. Part of their life was sharing with people what they thought. They weren't pushy, but they thought a remnant or small group of people would bring about a new kingdom. Over the sheep type."

"The sheeple," his wife Jackie expanded. Referring to Randy, she also says, "He was an all–American guy to the core. An angry, orientated farmer's kid."

In 1985, Randy and Vicki Weaver became involved in a still–mysterious dispute with some Naples residents named Sam Wohali, Terry Kinnison, and Scott Rohloff. As many friends have related, Randy could be volatile and argumentative, sometimes opening his mouth and speaking before fully considering how his thoughts would affect others. This sometimes led to disputes and breaches of friendship that could get nasty. Afterward, Randy would sometimes be befuddled that other people were angry with him, but he usually became convinced that any unpleasantness was entirely the other person's fault. Whatever lay behind it, in 1985 Randy and

Vicki Weaver filed the following curious document in the Boundary County Courthouse:

Thursday, February 28, 1985

To Whom It May Concern:

This statement is a legal affidavit. We hereby make a public notice on this date, that we, a married couple, Randall Claude and Vicki Jordison Weaver believe our physical lives to be in jeopardy. We are the parents of three small children whose lives are also in danger.

We are the victims of a smear campaign of our character and false accusations made against us to the Federal Bureau of Investigation and the United States Secret Service by some local residents who have a motive for my decease. The local residents are named:

Mr. Sam Wohali

Mr. Terry Duane Kinnison

Mrs. Nina Kinnison & Family

Mr. Scott Rohloff

We have had conversations with and explained our innocence and the motive for this conspiracy to have myself and my wife murdered by the federal government to the following officials:

Mr. Ron Smith, sheriff, Boundary County

Mr. Joe Allen, special investigator, Boundary County Sheriff's Office

Mr. Ken Weiss, FBI Agent, Coeur d'Alene

Mr. Glen Curtis, FBI Agent, Coeur d'Alene

Mr. Bob Andrew, U.S. Secret Service, Spokane, Washington

Mr. Ron Moellring, U.S. Secret Service, Spokane, Washington

I make legal and official notice that I believe I may have to defend myself and my family from a physical attack on my life.

There are witnesses from Deep Creek, Idaho, who heard this conspiracy being planned and who can be subpoenaed to give testimony. The U.S. Secret Service apparently does not care if I am innocent or not. There is evidence of my innocence but they continue to try to build an illegal case based on fraudulent evidence because they don't like my political beliefs or religious faith.

My accusers set me up as a criminal member of Aryan Nations. They accused me of having illegal weapons. They accused me of saying I was going to assassinate the president of the United States and the Pope. Very possibly a threatening letter was sent to the president with my name or initials forged. My accusers hoped that the FBI would "rush" my home with armed agents hoping I would feel the need to defend myself and thus be killed or arrested for "assault on a federal official." Fortunately bad weather (the first part of Feb. 1985), witnesses to this plot, and our God, the Lord Jesus Messiah, King of Israel, prevented a disaster.

These accusations are all lies and can be proven as such. My accusers have heard of FBI confrontations in North Idaho on the radio and in the newspapers and thus got their ideas for my death.

Randall C. Weaver (signature)
Vicki Weaver (signature)
[fully notarized Feb. 28, 1985, and officially filed on the same day with the Boundary County Court. File # 01463339]

A little later, a Naples resident named Steve Tanner, with whom Randy Weaver had worked on construction projects, accused Randy Weaver of stealing $30,000 Tanner had entrusted to him. Randy always proclaimed his innocence, but years later Steve Tanner was still bitter about the incident and convinced that Randy Weaver had stolen his money and acted dishonorably, and that he had behaved dishonorably toward Terry Kinnison and others as well.

Tanner was able to show people an undated, handwritten receipt saying: "I, Randy Weaver, sold Terry Kinnison one-half interest in 20-acre parcel located on Ruby Creek in section 23. No deed has been transferred, for sum of $3,000," with signatures by Randy Weaver as "seller" and Terry Kinnison as "buyer." There was also a notice filed by Terry Kinnison and his wife Nina in the Boundary County Court, in March 1985, to the effect that Terry Kinnison and his wife had advanced $3,000 to Randy and Vicki Weaver in exchange for a half-interest in the property on Ruby Ridge.

In 1988, Randy Weaver ran for sheriff of Boundary County on a platform of restoring power to the local people and protecting them from the federal government. "The federal income tax is the most cunning act of fraud that has been perpetrated against Americans since the introduction of paper money and the credit system," he declared. He didn't say what he would be able to do about it as sheriff. He did hand out "get out of jail free" cards as a campaign tactic, promising that people arrested for nonviolent crimes would get a second chance from him as sheriff.

Tony Brown says that although he didn't really expect to win, Randy Weaver was quite serious about making the race. He wanted to use the campaign, says Tony, as an educational vehicle to tell people about the primacy of the county in the scheme of things. About 70 percent of Boundary County is federal property, and disputes had arisen over enforcement of land–use policies (some arising from the way the federal government chooses to enforce the Endangered Species Act) on both public and private land in Boundary County. The county has power to refuse to enforce such laws, Randy contended, and federal agents should be required to get permission from local law enforcement before moving against county residents. He lost the race, getting about 10 percent of the vote in the Republican primary—perhaps in part because reporter Dean Miller of the *Spokesman-Review* reprinted some racist statements Randy made in unguarded moments. Friends and family believe his open advocacy of his radical ideas was a good part of what led the government to focus on him.

There were always a lot of bikers at the Aryan World Congress meetings. At a 1989 meeting, Randy Weaver met a biker named Gus Magisono, five feet eleven inches, 245 pounds, in a black Harley T-shirt and black boots. Magisono was especially friendly to Randy, and kept in touch with him after the congress was over. By the fall of 1989, Randy was especially pressed for money, finding it hard to get enough together by doing odd jobs for farmers, and cutting and selling wood. Magisono said he could make some money selling guns. He expounded to Randy what he thought the mistakes the Order 1 and Order 2 groups had made, and said he was in touch with people who planned to do it better but they needed sawed-off shotguns. Randy had never sold a sawed-off shotgun in his life, and Magisono testified later that he was reluctant about breaking the law. But eventually Magisono talked him into it. Randy pulled his pickup next to Magisono's car, and pulled out his Remington pump-action shotgun from a case. Magisono touched the barrel at about the thirteen-inch point. "About here," he said.

The federal law restricts the sale of shotguns with a barrel shorter than eighteen inches, although it can be done by a federally licensed firearms dealer who pays a transaction fee of two hundred dollars.

There is dispute about whether Randy Weaver actually delivered the two shotguns sawed off a week later—for which Magisono paid him three hundred dollars, with one hundred dollars more promised later—or whether Magisono later sawed them off himself. Magisono later said that Randy told him he hoped they would be resold to inner-city gang members, so more black people would be killed.

But the burly biker to whom Randy Weaver sold those two shotguns wasn't really named Gus Magisono. His real name was Kenneth Fadeley. The Bureau of Alcohol, Tobacco and Firearms had busted him earlier for gunrunning and offered him clemency if he could sign up more people to do undercover work or arrange more busts.

Eight months later came the offer that would be difficult to refuse. Randy Weaver was approached by two BATF agents, who told him he could avoid arrest for the sawed-off shotgun charge by agreeing to spy on the Aryan Nations in Hayden Lake. They told him they didn't have a warrant, but that they had incriminating tape recordings of his dealings with Fadeley-Magisono. They told him he could lose his truck and his property if he were arrested and convicted on the firearms charge.

But Randy Weaver refused to become a government spy. Instead, he phoned the Aryan Nations to warn them that the feds were trying to infiltrate the organization. They told him that they were well aware of that, that they knew there were several agents in the organization now. They could usually recognize an agent, they said, because they tended to be militant in an exaggerated way, always urging others on to violence or some outrageous action.

Vicki Weaver also sent the following letter to Richard Butler at the Aryan Nations:

June 12, 1990

> TO: Aryan Nations & all our brethren of the Anglo Saxon Race.
>
> This evening at approximately 6:15 P.M. at Deep Creek, Id. two U.S. Treasury agents (Gunderson & Barley) followed Randy & Vicki Weaver to the home of friends. (They were driving a Forest Service Rig.) When the woman of the house went out to her yard, they told her they wanted to talk privately with Randy. She thought they were locals—he went out.
>
> They threatened him with federal firearms charges & prison time and the confiscation of our truck. They said they didn't have a warrant yet. They said they want him to join their team and that he must come alone to the Courthouse in Spokane tomorrow at 11:00 A.M. Randy said, "NO WAY!" THEY SAID, "OH YES, THAT'S THE WAY WE DO THINGS."
>
> This letter is to let you know what is happening. Randy & I live on County Rd. 132 at the 3,000 ft. level. Randy & I & the children are ready to stand for the truth and our freedom! We cannot make deals with the enemy. This is a war against the white sons of Isaac. Yahweh our Yashuya is our Savior and King. The decree (Genocide Treaty) has gone out to destroy Israel our people. If we are not free to obey the laws of Yahweh, we may as well be dead!
>
> I don't know if they'll push this or not it may be a royal bluff. They claim they have "taped conversations" that incriminate Randy. Nothing else but accusations. We have decided to stay on this mountain, you could not drag our children away from us with chains. . . .

Six months after that, in December 1990, Randy Weaver was indicted on federal firearms charges. On January 5, 1991, the Weaver family composed the following letter directed to those who enforce the laws of the federal government:

"*And judgment is turned away backward. And justice standeth afar off. For truth is fallen in the street. And equity cannot enter. Yea, truth faileth; and he that departeth from evil accounted as mad; and Yahweh saw it and it displeased him that there was no judgment.*"

We, the Weaver family, have been shown by our Savior and King, Yahshua the Messiah of Saxon Israel, that we are to stay separated on this mountain and not leave. We will obey our lawgiver and king.

You see the mighty One of heaven knows his people. You are servants of lawlessness and you enforce lawlessness. You are on the side of the One World Beastly Government. Repent, for the Kingdom (government) of Yahweh is near at hand.

Choose this day whom you will serve. As for me and my house—we will serve Yah-Yahshua the King.

Whether we live or whether we die we will not obey your lawless government.

On January 17, 1991, Randy and Vicki were driving down the rutted, winding road leading from their property—some stories report that they were headed into town for supplies, others that they had been alerted that somebody might need help along the road. They saw a pickup truck with a camper shell parked on the bridge, blocking it, that traversed a small stream near the Raus' house. The hood was up and a man and a woman, apparently in trouble, were looking at the engine. Randy and Vicki stopped to help. As Randy began to look under the hood, a pistol was pressed against his neck. Federal agents piled out of the camper shell, and he was soon surrounded. Vicki was thrown facedown into the slush by the side of the road and searched. The agents took a small handgun she had in her purse (it was later returned, since it was legal and legally owned). Randy was arrested and taken to the Boundary County jail. There he posted a $10,000 bond, with his property as surety. He returned home.

Randy's court date was originally set for February 21, then reset for February 20 for the convenience of the BATF. But the official notice sent out by probation officer Karl Richins to the Weavers had the date of March 20. Richins later testified that when it became evident that Weaver had been sent the wrong date for his trial and notified his superiors, he was taken off the case and told not to correct the mistake.

When Weaver did not show up for the court date on February 20, Assistant U.S. Attorney Ron Howen, who was handling the case, went before a grand jury on March 14, six days before the date Randy Weaver had been given in the notice mailed to him, and sought to have Weaver declared a fugitive from justice, subject to arrest. A deputy court clerk testified that he told the judge in the weapons case, Harold Ryan, about the mistake regarding court dates before Ryan went ahead and signed the arrest warrant for Randy Weaver for failure to appear.

From the tone of letters that had already been sent from the Weavers to various authorities—including another letter from Vicki Weaver dated February 3, 1991, saying the Weavers would not bow to the government and peppered with phrases like "the tyrant's blood shall flow" and "war is upon the land"—it is quite possible that the mix-up over dates mattered little. Randy and Vicki Weaver had apparently decided that Randy would not show up for court under any circumstances. Randy later told friends that he was convinced he would be railroaded, that government witnesses would lie under oath, and that he would be convicted whether guilty or not. Considering that he had been entrapped by an undercover agent into sawing off the shotguns in the first place, that might not have been an unreasonable expectation.

For the next sixteen months, the Weavers did stay on their mountain, growing and canning their vegetables, and hunting for meat. Since Randy was the one with the arrest warrant hanging over him, on most days he didn't even venture out of the cabin.

Friends who knew of their plight sometimes brought them food and other supplies, or brought their children up to spend time playing with the Weaver children. From time to time, the Weavers were reminded that they were being watched. Helicopters or airplanes would sometimes fly very low over the property.

On one occasion, on April 18, 1992, Geraldo Rivera tried to interview them and flew a helicopter very near the cabin. Some newspapers wrote that on that occasion the Weavers had fired on the helicopter. But the only evidence for that was a "popping sound" a cameraman heard over a headset tied to a boom microphone hanging outside the helicopter. Some friends, the Nicklaus family, were visiting the cabin that day, and they joined the Weavers in denying the story. Karmin Nicklaus recounted the story:

> *My stepdad and I had gone up there. We're sitting there in the house and this helicopter began flying over real low. The kids had ran outside, to see if it was the same helicopter that had been flying over days before. Everyone went outside to look except Vicki and I. I watched from a picture window; it was flying real low. I mean, you could distinctly see what everybody in the helicopter was wearing. A guy was hanging out of the window with a video camera taking pictures. It circled overhead a few times and then hovered for a few minutes. It then dove down toward Deep Creek, hovered for a few more minutes and left.*
>
> *There were no gunshots, and I could see everyone outside; no one pulled their gun. This all took place on Saturday, April 18 and on the following Thursday [April 23] the* Spokesman–Review *reported that the Weavers shot at the helicopter. When I read that I immediately got ticked-off because I knew it was a lie.*

The Nicklauses were one of several families that visited the Weavers during the time they stayed at Ruby Ridge, sometimes bringing food and supplies. On one stormy day, Karmin came to visit but was not greeted, as was usually the case, by a family member at the rope gate. She wondered what was wrong. As she walked up the driveway toward the cabin, no dogs barked and nobody came out—most unusual. As she approached the porch, she wondered if perhaps they were all dead, or if she was walking into some strange situation. Should I yell to get their attention so as not to get shot? she wondered. Or should I just knock? When she knocked, Vicki opened the door and began weeping. "Do you know," asked Vicki as the tears trailed down her cheek, "how long it's been since someone has knocked on my door?"

It was a tense but tolerable existence. The Weavers had spent most of the last several years at the cabin anyway. They were constrained in that they weren't able to go to town for supplies as they had done before, but friends brought supplies. They wavered between the hope that the feds would tire of the game and give up, go after somebody else, and the fear that sooner or later it would all end in a confrontation from which none of them would escape alive.

Karmin Nicklaus said later that the Weavers didn't expect the battle of nerves to end well. "They believed the feds were going to come up there and take them out," she said. "The feds showed them that when they came up with the big helicopters. Vicki knew the day the feds set up their microwave cameras that they were going to come up there and take them out. They believed that they would all be killed."

In October 1991, a new baby daughter had been born to the Weavers, whom they named Elisheba. The baby was born in what the family called the birthing shed, some fifty feet from the cabin. Following their understanding of Old Testament laws about cleanliness and uncleanness, Vicki and Sara would stay in the birthing shed during their menstrual periods, and the shed rather than the cabin itself was considered the proper place for childbirth.

By August 1992, baby Elisheba was ten months old. Her young life, indeed, the lives of the whole family, were to change drastically and ineradicably.

How the Government Got to Ruby Ridge

A FTER RANDY WEAVER REFUSED TO BECOME AN UNDERCOVER INFORMANT for the Bureau of Alcohol, Tobacco and Firearms, it was at least possible to imagine that the government could have left him alone. He had, after all, been entrapped into sawing off and selling two cheap shotguns to an undercover informant. The agency could have let the matter drop or kept the tapes of the encounter as something to hold over his head at a future date. Randy and Vicki Weaver may have espoused radical ideas, but they had chosen to express them by withdrawing from society. As such, they hardly posed a serious danger to other people.

But something about the refusal to become an informant, perhaps coupled with the fact that Randy had become a public figure in a minor sort of way by running (and losing) for sheriff of Boundary County, made the BATF decide that this man, perhaps as an example to others, should be pursued. So the indictment was brought against him and, as we have seen, the Weavers decided to stay at their mountaintop home on Ruby Ridge rather than appear in court. Whether they would have made this decision before a warrant was issued had they known the correct date might be debated. But once they decided, that was it.

At this point, the BATF might once again have backed off a bit, or put the Randy Weaver case on a back burner. The firearms charge was, after all, a misdemeanor, not a felony, and while failure to appear is treated seriously in most courts, it's not the same as a felony. The BATF could have notified the local sheriff that a federal fugitive was living in the area, asked him to apprehend him when it was convenient, without necessarily going too much out of his way. From the standpoint of public safety, the Weaver family hardly represented a serious threat. They had placed themselves in self-imposed exile, perhaps more isolated from the rest of northern Idaho society (except for a few friends) than if they had actually been in jail.

But going after white separatists and purported right-wing crazies had been good for Ron Howen. And while some Idaho residents were inclined to be sympathetic to a Bible-spouting Christian Identity believer who distrusted and hated the government, not all Idaho residents were. Some residents thought such people were dangerous and should be controlled or neutralized, and not everybody who thought that way was a stickler for due process or the concept of a person being innocent until proven guilty beyond a reasonable doubt.

Shortly after Richard Butler established the Aryan Nations encampment near Hayden Lake, as chapter 2 outlines, a group of Kootenai County residents formed the Kootenai County Task Force on Human Relations. In addition to speaking out, exposing, and denouncing the kind of ideas Butler taught at his services and sessions, they also demanded action from local, state, and federal law enforcement agencies—often demanding not only law enforcement activity in response to overt actions, but response to threats and sometimes even to the very hatefulness of the kind of rhetoric Butler and his followers employed.

When the militant group calling itself the Order went on its spree of violence in 1984, culminating in the murder of Denver talk show host Alan Berg, a lot of people in Idaho and elsewhere in the Pacific Northwest changed their attitudes about these white racist, white supremacist, or white separatist groups. It was one thing to be aware that a leader was gathering followers with inflammatory rhetoric. That might even be viewed as quaint or colorful, a tribute to the real diversity you get when you allow freedom of speech. And even a swastika painted on a building or store once in awhile, while certainly frightening to those victimized and evocative (probably intentionally so) of a much more horrid persecution that might follow, could also be viewed from a certain perspective as childish vandalism from people who might bear watching but were essentially displaying their own infantilism more than real menace.

But the Order robbed banks, planted bombs, and killed people. Its leader Robert Jay Matthews wrote: "I realized that white America, indeed, my entire race, was headed for oblivion and turned the tide." He acted. There is some evidence that federal undercover agents pushed this existing militancy toward ever more violent and outrageous actions, in part to make sure that arrests would lead to convictions on charges serious enough to warrant serious prison time, and in part to create fear and distaste for such groups among the general public. But whatever the internal dynamic of the Order's spree of crime and violence, by the time Robert Matthews was killed in a fiery shootout with police and federal agents on Whidbey Island in Washington, the Kootenai County Task Force on Human Relations was no longer alone in its concern and determination to do something about what was perceived as a growing number of white separatists and white supremacist and neo-Nazi groups in northern Idaho.

In a word, Nazis in the neighborhood weren't good for business, especially when they were perceived as likely to be violent. Developers and newspaper publishers began to rally around the cause of controlling the racists. In 1991, the task force produced a documentary called *Stand Up to Hate Crimes* celebrating the group's first ten years of existence. In it, Marshall Mend, a local real-estate developer, explains: "We had three problems. One, our community's image was being destroyed by the media; two, we saw minorities being discouraged from moving to the area; three, we saw these same articles encouraging racists, bigots, and other hate groups to move into our area."

Taking on Robert Matthews's Order in 1984 was essentially an FBI operation. In 1986, when the Order 2 was formed, an interagency task force involving the BATF, Secret Service, and state and local police agencies was mobilized.

The task force was also active on the state level, working with state legislators in Boise to get anti–hate crime laws passed. Incidents of racist graffiti in Coeur d'Alene declined dramatically. Whether out of the commonplace desire for something new or because of a growing perception that they were not welcome or comfortable in that part of Idaho, many of the angriest young men at the Aryan Nations started to move to the flats of Sanders County in Montana, some sixty miles away, where yet another popular leader was gathering followers together.

All this drew attention from respectable opinion outside northern Idaho. In 1987 the mayor of Coeur d'Alene traveled to New York City to accept an award for civic achievement and advancement of humanitarian causes from the Raoul Wallenberg Committee of the United States (Wallenberg being the Swedish diplomat who used his access to diplomatic papers to save thousands of Jews from being sent to Nazi extermination camps during World War II and was almost certainly captured and imprisoned by the Soviets after the war).

Meanwhile, the FBI was beefing up its forces and its capabilities throughout Idaho, but especially in the north. It was convinced that this white supremacist phenomenon was serious and potentially dangerous business. Wayne Manis, former special agent–in–charge of the FBI's Coeur d'Alene office, says he believes that the agency was up against "without a doubt the best organized and most serious terrorist threat that this country has ever seen."

A little apocalyptic and overstated? Shortsighted and without much of a historical memory? Almost certainly. But if that was the mindset among federal officials during the late 1980s, when they perceived themselves as cleansing northern Idaho from these dangerous "terrorists," as they watched Randy Weaver run for sheriff on a promise to try to keep the federal government out of the county and encourage people to resist the Internal Revenue

Service, and as they watched him decide not to show up for court—knowing, if they did even a tiny bit of homework, that he was a former Green Beret trained in demolition weapons and tactics and a topflight marksman—then perhaps—perhaps—we can understand the response to a citizen who had never before been arrested or shown any inclination toward lawlessness failing to appear on a misdemeanor weapons charge.

Assistant U.S. Attorney Ron Howen, who had been involved in the Order 2 prosecutions, and the prosecution of an Idaho tax resister named Claude Dallas and not had his career damaged by the association, went to a grand jury to get a warrant for Randy Weaver's arrest on failure to appear in court on March 14, 1991, six days before the date on the notification Weaver had received. In the later federal court trial, Karl Richins, a probation officer, testified that when it became evident to him that Randy had been given the wrong date, he (Richins) was taken off the case and told to do nothing to correct the mistake. Ronald Haberman, court clerk, testified that he told Judge Ryan of the mistake in court in February 1991, but that the judge went ahead and issued the bench warrant anyway.

Now the authorities had the legal justification (whether it would have stood up in court if they had simply arrested Randy Weaver and brought him in or not is another question) they needed to arrest Randy Weaver. The question was, How were they to accomplish the arrest?

About this time, Vicki Weaver sent a letter to Howen's superior, U.S. attorney for Idaho Maurice Ellsworth, filled with apocalyptic biblical quotations and promising that the Weaver family had no intention of obeying the lawless government. Ellsworth turned it over to the U.S. Marshals Service, the federal agency charged with tracking down and bringing in federal fugitives for trial, for a "threat assessment."

The threat assessment on the letter concluded that it was a veiled threat against the government in general, not a threat against any particular individual, and therefore of a low level of interest. But the U.S. Marshals Service went beyond the letter to provide a threat assessment on Randy Weaver himself, supposedly based on an investigation.

The U.S. Marshals Service is the descendant of the federal agency that provided the fabled marshals to so many towns of the Old West. It is, in fact, the oldest branch of law enforcement in the federal government, founded by George Washington in 1794.

Today, the duties of the 2,700 or so deputy U.S. marshals are to protect the federal judiciary, escort federal prisoners, seize the assets of convicted felons, escort sensitive military equipment, maintain the federal Witness Protection Program for witnesses who testify against organized crime figures and need to establish new lives with new identities, and to capture fugitives from justice. It is in this latter capacity that the marshals had been keeping track of Randy Weaver and trying to figure out how to bring him into court or otherwise deal with him.

Most of the duties of the U.S. Marshals Service are relatively prosaic and routine. But Jeff Fahey, who researched the agency in preparation for playing hard-charging but vulnerable and human Marshal Winston McBride on the ABC show *The Marshal*, says, "They're the cowboys of the law enforcement agencies, the loners, and they like to feel that way." Maybe it has something to do with the legendary character of the U.S. marshals of the Old West. Perhaps that helps to explain, a little bit, what happened at Ruby Ridge.

Deputy Marshal Ron Mays, in his threat assessment, said he had heard that Randy Weaver was growing marijuana and had been involved in bank robbery. The report spoke of heavy-caliber guns mounted on tripods around the "compound." It said Randy was a member of the Aryan Nations, that he had threatened the life of the president, and that he was likely to shoot officers on sight. It said the fortified house had blackout curtains, that Randy had spoken of fleeing to Canada. Randy and his dog were said to patrol the perimeter of the property regularly, looking to shoot officers. It said that after having had Special Forces training, Randy had become a loose cannon, that he had planted explosives on his property and in places surrounding it that could be detonated from remote locations. Mays also said he had heard that the Weaver residence was isolated, with a two-hundred-yard clearing on all sides to make it difficult to approach.

None of these stories were true, but the report created a picture of a dangerous, desperate, well-prepared man who could prove very difficult to bring to justice. Whether the U.S. Marshals Service really believed much or any of this or not is almost impossible to determine at this juncture. To give them the benefit of the doubt, they proceeded as if they believed it was a valid assessment.

Marshal Ron Mays was told by Idaho's chief deputy inspector of the U.S. Marshals Service, Ron Evans, not to initiate any contact with Randy Weaver or with any other agency without getting prior approval. Mays later testified that he went ahead and initiated contact with the BATF, the Veterans Administration, and the Boundary County sheriff after preparing the assessment, so as to coordinate a plan. Meantime, however, Gerard Hoffmeister, the court-appointed attorney who had been selected to represent Weaver on the weapons charge, was telling Evans that he believed he could persuade Weaver to surrender himself voluntarily. Evans sent a memo to this effect to his boss in Washington, D.C., Antonio Perez, chief of enforcement for the U.S. Marshals Service and the number-three man in the agency.

Deputy Marshal Dave Hunt, perhaps anticipating that Weaver would not show up, had been leading surveillance of the property even before the February 20 court date. He and others tried to determine who everybody was who visited the Weavers, by recording the license numbers of cars or other vehicles that drove up the lone road to the property. Hunt testified later that his purpose was to try to identify who knew the Weavers, so he could try to convince some friend or acquaintance to cooperate in getting Randy to turn himself in, and in fact he did contact several people over the next few months. Although he acknowledged that he didn't understand the Old Testament quotes Vicki had used in her letters, he said later that the letters caused him to believe that Randy was very dangerous.

In March 1991, Marshal Hunt enlisted Ruth Rau and her husband Wayne in the surveillance operation. The Raus, the Weavers's nearest neighbors—living about a mile away, by the side of the only road leading to the Weaver property—had already cooperated with the BATF, beginning around August 1990. Although the Weavers and Raus had a reasonably cordial relationship for about five years—their children played together, and on occasion they would have one another over for dinner—the relationship turned very sour in about 1989. The Raus claimed that the Weavers had cheated them in some transaction, and that when called on it, they turned hostile, having the kids march up and down the dirt road in front of the Rau house in Nazi uniforms, issuing threats, and engaging in petty vandalism. The Weavers claimed the Raus were to blame. Whatever the truth of the matter, the neighbors were feuding, and the federal agents took advantage of the fact.

The Raus, like most families back in the woods, didn't have a telephone. So the U.S. Marshals Service arranged for one to be installed. They paid the Raus about $1,200, including a $500 charge to have the phone line brought about a quarter–mile to the house from the nearest trunk line. The marshals also paid for a $1,500 insurance policy on the Rau house because they and the Raus feared that the house might be burned. The marshals installed what is called a pin register on the phone to record the numbers of all incoming and outgoing calls.

Most of the other people approached by Dave Hunt or other marshals wanted nothing to do with the feds, although some of them agreed to transmit messages. One of Randy's friends was asked what it would take for Randy to surrender voluntarily. He reported back that Randy would surrender if the BATF would admit it was wrong to set him up on the original weapons charge, if they would return the pistol they had taken from him when he was first arrested, which had never been returned, and if the sheriff would give him a written apology for calling him a paranoid in court.

The marshals wanted criminal charges filed and warrants sworn for the whole family, especially for Vicki Weaver, whom they considered the leader and the real strength of the family. On several occasions, they urged that friends who brought the Weavers food and supplies could and should have criminal charges of aiding and abetting a fugitive brought against them. But Assistant U.S. Attorney Ron Howen refused. He doubted any charges could be brought against Vicki that would have a chance of sticking, and he said that people bringing supplies to the cabin could argue that they were supporting the family, not Randy himself.

It has been reported that Hunt offered a friend of Randy's named Alan Jeppeson $20,000 to help arrest Randy, and Jeppeson told Hunt to go to hell, but Hunt denied this story in court. Hunt did testify that he offered an acquaintance of Randy's named William Grider, whom he had been using to carry messages to Randy in hopes of getting some kind of negotiations going that would lead to surrender, $5,000 to help him arrest Randy. Grider refused, but according to Hunt said that for that kind of money he could kill Randy and tell Hunt where to find the body. Hunt didn't know if he was serious, and didn't follow up on the offer, nor did he tell any of his superiors about the conversation.

Dave Hunt at length became convinced that these efforts to try to reach Randy and arrange a surrender through a third party were going nowhere. He later testified that he came to believe that Randy was manipulating his go–betweens, that he really didn't care about his cabin or the safety of his family, that he wasn't sincere in negotiating. In October 1991, baby Elisheba was born to the Weavers, with Randy assisting in the birth. Marshal Hunt at that point decided that with negotiations making no headway, he would let the family endure another winter in their remote and uninsulated cabin, and see if Randy's attitude had changed by the next spring. Another factor was that with winter coming on—a serious season in those northern latitudes—continued personal surveillance would be very difficult.

Spring came, and Randy Weaver's attitude, insofar as Marshal Hunt could determine through various third parties, hadn't changed substantially. Hunt thought it was time for a more aggressive approach. He wanted to bring in the electronic surveillance unit of the U.S. Marshals Service, with cameras and other devices, so that he and other agents wouldn't have to spend so much time spying in the hills, and so that there would be less chance of anyone being discovered. For the expensive electronic surveillance equipment to be activated, however, the Weaver situation would have to be declared a "major case." Thus, on March 11, 1992, Ron Evans, chief deputy marshal of Idaho, submitted a formal request to the electronic surveillance unit back in Washington, D.C., for authorization to declare the case major and bring in the high-tech gadgets.

Obviously, in the eyes of those most intimately involved with it, the Weaver case had become something more than simply a misdemeanor weapons charge arising from an entrapment scenario. Hunt and others later testified that they had never seriously considered simply walking up to the front door of the cabin with a warrant, knocking, and demanding that Randy Weaver come with them. They said their assessment was that the risk of an armed, potentially violent confrontation was too great.

Deputy Marshal Jack Cluff, also working on the Weaver case, had earlier in the spring gotten a message to Randy Weaver, through a third party, to the effect that if he did not surrender, the marshals would come to the cabin, arrest both him and Vicki, and take the children. That hadn't seemed to make much of an impression. Displeased with informal negotiations that seemed to be going nowhere, Howen issued an order that any future negotiations would have to be conducted through an attorney rather than through various acquaintances.

So, on March 3, 1992, a few days before the formal request for electronic surveillance equipment, Marshal Cluff and Ron Evans drove up the road leading to the Weavers' property to look for sites to install cameras to monitor all traffic up and down the road. As they moved onto the Weaver property, they were approached by three people and a big yellow Labrador dog. The three were carrying hunting rifles. The oldest male, whom the agents recognized from photos as Randy Weaver, told them they were trespassing and asked them what they wanted. Quickly coming up with a cover story, they said they were looking for property to buy. Randy told them to leave, go into town and find a real-estate agent, and then come back. A piece of property adjacent to the Weavers'—beyond even the dirt roads and without any access to water or electricity—had been on the market for several years without attracting any legitimate prospects, although a few potential buyers had heard about it and inquired at the Weaver cabin and been told very much what Randy told the federal marshals. All reported that the Weavers were friendly and helpful.

In the subsequent federal trial, Evans testified that he couldn't tell if the dog was vicious or friendly, because all he could see from the car was its back. Gerry Spence, Randy Weaver's attorney, then showed the marshal a transcript of Evans's previous testimony to the grand jury. In that testimony, he had said that the dog was running alongside the vehicle nipping at the wheels. He had also said he was unable to determine if the girl, who was one of the three people, was carrying a gun, while in the actual trial he was sure all three had guns. "Which time were you telling the truth?" asked Spence. "Both times," replied Evans.

The meeting to decide whether to escalate the Weaver situation to "major case" status took place either March 26 or March 27 at the U.S. Marshals Service headquarters in Washington, D.C. It took fifteen upper-echelon people, including a public information specialist (aka public relations person) several hours to make the decision. When G. Wayne "Duke" Smith, number-two man in the Marshals Service, was asked at the subsequent trial whether it usually took fifteen people and a public relations specialist to declare a case a major case, he was not required to answer.

Beginning in April 1992, the more aggressive, electronically enhanced surveillance of the Weaver family began in earnest. Led by site inspector Art Roderick, a team of six marshals was assigned to the Weaver case. The team rented a condo at a ski resort, figuring that at a resort their comings and goings would not attract undue attention. Just to be sure about privacy, however, they rented an entire building. They had their equipment shipped to Spokane, Washington, across the state line and some ninety miles from Naples, so as to be out of the immediate area. The equipment included electronic listening devices, video cameras, a pin register for recording telephone numbers, bullet-proof vests, full camouflage gear, two automatic weapons, and other guns.

The six-man team, consisting of marshals Art Roderick, Dave Hunt, Warren Mays, as well as Mark Jergensen, electronic specialist William Hufnagle, and emergency medical technician Ron Libby, got busy. They set up electronic spying sites with video cameras on two sides of the Weaver house, one two-thirds of a mile from the house and the other about three-quarters of a mile away. They arranged to have a Medi-Vac helicopter, with a crew of six, made available from Fort Lewis, Washington. Using the helicopter and later a Cessna 172 airplane that they rented, they made several flyovers of the Weaver property to take aerial photographs. There was a house next to the Rau home from which Bill Grider (whom Dave Hunt had tried to use as a go-between with Randy Weaver) had some time before been evicted by the IRS. The marshals took over this house and made it a field headquarters. They had a phone line run to this house and installed a generator for electrical power.

Whenever the marshals went onto the Weaver property or anywhere near it, they were armed and in full military camouflage regalia. Even so, they seldom went very close to the house for fear of being detected. On one occasion, they brought a million-candlepower infrared light for night work, but when they went toward the house after midnight, they couldn't get the light to work. They sometimes rented a commercial helicopter for aerial reconnaissance, out of concern that the same aircraft shouldn't be flying over the area repeatedly.

The Medi-Vac helicopter the team acquired was specially equipped with what was called a "jungle penetrator," a basket and hoist device for rescue in locations where it was not possible to land. Later in the trial, Marshal Roderick testified that he had requested the medical helicopter because of the roughness of the terrain, which created the possibility that one of his agents would fall or otherwise need assistance. His request document, however, said that the primary reason for requesting the chopper was "because of the high risk of violence." The two medical officers on the team were specially trained in tactical operations.

During the months between April and August, the six-man team went over dozens of possible scenarios for apprehending Randy Weaver and his family. At one time, Roderick had wanted to use an XR-5000 "stun gun," which would incapacitate Randy and require that he be taken to a hospital in Spokane by the Medi-Vac helicopter. Then, because the fugitive would be in another state, a removal hearing would be required, during which time no release or bond would be possible.

The agents surveyed a landing zone above the Weaver property where the chopper could sit until it was needed in some kind of tactical operation. They ascertained that the yellow dog almost always slept outside the cabin, which would create a problem for nighttime reconnaissance or operations. They ran three thousand feet of wire from the house where they had set up the generator to power their surveillance cameras. Later, they bought solar panels and batteries to power the cameras.

The marshals considered cutting the Weavers' water line—the cabin got water from a nearby spring and a gravity-feed pipe system—and forbidding friends to take any food or supplies to the cabin. They had ascertained that because of the Weavers' religious beliefs, women having their menstrual cycle were considered "unclean," and the Weaver women spent those days in the birthing shed. They devised a plan to sneak up on the shed while sixteen-year-old Sara was there alone, "capture" her, and turn her over to the county sheriff. The fact that there was no arrest warrant for Sara somewhat complicated that scheme.

Marshal Roderick had discovered that when real-estate prospects showed up, the Weavers were usually friendly and helpful. So he devised a plan to have marshals pose as real-estate prospects. It included having five two-man teams in full camouflage hidden in various spots near the property in case they were needed for backup. When a man and a woman, who seemed obviously nervous, did show up to ask about property, as Vicki later told her friend Jackie Brown, Randy was not in sight. But Vicki, elaborately polite and solicitous, invited them in for coffee. They hesitated, looking around, but finally came in. Vicki was, if anything, overfriendly, and full of information about real estate, but she just didn't know where her husband was just then, probably puttering around somewhere. The more obviously nervous the prospects seemed to be, the sweeter and more helpful Vicki acted. Later, she had a good laugh with Randy and with Jackie about the whole episode.

All told, some 160 hours of videotape were shot, showing members of the family outside, doing chores, playing, tending the vegetable garden, and almost always carrying guns, including the older children. Later on, during Randy Weaver's trial, the prosecution and defense reached a bargain about the use of this tape. The prosecution and defense both had access and got to show the jury one full day of edited video. The prosecution showed scenes with the adults and children carrying guns. The defense showed the family playing and doing chores, greeting a visitor with a daughter with whom the Weaver children then played, riding bicycles, batting rocks with a stick. The prosecutors asked the marshals what percentage of the time the adults were carrying guns. Gerry Spence asked what percentage of the time the big yellow Labrador's tail was not wagging.

All this surveillance was costing the taxpayers about $13,000 a week. Sooner or later, something would have to come from it. Antonio Perez, chief of the U.S. Marshals Service Enforcement Division (number-three man at the agency), testified that a tentative plan had been drawn up by June, but that implementation was delayed because Henry Hudson was only acting director of the service, and the top brass didn't want to put the plan into operation until he had completed his Senate hearings.

Exactly what this plan consisted of is still not known. Antonio Perez insists that his explicit orders were that there should be "no confrontation." Some notes were later produced at the trial that talked about the necessity to "take out" the dog. The federal authorities seemed to have little faith or trust in local officials to be cooperative. A note, apparently from Perez, was introduced into evidence that said "Approach Sheriff!!! Offer him some money." And the six officers who had been on the Weaver case for months were supplemented by marshals from the U.S. Marshals Service's Special Operations Group.

Henry Hudson was confirmed by the U.S. Senate as director of the U.S. Marshals Service on August 12, 1992. Nine days later, six men from the U.S. Marshals Service, armed and decked out in camouflage, entered Randy Weaver's property early in the morning, on what officials of the agency still insist was only a reconnaissance mission.

CHAPTER 4

The Standoff

THE SHOOTING AT THE Y, SOME FIVE HUNDRED YARDS FROM THE WEAVER cabin, on Friday, August 21, 1992, precipitated a standoff that was eventually to capture nationwide attention. On that first day, a U.S. marshal had been killed, as well as a young boy who had just turned fourteen. On the second day, the boy's mother was killed and his father and friend were wounded. The standoff that ensued was not to be resolved for another nine days. The local media covered the story as fully as possible, given that they were dependent on FBI spokespeople for most of their information. The standoff at Ruby Ridge led most television newscasts in the nearby towns of Portland, Oregon, Spokane and Seattle, Washington, and Coeur d'Alene and Boise, Idaho. The story was front-page news in most area newspapers, with Marshal William Degan's death having just been announced. In other parts of the country, the story was generally relegated to the back pages.

During those nine days, Randy Weaver, Kevin Harris, Sara Weaver, Rachel Weaver, and Elisheba Weaver remained in the small cabin, with Randy getting better and Kevin getting worse. The cabin was surrounded by federal agents, deployed in the surrounding woods, eventually with lights shining day and night, making it difficult for the Weavers to get regular sleep. About a mile down a twisting dirt road, on the meadow across the road from the Rau home, was the federal command center, an ever-growing "tent city" that eventually housed at least four hundred agents and dozens of vehicles. Eugene Glenn, FBI special agent-in-charge at the Salt Lake City office, was in overall charge as on-scene commander, with Richard Rogers commanding the FBI Hostage Rescue Team. Down at the roadblock, where Ruby Creek Road intersects the main paved road, was a crowd of reporters, protesters, friends of the Weavers, and people keeping vigil. From the roadblock area, the protesters could see the Weaver cabin, on a ridge about three miles away, but the cabin was too far away to see with any reliability just what was going on there. Some people stayed at the roadblock for the entire eleven days of the Weaver event, while many more came and went.

At both the federal staging area and the roadblock, portable generators were set up, at first by the federal agents and later by some of the protesters or vigil-keepers who had decided to stay for the duration. Powered by gasoline motors, they furnished a constant whining background noise for the ensuing standoff, sometimes making it necessary to shout to be heard.

Saturday, August 22: Day Two

During the day, before the shooting at the cabin in the late afternoon, the roadblocked bridge seemed almost crowded as military and Red Cross vehicles moved into the "staging area" near the Rau home, soon informally dubbed "Federal Way." Armored personnel carriers, automatic weapons, helicopters, explosives, and a mechanical robot fitted with a telephone were among the equipment brought to the remote meadow. Before long enough law enforcement personnel, from the Idaho State Police, the Bonner County Sheriff's Department, the FBI, the Bureau of Alcohol, Tobacco and Firearms, the U.S. Marshals Service, and the Idaho National Guard had arrived so that two hundred people were on duty per shift, twenty-four hours a day.

Down at the roadblock, the number of concerned neighbors and friends grew also—to about thirty by the end of the day Saturday—and their mood became increasingly angry and impatient. Signs and flags began to appear.

Among the angriest was Bill Grider and his wife Judy, who had been acquaintances of the Weavers for several years. The Griders had been among those who had brought food and supplies to the Weaver family during the eighteen months that Randy Weaver was officially classified as a fugitive. The relationship seemed to have cooled in the last months before August, probably because Bill Grider was carrying messages from the U.S. Marshals Service to Weaver, and Weaver began to wonder which side he was really on. Once the Ruby Ridge confrontation had begun, however, Bill Grider became one of the most enthusiastic and aggressive protesters. That led some other protesters, like Bill Rich, an entrepreneur from Portland, Oregon, who was a local coordinator for Populist Party presidential candidate "Bo" Gritz, to wonder if he wasn't, so to speak, protesting too much—serving as something of an *agent provocateur*, spurring other protesters to excess and perhaps seeking to spark an incident that might serve as a pretext for a tough crackdown. "He would charge at the officers' line, cursing and getting in their faces very aggressively," Rich said later. "Nobody else could get away with that kind of deliberately provocative action, and most of us, angry or upset as we might have been, had no interest in it."

Such thoughts and concerns added to the natural tension among those who assembled at the Ruby Creek bridge and stayed there, for whatever reason. Some of the neighbors who had been forcibly evacuated from their homes spent a great deal of time at the roadblock, some out of curiosity and some out of concern. Other local people joined the crowd. As news of the standoff spread, through the news media and through private communications networks, especially among organized "patriot" groups, people came from other cities and states. Rich and a few others, including former BATF undercover operative Don Stewart, who had become convinced over the years that the agency he had done work for had veered out of control, came from Portland. Some skinheads, people who shave their heads, wear black, proclaim the importance of "white power," and in some cases wear swastika armbands and other Nazi paraphernalia, arrived from Portland, Utah, and Las Vegas, and made themselves visible out of proportion to their numbers or influence. Some local friends of the Weavers kept the vigil. And some people from surrounding areas who had no particular interest in or sympathy for the Weaver family's beliefs but felt they were being abused by the government came to demonstrate their disgust at what "their" government was doing for varying periods of time.

John Trochmann, his brother Dave, and his nephew Randy were veteran patriot activists who would go on to found what they would call the Militia of Montana—in part they said to prevent future Ruby Ridges. They were fascinated by their conviction that agents of the New World Order were spinning constant conspiracies to take over the United States, make it a subdivision of the United Nations, and subvert American liberties. Along with John's wife Carolyn and other family members and supporters, they came from relatively nearby Noxon, Montana. Carolyn soon took over cooking chores for the crowd that came to number 150 or 200 per day, collecting money in a coffee can, directing people to buy provisions at nearby stores, and cooking three meals a day on portable propane stoves or over fires for all those who wanted to partake.

With so many people assembled, most of whom had not known one another before, each with his or her own particular agenda or reason for being there, tensions and suspicions, often tempered by and coexisting with a feeling of solidarity and mutual purpose, were inevitable. These people were facing armed state or federal law enforcement officers, some of whom occasionally pointed weapons at them across a piece of crime-scene tape, worrying about what was happening at a remote cabin some three miles away, and sometimes grudgingly getting to know one another. The authorities told them little or nothing about what was happening up at Ruby Ridge, and many of these people would have believed little or nothing from federal authorities anyway. Rumors flew. The feds were planning to blow the whole family away or burn the cabin. Or, they had already done so, and were just trying to figure out a way to put the best face on what they had done. Nothing much had really happened or was likely to happen. Reliable information was scarce, but theories and speculation were plentiful.

Eddie Farr was a volunteer for the Red Cross Disaster Action Unit, which was called to provide food for the law enforcement personnel, setting up an encampment at the meadow across from the Rau home. He arrived with other volunteers on Saturday to help set up a food tent. That first day, the Red Cross brought food from a Red Cross warehouse in Spokane, but in the days to follow most of the food came from restaurants in Bonners Ferry. Farr observed an extensive camp being set up. Assistant U.S. Attorney Ron Howen, who had brought the original firearms indictment against Randy Weaver and would later act as lead prosecutor, had a thirty-foot recreational vehicle as a headquarters. Farr watched three members of the Idaho National Guard work an hour and a half digging a trench for an antenna for Howen's trailer so he would have secure communications.

New vehicles and supplies arrived all through Saturday. Eventually, some 250 vehicles were brought in, including armored personnel carriers, the humvees, thirteen eventually, jeeps, trucks, and vans. People built wooden shower facilities, portable restrooms were brought in, and additional RVs, including one for Eugene Glenn, parked adjacent to Ron Howen's headquarters. Generators were brought in and set up, along with fuel to power them. Most of the officers were dressed either in camouflage or in black. Farr noticed that while many different uniforms, from state, local, and federal agencies were in evidence, almost nobody wore a badge or a name tag. The atmosphere on Saturday was tense and uncertain, according to Farr.

Back at the bridge, a half-dozen agents stood on or patrolled the crime-scene tape that kept spectators out. A fire line was established on the federal side of the bridge. Monofilament fishing line was strung from tree to tree at about waist height, and soft drink cans filled with small pebbles were attached to it with electrical tape at intervals of twenty to thirty feet so that if anyone should cross the creek after dark, they would almost certainly make enough noise to attract attention. A well-traveled trail ran from the left side of the bridge about a third of a mile along the mountainside, in steep terrain. Agents armed with shotguns stationed themselves along the trail, digging out small level spaces at regular intervals so they could stand or sit and keep a close eye on the crowd gathering on the other side of the bridge.

Among those who arrived on Saturday were Barbara Pierce, mother of Kevin Harris, and her husband Brian, Kevin's stepfather, a paralegal who worked for the Spokane County prosecuting attorney's office. By evening, a light rain was falling, and the Pierces had no official word about their son. Finally, after eighteen hours of waiting, "cold, tired, and hungry," as he later told a magistrate, Brian Pierce became frustrated. "I had enough. I asked to talk to the officer in charge. They said I had to go to town [Bonners Ferry]. I told them if I stepped across the line, I guaranteed someone would be there to talk with me. An officer said I would be arrested, but I could go for it. I guess I went for it. I stepped across the line." Brian Pierce was arrested, charged with obstructing and delaying a law enforcement officer in the line of duty, taken to the Bonner County jail, processed, and later released after friends and family paid the bail of three hundred dollars.

Sunday, August 23: Day Three

By Sunday, the crowd on the public side of the bridge had grown considerably, reaching some two hundred people by evening. Although no authoritative news had been given them, many in the crowd believed that Sammy Weaver had been killed as well as Marshal Degan. On Sunday, before the law enforcement officials had the area completely secured, a few protesters, along with a cameraman from a local TV station, said they managed to slip behind the law enforcement lines and make their way to the

Weaver cabin and later to the federal staging area. One of the protesters, a Vietnam veteran, says he saw law enforcement agents place a satchel grenade, an explosive device that can be triggered by a gunshot, on an outside wall of the Weaver cabin. When they got to the federal staging area, these witnesses say they saw a twenty-gallon drum on the seat of a helicopter being filled with diesel fuel. When the pilot of the helicopter took off, the three ran from their hiding place in the bushes and waved at the helicopter with their video camera to let the pilot know he was being taped. The pilot circled the Weaver cabin a few times, then returned to the staging area, having done nothing.

Mike McLean, a reporter for the *Bonner County Daily Bee*, was one of the reporters who undertook this reconnaissance mission, along with Tom Grant of Spokane's Channel 2 news. He confirms that they got near—within a half-mile of—a fuel truck, and saw people loading what seemed to be fuel into some kind of cylindrical containers that were then put in the helicopter. The helicopter took off, then circled the Weaver cabin. Then it veered away. McLean believes that its occupants had spotted his car parked on a back road near the cabin area and started inspecting the woods to try to find the occupants of the car. When it became obvious that the helicopter was looking for them, they moved away from the trees where they were hiding, waved their cameras—McLean had a 35 millimeter camera with a 600 millimeter lens—and the helicopter landed immediately. McLean's memory, however, is that agents on the ground had attached something—he isn't sure whether it was an explosive device or not—to one of the outbuildings, not to the cabin itself.

This incident convinced many people that the federal agents planned to burn the Weaver cabin to eliminate any witnesses, and that the plan was stymied by the witnesses with a video camera. Others who were at the roadblock at the time speak of a helicopter hovering near the cabin, and a videotape shot from the roadblock area shows this action. But not all the protesters believe there was a federal plan to burn the cabin, that this was simply an instance of harassment or surveillance of those hunkered down inside the cabin.

Inside the cabin, few of the inhabitants so much as moved for several days. Baby Elisheba was taken from her dead mother's arms and Vicki's body was covered with a sheet and left on the kitchen floor. Randy Weaver's shoulder wound was superficial, and he treated it by pouring cayenne pepper on it. Kevin Harris's wounds were more serious. A bullet and fragments from Vicki's skull had hit him in the chest, and the wound became seriously infected. He became weaker as the days wore on. Sixteen-year-old Sara Weaver took charge, crawling on her belly to the kitchen to get canned food and comforting the younger children. The baby, still nursing, cried "mama" inconsolably and Randy Weaver rocked her and said, "I know, baby. Mama's gone." Everybody tried to stay low so that they couldn't be seen through the windows.

The traffic across the bridge leading to the federal staging area continued unabated. On Sunday, large earth-moving equipment was brought in, as well as trucks carrying huge beams. Most of the people at the roadblock thought the federal agents were planning to smooth the road to the Weaver cabin to allow more vehicles and equipment to be brought as close to it as possible.

This evening FBI agents went into the birthing shed and found Sammy Weaver's body. One FBI agent is said to have cried out in horror, "My God, they're killing their own!" It is possible that some of the FBI agents were genuinely surprised at this discovery, that the marshals had not told the FBI that Sammy had been killed, but the evidence available to the public on this point is unclear. Sammy's body was removed and sent to Spokane for an autopsy, and on Monday news of his death was released to the media and to the protesters and others keeping vigil at the bridge.

Monday, August 24: Day Four

On Monday, Kevin Harris was formally charged in federal court for the murder of Marshal Degan and Randy Weaver was charged with assaulting a federal officer. Brian Pierce was brought before Magistrate John Lester in Bonners Ferry on the obstruction of a law enforcement officer charge arising from crossing the crime-scene line on Saturday. He pleaded guilty to the charge, a misdemeanor with a possible fine of $1,000 and up to a year in jail. But Magistrate Lester said the standoff at Ruby Creek was not a matter for his court to adjudicate. He withheld the judgment against Pierce, meaning he would have no permanent record if he obeyed the law for one year and fined him $150, including court costs.

Explaining his behavior to the judge, Brian Pierce made a simple plea: "I just want to know if my son is dead, alive, or if you're going to blow his head off as soon as he pokes it out." The local magistrate couldn't answer the question.

At the roadblock, the announcement of Sammy Weaver's death stirred anger among the crowd. FBI agent-in-charge Gene Glenn said, "Samuel's death is a tragedy. We are taking every reasonable precaution to prevent death." But few people were mollified. Hand-painted signs with messages like Baby Killers soon appeared. Most of the people in the crowd, which now numbered between 150 and 200—cars were parked along the side of the road for a half-mile in either direction—believed the marshals had tried to provoke a confrontation. "The federal marshal was invading someone else's property and he may have shot someone else's dog," said Sean Maguire, a local resident. A man who identified himself to reporters only as Jay M. said, "Those motherfuckers want to do it. They want to provoke an armed confrontation."

Hand-painted signs, some painted on lids torn from cardboard boxes, proliferated at the roadblock. They included messages like, This Is Freedom?, Government Out of Control, This Has to Stop, Feds Go Home, Come Stand with Us, Tell the Truth Media, Leave Them Alone, Government Lies and Patient Dies, and FBI Burn in Hell, along with various religious messages. Whenever a vehicle would come to the bridge to be admitted, it would be surrounded by protesters chanting "shame on you," urging the driver to turn around and not be a part of this.

A few more skinheads had arrived at Ruby Creek and were attracting attention both from the crowd and the media. A later study of newspaper accounts of the standoff showed that almost half the photos of the crowd featured skinheads. They were certainly the most colorful members of the crowd—perhaps more inherently interesting than the older women who made up most of the group—but witnesses say that fewer than a dozen skinheads were ever in evidence. Chris Temple, a Montana financial analyst and newsletter publisher who moonlights as a reporter for the California-based Christian Identity newspaper *Jubilee*, arrived Sunday night and helped to circulate petitions protesting the federal government's activity and pleading with the feds to leave. Of those who signed them, he says about 75 percent were relatively local residents—within a radius of sixty to seventy miles from Naples. Some political activists of various stripes—mostly from self-styled patriot or constitutionalist groups—came to Ruby Creek from Montana, Washington, Oregon, and Utah. But most of those who gathered were from the immediate area. Few were outright supporters of the Weavers or their political or religious beliefs, but instead were upset at what they viewed as government overreaction to a minor offense.

In Marin County, California, Kirby Ferris, a columnist for a weekly newspaper with a constitutionalist slant, after a sleepless night spent pondering the Sunday *New York Times* coverage of the Weaver standoff, was busy on the telephone. The *Times* story had mentioned that Randy Weaver was a former Green Beret, and, as Ferris wrote later, "a single name popped into my mind: Lt. Col. James 'Bo' Gritz."

Bo Gritz is the flamboyant, controversial former Green Beret who is believed by many to have been the model for the character in the *Rambo* movies. As a Green Beret in the army's Special Forces, he had earned sixty-two decorations for valor during the Vietnam War and had served in the army for some years afterward. He was commander of the U.S. Army Special Forces in Latin America and later chief of special activities for the U.S. Army General Staff at the Pentagon. During his tours of duty in Southeast Asia, he claims to have visited Khun Sa, a Burmese resistance fighter and opium warlord in the Golden Triangle area. He was shocked, he says, to learn from Khun Sa that some high-level American officials were among his best customers. Later, he says that he learned that the CIA was involved in cocaine trafficking in Latin America to finance its own covert operations. Whether these allegations are true or provable or not, Gritz became convinced they were, and thus began his estrangement from the government.

Gritz became prominent in the early 1980s when he led several trips into Vietnam and Cambodia in search of Americans missing in action (MIAs) who, he believed (along with many Americans), had been left behind by the American government at the end of the war. His trips, some financed by family members of prisoners of war and MIAs, did not turn up any live Americans, but attracted a great deal of attention.

An imposing, charismatic presence with sandy, now greying hair, a mustache, ever-present sunglasses, and a powerful military bearing, Gritz had gradually become associated with right-wing populist political movements and believers in conspiracy theories. From his headquarters at a Nevada ranch, he conducted seminars and what he called SPIKE (Specially Prepared Individuals for Key Events) training around the country. In 1992, he ran for president, on the ballot in many states as the candidate of the Populist Party and in some states as the candidate of another local party affiliated loosely with the populist cause. He had a strong network of supporters in the west and especially in the Pacific Northwest. People driving through Utah, Idaho, Oregon, or Montana in that year might have seen almost as many Gritz for President or God, Guns, and Gritz signs as signs for the major political party candidates.

Although he is not an Identity Christian, Kirby Ferris was familiar with an Identity church called America's Promise Ministries in Sandpoint, Idaho, about thirty miles south of Naples. As he later wrote in his book, *A Mountain of Lies*:

> *It was reported that Randy Weaver embraced Identity beliefs. I thought that someone at the church just might be able to get through to Weaver. I called the church and told them that I really thought that Bo Gritz might be able to help in the crisis that was building. The idea was met with enthusiastic agreement.*

Then I contacted Bo Gritz's campaign offices in Phoenix and "lobbied" for the Gritz people to connect with America's Promise. Then I called Idaho again and asked them to keep trying to reach the Gritz people. Sometime later Monday afternoon I was informed by America's Promise that the connection had been made.

Then I began calling the U.S. Marshals offices in San Francisco, Boise, and Washington, D.C. I did the same with the FBI. I made a "sales pitch" to anyone who would listen to me . . . Randy Weaver had to know who Gritz was. What Green Beret wouldn't know about Bo Gritz? Over and over again, I told the FBI and U.S. Marshals offices that if anyone could get Weaver down off that hill without further bloodshed . . . it would be Bo Gritz.

Kirby Ferris wasn't the only person busy on the telephone during the standoff. Activists in the patriot movement or in various populist movements around the country were activating telephone trees, sending faxes, or calling radio talk shows. Tony Brown, Jackie's husband, said he often found it depressing or demoralizing to be at the bridge, so he would go home, call acquaintances, or be on radio talk shows around the country, talking about the Randy Weaver case. Although the major national media didn't cover the case anywhere nearly as extensively as the local press did, people who had a special interest in the case and knew which radio talk shows had a similar interest were able to get periodic detailed updates.

In addition to framing the announcement of the discovery of Samuel Weaver's body on Monday, the federal forces surrounding the Weaver cabin made efforts to establish contact and communications with Randy Weaver and the remaining members of his family. They shouted through the walls of the cabin and used bullhorns, but got no response. An armored vehicle brought a specially designed robot with a telephone onto the cabin's porch, right outside the door, informed Randy it was there, and pleaded with him to pick up the phone and be in contact with FBI hostage negotiators to work out a way to end the situation peacefully. There was no response from inside the cabin, perhaps in part because the robot also had a shotgun barrel right next to the telephone. Federal officials later said that the shotgun was not loaded, that the barrel was simply part of the standard equipment on the robot, designed to make it useful for a variety of situations. But after what Randy had just experienced, he was taking no chances.

Tuesday, August 25: Day Five

On Tuesday, based on a report aired by a Spokane television station, KHQ–Channel 6, the rumor became widespread that Kevin Harris was dead. Although the TV station said it had confirmed reports of Harris's death, Gene Glenn adamantly denied the report. Barbara Pierce was torn, confused, and heartsick. In a news conference at the roadblock site, she said that the federal agents had refused to talk to her about her son's condition. "I demand as a mother the body of my dead son," she said. "I have a right to that. I expect nothing less." She said she was pleading with federal officials to allow her to meet with her son if he was still alive in hopes of avoiding a violent end to the situation. Special agent Glenn said that a possible meeting with the Pierce family was "something we are working on."

Early in the morning, a rumor spread through the crowd, perhaps started by federal agents as some suspect, that all of the family was dead except for either Vicki or Sara and the baby. The story was that either Vicki or Sara, along with the baby, was out in the woods, that a search was underway and that was why other roads had to be blocked. Blocking those roads also had the effect of preventing any news organizations from having a vantage point from which they could videotape or photograph the Weaver cabin, as a few had occasionally been able to do up to that point.

Later in the morning Rico Valentino, who had been a fixture at the Aryan Nations compound in Hayden Lake during the late 1980s, showed up at the roadblock. Valentino had turned out to be an FBI informant who had money to throw around and had implicated three other Aryan Nations members in an alleged plot to blow up a gay bar in Portland. Valentino was accompanied by a couple of other people who looked to Chris Temple like obvious plainclothes officers, and he tried to ingratiate himself with the crowd. Most of the people quietly demonstrated that they wanted nothing to do with him, and after about an hour he left.

State and federal officials arrested five skinheads from Portland whom they found in a pickup on one of the back roads near the Weaver property on concealed weapons charges. Six weapons, including rifles with bayonets, were reportedly found in the vehicle. The charges were later dropped, but the incident added to the feeling, on both sides of the crime-scene tape, that this was a volatile situation in which almost any miscalculation, any shot fired could lead to a large-scale, tragic confrontation.

It appears that after Saturday, or at least after Sunday, the federal officials on site had decided to treat the Weaver standoff as a hostage situation. The first two days had left three people dead, and despite what might have been bravado from some of the agents, the leaders didn't want any more casualties. The Weaver cabin was fully surrounded; there was virtually no chance any of those inside would be able to escape. Usually, in such a situation, people trapped in an untenable position become gradually more amenable, perhaps over a period of days, to some form of negotiations. There is some evidence that the government might have considered, and perhaps even begun to implement, a more aggressive end to the standoff, if what happened with the helicopter was really an attempt to burn the cabin. However, after a couple of days, the federal officials hoped that eventually Randy Weaver and the others would come to see that the only way out was to surrender peacefully. The major problem was that the people in the cabin, already predisposed not to trust the government, were not inclined to believe any promises about a peaceful end to the standoff.

Later in the day, a small contingent of skinheads from Utah and Nevada arrived at the roadblock. One Weaver supporter was of the opinion that "this new group of skinheads was a lot different from the other ones. They helped us keep the camp orderly and maintained."

Wednesday, August 26: Day Six

By Wednesday, according to Tony Brown, morale among those at the roadblock was low. The number of people varied from one hundred to three hundred, with many local people coming around for a few hours, leaving and coming back later, some staying all day. Many camped out, some in tents that began to be put up near the creek, some sleeping in their cars. Late August in northern Idaho is the end of summer and the beginning of fall. The days were moderately warm and the nights cool, but not so cold as to bother most people with a blanket or warm clothes. But people who had been at the roadblock since Saturday, with only the news of Sammy Weaver's death and endless rumors and speculation to break the tension and uncertainty, were becoming fatigued and restless. Rumors were flying that Bo Gritz would be arriving that day, which pleased some of the crowd and displeased others.

Ed Farr, the Red Cross volunteer, was called to deliver food to the federal officers, the first time he had been to the federal compound since Saturday. He was surprised at the change, at how much larger and more extensive it had become. There were 250 vehicles in the meadow now, including bulldozers and earth-moving equipment, and more tents and more permanent-looking structures. He heard several federal agents, dressed in black and carrying automatic weapons, speak openly about how, "When I get up there I'm going to waste them all." He noticed that a couple of the tents had signs that read Base Camp Vicki. The public hadn't yet been told of Vicki Weaver's death, so on that day he was only puzzled about the possible significance of the nickname.

Late in the afternoon Bo Gritz arrived at the Spokane airport, about a two-hour drive from Naples. He had previously made a taped appeal to Randy Weaver for the FBI office in Boise, which had not been played for Randy. Interviewed by Spokane news media at the airport, Gritz said, "I told Randy [on the tape] that if he did remember me, that he'll know that I'm someone whom he can trust, because we have a common brotherhood in Special Forces. And that, before I was anything, I was a Christian, which I believe he is."

(While it is possible that Randy Weaver and Bo Gritz might have met briefly at Fort Bragg in 1969, Gritz had not been Weaver's commanding officer, and neither of the two now remembers being previously acquainted. Randy Weaver did have one of Bo Gritz's campaign posters in his cabin.) Gritz also said, "If the FBI won't let me go up there and try to talk to a person that I have a rapport with, face to face, then it shows their belligerency in this matter."

Gritz was met by Pastor Dave Barley of America's Promise Ministries in Sandpoint, and Barley drove him and his friends to Naples. He was accompanied by one of his campaign chairmen, former Arizona state senator Jerry Gillespie, and former Phoenix police officer Jack McLamb, who since his retirement had become a patriot activist, a close associate of Bo Gritz, and publisher of a newsletter called "Aid and Abet." Gritz immediately went to the crime-scene tape and asked to speak to Agent Gene Glenn. He was told that Agent Glenn was very busy and didn't have time to talk to him. Agent Glenn was to be too busy to talk with Gritz for almost two days.

Back at the cabin, federal agents did play recordings of appeals to Randy Weaver from friends and relatives of Weaver and Harris, including Barbara Pierce. They also got the first response of the standoff from inside the cabin, a male voice believed to be that of Randy Weaver shouting something as a remote-controlled robot moved the telephone from a place about twenty-five feet in front of the cabin to the cabin's porch, under a window. Glenn said that "any response after no response for days is a positive toward what we hope will initiate a dialogue," but he noted that the comment was not conciliatory. "Defiance would be a little strong, but it's closer to accurate than 'positive,'" he said of whatever the male voice had shouted.

Inside the cabin, the inhabitants, still afraid to move around very much or to stand up so they might be seen through a window, were busy putting their own recollection of events on paper. Randy and Kevin Harris had been wounded to the extent that they were unable to use their writing arms, so they dictated the chronology to Sara, who wrote it down:

Wednesday, August 26, 1992

Approximately 11:30 Friday morning, August 21, 1992, the dogs started barking like they always do when strangers walk up the driveway. Randy, Kevin, and Sam ran out to the rock with their weapons. Randy was carrying a double-barrel 12-gauge shotgun. Kevin was carrying a .30-06 bolt-action rifle. Sam was carrying a .223 mini-14. When they got to the rock our yellow dog Striker was down at the pumphouse barking up into the woods. Sam said he heard something or someone running west, so they followed. Sam and Kevin followed Striker. Randy dropped down on the old logging road headed west.

I (Randy Weaver) didn't have any idea what we were chasing, but was hoping it was a deer. When I (R) reached the first fork in the logging road, a very well camouflaged person yelled, "Freeze, Randy!" I immediately said "Fuck You" and retreated 80–100 feet toward home. I realized immediately that we had run smack into a ZOG/NEW WORLD ORDER ambush. I stopped to see if I was being followed.

About that time I heard a gunshot and Striker yelped. Then I heard two more shots and Striker stopped yelping. I (R.) started yelling for Sam and Kevin to return home, and that they (THE FEDS) had shot Striker. I also fired my shotgun once into the air to draw attention to myself praying that would help. I replaced the empty shell with a new one, shoving it (the shell) past the extractor, jamming my shotgun. I drew my 9mm handgun and fired 3-4 rounds up into the air and I yelled for Sam to return home. Sam responded and said, "I'm coming DAD!" I then walked backwards up the hill toward home yelling to Sam and Kevin to come home. All the while I heard many shots ringing out from the direction of the ambush. By the time I reached home I still hadn't seen Sam or Kevin coming home and they didn't respond anymore when I called to them. A few minutes later, Kevin came walking home. We asked him if he'd seen Sam. Kevin said, "Yes, Sam's dead."

Me (Kevin Harris) and Sam followed Striker through the woods, until we came out on the road that forks off the one

Randy was on and runs north. We (K & S) headed south toward the same road Randy was on. Striker reached the corner first, then Sam, and then me (K). A camouflaged person was in the road and he shot Striker. Sam yelled, "You shot Striker, you sonofabitch!" And they pointed a gun at Sam. Sam opened fire. I (K) took cover beside a stump and Sam headed up the road toward home. It appeared as though Sam had been wounded in the right arm. Also Sam yelled "Oh shit! Kevin come on!" and headed home. The men were still shooting at Sam, so I shot one of the sons of bitches. After they killed Sam, one of the FEDS jumped out of the woods and for the first time declared he was a federal marshal. The feds then grabbed their wounded and left. I (K) then headed home up the road and spotted Sam's body laying in the road without a doubt shot in the back. I checked for a pulse and didn't find one, so I (K) proceeded home.

When Kevin got home and told us Sam was dead, Kevin and I (Randy) and Vicki walked back down to get Sam's body. We brought him home and laid him in the guest shed. We cleaned his body and wrapped him in a sheet. We also brought Sam's rifle home and that is the weapon I (R) am using now. We left NO WEAPON with Sam's body, as was reported on the local news. From that point on we have never left the knoll, and prepared to defend ourselves here.

On August 22, 1992, Saturday, the next day sometime late afternoon, we heard our two remaining dogs start barking. Kevin, Sara, and I (Randy) left the house to check the north perimeter. We didn't see anything, so I (R) was going into the guest house where Sam was to see him one last time. As I (R) reached up to unlatch the door, I was shot from the rear and hit in the upper arm. The bullet exited through my armpit. Yahweh-Yahshua has almost totally healed it on the day of this writing.

When everyone heard the shot, Kevin and Sara came around behind me (R) and we headed for the house in this order: Randy–Sara–Kevin. Vicki came outside the door and yelled: "What happened!??" Randy yelled, "I'm hit!" Vicki was holding open the door for us to get in the house, Elisheba in her arms. A shot rang out and Vicki fell to the floor.

She had been hit in the head and she died instantly. (She fell in such a way Elisheba was not harmed. Praise Yahweh!) At the same time, Kevin fell through the door into the kitchen. As near as we can tell, Kevin was struck with the same bullet that hit Vicki, leaving a very large wound on his left upper arm, and penetrating his chest. There are also several small fragment wounds on his arm. Needless to say, we understand snipers are everywhere. They killed Sam, wounded Randy, killed Vicki and wounded Kevin. The feds totally covered up the murder of Gordon Kahl and Gene Matthews amongst numerous other cover-ups especially against White Racialists and/or Tax Protestors. If they think that we are going to trust them (we didn't trust them before they shot us), they're crazy! Yahweh is starting to heal Kevin. We constantly pray he'll be okay. Since Vicki, Kevin, and I (R) have been shot we haven't left the house and do not plan to unless we are starved out. Then we will most certainly take the offensive. It appears as though the feds are attempting to draw fire from the house as an excuse to finish us all off. If they even so much as crack a window pane on this house with a robot, telephone, gas grenades, etc. it's all over with.

Our heartfelt thanks goes out to all our sympathizers. Our faith is in our creator Yahweh-Yahshua the Messiah. We do not fear the ONE WORLD BEAST government. They can only take our lives. Only Yahweh can destroy our souls. Samuel Hanson Weaver and Vicki Jean Weaver are martyrs for Yah-Yahshua and the White Race. Even if the rest of us die, we win. Hallelu-Yah! Keep the Faith. To all our families and brethren, We love you. Hallelu-Yah!

Randy Weaver (signature)
Kevin Harris (signature)
Sara Weaver (signature)
Rachel (signature)
Elisheba (printed)

Thursday, August 27: Day Seven

On Thursday, what was viewed up to then as the biggest break in the case occurred when Randy Weaver responded to his sister, Marnis Joy, who had been brought out from Iowa, as she yelled through a bullhorn. Randy didn't offer much more than an acknowledgment of his sister's presence, but that was more than had been heard from the cabin before.

At noon, radio commentator Paul Harvey made a personal plea to Randy Weaver through his radio show. It had become known that Randy Weaver regularly listened to Harvey's show. "I am talking to you personally," said Harvey to Randy and 23 million other listeners. "A telephone has been left right outside your door on the porch. Reach out and pick it up. Nobody will shoot. Your family wants to know what to do with Samuel's body; and also, I will arrange for an attorney in Spokane to represent you, and/or whomever, in the death of Deputy Degan. You can negotiate an end to this standoff right now. And believe me, Randy, you'll have a much better chance with a jury of understanding homefolks than you could ever have in any kind of a shootout with two hundred frustrated lawmen."

Harvey also said, "Randy, if you are listening, do not have anything to do with the people coming up to see you. They are there for political ambition. Please pick up the telephone outside your cabin and call me and talk to me, and I'll make sure you get the best lawyer in the country."

Randy didn't listen to Paul Harvey that day, nor did he respond in any way to the appeal.

Bo Gritz, still frustrated that he was having no success contacting Agent Glenn, began work on a citizen's arrest document. At a news conference that evening, he said, "To me, Randy is a skilled soldier, he is obviously determined, as is his family, and I think that he could cause loss of life, and I don't think anyone wants that except maybe the bureaucrats who would like to see this thing escalate to a FEMA [Federal Emergency Management Agency] case. You've got an area up here with a lot of independent people, and I think they'd love to come in here and contain this area, and try to pacify it."

It was probably that night—she doesn't remember the exact day, as they tended to blend into one another—that Niaoka Threlkeld, one of Kevin Harris's sisters, had an ironic encounter. She had been at the bridge since Saturday, not acknowledged or recognized by anyone in authority, worrying about her brother and sleeping in her car, as many of the protesters and vigil-keepers did. She was stopped one night by several carloads of police who started giving her a hard time about a burned-out headlight. As they were hassling her, a car pulled up and an imposing, six-feet-four man got out and asked what was happening. Niaoka identified herself, explaining that she was Kevin Harris's sister, and tried to explain what was happening. FBI special agent Mark Thundercloud, a Native American, pulled out his badge and told the police to quit bothering her and move on. They did.

Then Thundercloud asked Nioaka where she was staying. She told him that she and several family members were sleeping in the car. Thundercloud then pulled out his motel room key and insisted that they all go there. He would be pulling all-night duty that night anyway, he said. He also loaned them his sleeping bag. Fifteen people ended up sleeping in the room that night, all of them getting a hot shower for the first time in days.

Friday, August 28: Day Eight

On Friday, Aryan Nations leader Richard Butler showed up at the roadblock. Most of the protesters didn't pay much attention to him or to the handful of followers he had brought with him.

Bo Gritz and his compatriots—an associate named Eric Lighter from Hawaii, who had been involved in a tax protest against federal officials and John Salter had arrived with documents outlining various alleged federal outrages and cover-ups—were working on a citizen's arrest document. Toward evening, Gritz and Jack McLamb approached the roadblock and announced they were there to perform a citizen's arrest on Gene Glenn, Cecil Andrus (governor of Idaho), Henry Hudson (head of the U.S. Marshals

Service), and William Sessions (head of the FBI). Nobody responded. McLamb then placed the document under a rock on the other side of the crime-scene tape, which he said constituted legal service.

Whether it did or not, an agent at the roadblock did take a handwritten note from Bo Gritz for Agent Gene Glenn and agreed to deliver it. The note read:

> *SA Gene Glenn:*
>
> *We aren't trying to make your task more difficult. We want to help. We believe that we can convince Randy to come out with assurances of fair treatment for himself and Kevin and security for his family. We appreciate your use of Marnis Joy, Randy's sister, to communicate with him. Now that he has responded, we want to expand the conversation to include options that Randy will have confidence in and desire to achieve.*
>
> *Our "citizen's arrest" is not designed to harass you or the others cited. We want you to know that as citizens, we demand you be accountable for your actions in this matter. We believe there have been two wrongful deaths thus far. Responsibility needs to be fixed. Any further damage to persons or property must be avoided. We demand an opportunity to speak with Randy in the manner of Marnis Joy to insure that Randy knows there is a plan for his well-being.*
>
> *We appreciate the situation and understand your position and normal operational procedures. We feel in this case an exception should be allowed. If we are able to attempt communication with Randy, we are willing to respect his response. If he is willing to surrender under our terms, we want to accompany him and Kevin Harris to a place of proper holding.*
>
> *Our request is not complicated, contains no other agency than seeing Randy, Kevin, and the women safely out of this situation so that proper justice can be done. Your refusal will only further complicate our concern and ultimately cause more problems.*
>
> *We pray for your sincere consideration of our request.*
>
> *Forever your Brothers,*
> *Bo Gritz   Jack McLamb*

Whether it was the citizen's arrest, the note, or some other factor—Gene Glenn later said he hoped that "certain themes might work with Randy"—a few minutes later Bo Gritz was escorted to the staging area to meet with Gene Glenn. After some discussion, Gritz was driven to the cabin in an armored vehicle. Randy wouldn't let Gritz into the cabin, and Gritz was in no mood to try to force anything. He shouted at Randy and Randy shouted back to him through the plywood wall. The conversation was brief. Randy wasn't ready to leave the cabin yet, but he said he would be willing to negotiate with Bo Gritz or with Vicki's brother, Lanny Jordison. Randy also told Bo about the killing of Vicki Weaver and the wounding of Kevin Harris and Randy himself. Gritz tried to talk Randy into letting Kevin come out to receive medical attention, but neither Kevin nor Randy was ready yet for that step. They told Gritz that the wound was serious but that Kevin was doing okay. Randy read to Gritz most of the statement that he and Kevin Harris had prepared on Wednesday, explaining their version of events on Friday and Saturday. Gritz tried to persuade Randy to allow him to remove Vicki's body from the cabin, but Randy said his two daughters felt that shouldn't be done until the end of the Sabbath, which Christian Identity believers celebrate from Friday evening to Saturday evening.

About a half an hour later, the joyful mood of the crowd when they saw Bo Gritz quickly turned angry, then somber, when Gritz announced that Vicki Weaver was dead. This was the first time anybody had heard or suspected that any harm might have befallen Vicki, and the reaction was extremely emotional. "This is war!" shouted one skinhead. "As God is our savior," shouted Judy Grider, "you will never take another woman." Those who looked at the roadblock noticed that whereas there were usually a half-dozen or so officers along the tape, the law enforcement officials had quietly brought about one hundred officers into the immediate vicinity.

But the women present quickly joined hands in a circle and began praying, many sobbing openly.

"A wonderful woman has had her life taken and she is in God's hands," said Bo Gritz in his statement. "The glory is that the family isn't damaged any more than it is." He also expressed the hope that the ordeal would be over soon. "I think this will be over tomorrow. Randy wants to come down off his mountain with what's left of his family." Gritz also recounted the Weavers' version of earlier events, as laid out in the statement.

In his own statement, Gene Glenn was emotional about the death of Vicki Weaver but guardedly optimistic about the eventual outcome of the standoff. "We are very pleased with the progress that was in progress this afternoon," he told the thirty-five or so reporters who were on site. "We believe the dialogue will continue." He was also complimentary about Bo Gritz's role: "Bo has been very instrumental in the facilitation of this negotiation process," he said. "Bo Gritz has been able to establish dialogue with Randy. We've been unable to."

That evening, after the announcement of Vicki Weaver's death, was the most emotional time of the entire standoff for most of the 150 or so protesters who were there when Bo Gritz came down from the mountain; indeed, some of them said it was the most powerfully emotional experience of their lives. After the initial reaction of anger was quieted by Bo Gritz's admonition to stay calm and not to resort to violence, and some women joining hands for a quiet prayer vigil, each person had to deal with the shocking news in his or her own way. Some of them had been there off and on, perhaps for a few hours at a time, during the past few days. Some had been there, camping or sleeping in their cars, for almost a week, and they were tense, fatigued, and uncertain anyway. After the prayer vigil some people went home. Some people gathered around campfires with guitars, singing quietly, mostly hymns and religious songs. Few people got much sleep that night.

While some of the local newspapers the next day spoke of Vicki Weaver being killed in a "firefight" or "gun battle" rather than by a sniper attack, they all said she was shot as she was standing in the doorway of the cabin.

Saturday, August 29: Day Nine

Early Saturday morning, Bo Gritz was allowed to return to the Weaver cabin, this time in the company of Chuck Sandelin, a local

Baptist minister, and Jackie Brown, Vicki Weaver's closest friend. When they got to the cabin, after a short period of conversation, Randy said he would let Jackie into the cabin, but that he still preferred that Bo and Pastor Sandelin stay outside. "I had the weirdest mixed feelings when I knew I was going in," Brown said later. "There was extreme joy—this was what we had been trying to accomplish for a week now, and I very much wanted to see how Randy and the girls were doing. But there was apprehension, too. I knew that Vicki was dead, but I didn't know how I would be able to handle actually being in the same room with the body of somebody I had loved so much. I didn't know how badly Randy and Kevin were actually hurt, or what their state of mind would be. I wasn't afraid of what they might do; I had known these people for five years. But after what they had been through, how badly shaken would they be? How much would this horror have changed them?"

When she stepped through the door, the first person Jackie saw was Kevin Harris, lying on the floor. He smiled weakly. "I was glad to see that he was aware and he knew who I was," said Brown. "I had worked in a couple of hospitals, and I know that sometimes a bullet wound that's not treated properly can go bad suddenly. I could tell he was weak—and in retrospect it's something of a miracle he was still alive. But the longer I stayed in there, the more convinced I became that he wasn't getting better, and wouldn't get better unless he got better medical attention."

Next Brown saw Sara and Rachel and hugged them for a long time. "It was so good to see them after all that time. Sara especially was so strong, but she was still just a girl and you couldn't help worrying about her." For Brown, though, it was baby Elisheba who was the "itty-bitty miracle" of the reunion. She toddled around, playing with her blocks, coming over to Brown for awhile, then cheerfully going into another part of the room to play by herself. Sara and Rachel, she says, had to be good with the baby and they were. When Elisheba was hungry or sad, they would rock her in a very maternal, calming way, somehow not transmitting to her any fear or nervousness they might have felt, but soothing and comforting her. If Sara did begin to get upset while she was holding the baby, as began to happen a couple of times while Brown was there, she seemed to know that it was time to hand her to Rachel, who could take over the soothing and comforting until Sara calmed down again.

Brown confirmed that Randy's wound really had almost completely healed and that he was physically in as good shape as could be expected. But there were concerns. They had been living in fear and uncertainty for a week, having seen part of their family literally shot out from under them. For most of that time, they had stayed on the floor, sleeping in sleeping bags and crawling to the kitchen to get canned food. But the food in the kitchen was running out. The bulk food supplies were stored under the house, and they had been afraid to poke a head as high as a window, let alone go out. For most of the time since the previous Saturday, they had been convinced that none of them would come through this situation alive. Only since the day before, when they had talked to Bo Gritz, had they begun to imagine the possibility that it might end in anything other than their own deaths.

Randy gave Jackie the written account of the confrontation that he and Kevin had dictated to Sara on Wednesday and asked that she get it to friends and to the media. He said that he thought it was possible that Sammy rather than Kevin had actually fired the shots that had killed Marshal Degan. He talked about his concerns. He had begun to think about coming out—it made a difference that a friend had opened the door and walked in without any shots being fired—but he was still convinced that he wouldn't be able to get a fair trial, that he'd end up serving some long sentence and the family would be broken up while he was in jail, and that he would lose his house and all his property.

He was also concerned about Kevin. He feared that his lung had collapsed and might be filling with blood. Gritz was able to get a federal medic to approach the cabin. While Randy still wouldn't let him in the cabin, he was able to ask questions and trade information by shouting through the walls. The medic offered some advice for temporary first–aid measures, and sent in some medicine and fresh bandages. Bo Gritz was concerned about Kevin and told

Randy so. "I'm on your side," Gritz said. "But if I were the authorities, I'd hang you for murder if you let that boy die. It can be prevented. And you'll need him as a witness."

Randy and Kevin, however, still weren't ready to come out. Neither were Rachel and Sara. In an interview later, Sara said she held out the longest against coming out. She believed the federal agents would never let them leave the cabin alive. After several hours, Brown and Gritz left the cabin and returned to the roadblock. There they told the crowd and the press more about Randy's version of the confrontation and related the concerns he still had:

"The concerns are these," said Gritz. "They feel that they are the ones who are the victims of criminal action, and when I talked to Randy about that, he said, 'Bo, I cannot go into the Babylonian courts and get a fair trial.' He has said he was set up on that weapons charge, and that he can prove that he was set up. But he's not sure about going to court. Still, if we can get a real champion that he has faith in, I believe that with that arrow in his quiver, that he might be very willing to come down here and shoot it. If Randy had any idea of fair treatment, I think he'd be down here."

In his radio broadcast the previous Thursday, radio personality Paul Harvey had said that if Randy turned himself in that he [Harvey] would pay for a lawyer. On Friday, Harvey contacted Spokane attorney Roger Peven, who agreed to offer free initial legal counsel on the original weapons charge and on any charges stemming from the standoff. "I said I don't care about fees right now," said Peven. "Getting everybody off the mountain alive is what's important to me.

"I know [Weaver's] worried, as anyone would be with two hundred rifles pointing at him," Peven continued. "He would have no worries that he would get the best representation."

Peven is a respected attorney, but Bo Gritz had another idea. On Saturday afternoon he called and secured a conditional promise from Gerry Spence, the famed Wyoming defense attorney and author, who had successfully represented clients ranging from the family of Karen Silkwood to Imelda Marcos, to give serious consideration to representing Randy Weaver if he agreed to come down from Ruby Ridge and turn himself in. It wasn't an ironclad promise. Spence considered what he understood to be Randy's religious and political beliefs reprehensible, and he reserved the right to make a final decision about being his lawyer until after he'd met with Weaver and gotten to know him a little. But at least Gritz would be able to tell Randy that if he came down now there was a good chance he would be represented by a man many consider the best defense attorney in the country, a defense lawyer reputed never to have lost a case.

Later in the afternoon, Jackie Brown, along with Bo Gritz and Jack McLamb, went to the cabin again, to spend time with the children and to make a list of things the family needed right away. Randy would still only let Jackie into the cabin. She related that Agent Glenn had said that authorities had agreed that Randy could pick the homes his daughters would go to if he surrendered, and promised he would have an opportunity to testify before a grand jury regarding the standoff. She returned to the roadblock with a list that included ten gallons of drinking water, hydrogen peroxide, and baby items, including disposable diapers and formula. The crowd quickly gathered several hundred dollars in donations and sent somebody off to buy these things.

Sunday, August 30: Day Ten

By Sunday morning, the Weaver standoff was front-page news not only in the local newspapers, as it had been for a week, but in newspapers all across the country. Speaker of the House Tom Foley, who represented the district in which Spokane is located, was in Washington for the weekend and made comments on the case that stopped just short of criticizing the government severely for its handling of the case. Speaker Foley also offered a personal reflection: "It's a tragic situation—the loss of life of a U.S. marshal, a young boy, and apparently now Vicki Weaver. It's a sad, sad thing."

In the afternoon Gritz, McLamb, and Brown were all allowed into the cabin. After an emotional discussion punctuated by prayer, the decision was made to allow Gritz and McLamb to take Kevin Harris out of the cabin to a medical tent at the federal staging area. Harris was given first aid and then flown by helicopter—accompanied by McLamb—to a hospital in Spokane, where he was treated for his wounds and put in a hospital room under heavy guard. He remained there for two weeks.

Then Brown and Gritz removed Vicki Weaver's body from the cabin and turned it over to the Boundary County coroner. Brown returned and cleaned up the bloodstains and the rest of the kitchen as best she could. Brown and Gritz returned to the roadblock and informed the crowd—now grown to at least three hundred—and the media about what they had done. In a news conference, Gritz said, "We're going to press the case. We've got the best lawyer in the United States, and I believe you're going to see this family, while it's unfortunate there was great sacrifice, come out of this thing a winner, if you can be a winner having lost your son and your mom. But it will be, I think, a crusade for other people. I think that's what Randall realizes."

Agent Glenn was upbeat also: "I can't overemphasize how pleased we all are," he said after Harris surrendered. "We consider this a tremendous step forward. This is an upbeat time, and we are anxious for a final resolution." Everybody expected that Randy Weaver and his daughters would come out of the cabin on the following day.

As a back-up plan, however, in case Weaver and the girls were not prepared to leave on Monday, Gritz and Glenn worked out what they called "Operation Alaska." Gritz would be wired for sound by the FBI. If he and McLamb got into the cabin but were informed that the Weaver family wasn't ready to leave yet, Gritz would grab Randy and McLamb would subdue Rachel and Sara. Gritz would then shout "Alaska," whereupon federal agents would come in and take the entire family into custody. Gritz said he didn't want to do it this way, that he preferred that Randy walk out under his own power, with some dignity. But he believed that the FBI was getting impatient for a resolution.

After one of the negotiating sessions, Gritz found himself driving down to the bridge over Deep Creek with Jack Cluff, the U.S. marshal who had organized the eighteen-month effort to try to get Randy Weaver to surrender, before the siege and standoff. Cluff had been an army helicopter gun crew chief in Vietnam in 1968 and 1969, providing air support for a Green Beret unit training Cambodian soldiers. He had earned twenty-six air medals, each one requiring fifty hours of flying time. He had joined the U.S. Marshals Service after the war. Cluff and Gritz began swapping Vietnam stories, and realized they had served in the same unit in Vietnam, Special Forces B-36. Gritz had been Cluff's faceless but legendary "Commander Bo" when Cluff had been a helicopter gunship crewman providing air support for Gritz's ground maneuvers. "I'll be a son of a bitch," Gritz said, and impulsively leaned over to hug him.

Cluff later described the encounter as "really weird." Jim Aho, a sociologist at Idaho State University in Pocatello who has written extensively about "Christian Patriots," makes a case in his book *This Thing of Darkness* that the fact that Randy Weaver, Jack Cluff, and William Degan were all Green Berets—trained by the government to be efficient military tools and later to become enemies or antagonists—is not just ironic, but one of the more significant factors in the Ruby Ridge standoff. He quotes Cluff admitting that Gritz had been "a hell of a leader." "And yet, 'it dawned on me: God, you radical bastard. What happened to you?' Gritz had somehow transmogrified himself into one of the enemy. In the intervening years, he, too, had become an exponent of government conspiracies and millenialism, an advocate of armed survivalism," writes Aho.

Also, Sunday night Bo Gritz and Chris Temple, the financial analyst who was one of the Gritz campaign's coordinators in Montana, helped two skinhead acquaintances of Randy's—John Bangerter of Utah and David Cooper of Las Vegas—compose a letter to Randy. In it, they argued that enough damage had already been done, that it was time for Randy and the girls to come down, and that "the battle was in the courts, not up here on the hill." Gritz had this letter with him when he went to the cabin Monday morning.

Monday, August 31: Day Eleven

When Monday morning dawned, most of the crowd at the roadblock anticipated that this would be the day the standoff would finally end. Bo Gritz and Jack McLamb left behind an almost festive scene when they went up to the cabin.

When the two men got to the cabin, however, they found the door locked. They called to Randy, but Randy informed them that he and Sara had agreed, after reading the scriptures and doing some numerical analysis, that the proper day for them to come out of the cabin was September 9 and not before. Gritz and McLamb were crestfallen. They were reasonably sure, from their discussions, that the FBI and other federal agencies simply wouldn't wait that long, and they were afraid that the longer the situation dragged on the more likely it was that more blood would be shed. They explained this to Randy, but he and Sara were adamant.

Although the door to the cabin was bolted, Gritz was able to slip the note from the two skinheads under the door. Randy promised to read it.

After he read it, he wasn't entirely convinced, but was willing to talk some more. Finally, he opened the door and let Gritz and McLamb in. After some discussion, it became obvious that Sara was the holdout. She wasn't convinced that the government would keep its end of the bargain, which included an agreement that the family could walk out together, not held by agents, and that Randy would not be handcuffed until he got into a helicopter that was to take him from the scene. There was no deal made related to prosecution. Decisions about what charges might be filed in addition to the original firearms charge and the assaulting–a–federal–officer charge would be up to Ron Howen.

Finally Gritz and McLamb, reminding Randy and Sara that the FBI had already kept some promises, that Harris had not been harmed but given medical attention, and that it really was in the best interests of the federal agencies, given all the publicity, to have this situation end peacefully, convinced them that they should end the confrontation now. The family prepared to leave. Sara cleansed

Randy's wound one more time and put clean clothes on the baby. Randy, Sara, and Rachel took off the guns they had been wearing. Sara straightened up the cabin a little, and looked around it one more time. Then the four Weavers walked out of the cabin together. Randy Weaver wore jeans and a T-shirt. Sara and Rachel wore dresses. Despite the bullet wound in his shoulder, Randy carried Elisheba. Sara and Rachel held the hands of Jack McLamb. They walked to a helicopter waiting nearby. Randy hugged Sara and Rachel one more time, then laid down on a stretcher so an FBI medic could examine him. Then he climbed into the waiting helicopter, waved good-bye, and the helicopter took off. It flew to Sandpoint, Idaho, where a U.S. Marshals Service white Sabreliner jet was waiting to fly him to Boise. There he would get a checkup at a hospital and then be taken to the Ada County Jail, the county where Boise is located.

Bo Gritz and Jack McLamb then came down to the roadblock to explain to those assembled how the final surrender had gone. During the conversation, Gritz waved at the skinheads who had sent the note in a manner that looked to many people like a Nazi "sieg heil" salute, saying this was from Randy, and that Randy knew they would understand. Their note, said Gritz, had had a lot to do with convincing Randy to surrender. Viewing the video, it is difficult to tell whether the gesture was a salute or just an enthusiastic wave. But the incident has been one of the ongoing controversies surrounding the entire affair.

After the helicopter took off, Jeane and David Jordison were allowed up into the staging area, where they greeted their grandchildren tearfully. They had come out from Iowa and had already checked into a local hotel, where they took Sara, Rachel, and Elisheba. The first thing the girls asked for was pizza. They got it.

The Federal Version
and Media Reports

THE PRACTICAL RESULT OF THE ROADBLOCK ERECTED BY FEDERAL OFFICIALS IN cooperation with the local Bonners Ferry police, the Idaho State Police, and other authorities was that federal authorities on the first days of the Ruby Ridge siege had complete tactical control of the Weaver property and a wide area surrounding it. Nobody was able to get in or out without permission from federal officers. This meant that the news media had to rely almost entirely on what federal officials said, which, of course, was a significant handicap.

Only one reporter, Mike Weland from the *Bonner County Daily Bee* had actually been to the cabin, having conducted a lengthy interview with the Weaver family in May 1992. Reporters from other papers, who began assembling on Friday, August 21, could interview neighbors and other people with knowledge of the area, but that's not the same as having firsthand knowledge, not the same as having actually seen the Weaver property and the mountains surrounding it. So while some allowance might be made for bias or simply getting facts wrong after being told them in good faith—and some minor variations in news stories are surely attributable to such factors—most of what came out in the first few days of the siege came out as it did because that was the story federal officials were telling the media.

Mike McLean, a reporter for the *Bonner County Daily Bee*, was one of the first reporters on the scene. Working in his office in Sandpoint, he had heard sirens around noon, then heard a call for assistance on the police radio he monitored in the office. He got the location and drove up to the bridge over Deep Creek. By the time he got there, the Bonners Ferry police chief was at the roadblock, which was simply a yellow crime–scene tape stretched across the road. The chief told him that Randy Weaver had been involved in a shootout, that as far as he knew there was one U.S. marshal dead, a continuing firefight going on, and that people from the sheriff's office were debriefing the U.S. marshals involved. It was the beginning of what he later called "eleven days on adrenaline." Before long, more media representatives arrived, and all were told the same story.

Saturday, August 22 stories in the newspapers, mostly filed on Friday after Ruby Creek Road had been closed off, speak of the death of Marshal Degan and generally feature a quote from Henry E. Hudson, director of the U.S. Marshals Service, speaking from Washington, D.C.

"The group [of marshals] came under fire from the fortresslike Weaver home, apparently without warning, and Degan sustained a fatal gunshot wound," Hudson was quoted as saying in the *Idaho Statesman*. The *Seattle Post-Intelligencer* paraphrased the U.S. Marshals Service director, saying that Degan "was killed as he kept watch on the fortress home of Randy Weaver, 44." The *Post-Intelligencer* also ran the quote from Henry Hudson, who was a continent away.

The *Idaho Statesman* story then continues: "Five other deputy marshals were trapped on the ridge, the Marshal's Service said. Federal, state, and local law enforcement officials were on the way to rescue them, the agency said late Friday."

The *New York Times* story of August 22, filed August 21 from Naples, has it a little differently: "Only one of the deputies was hit, but five others were still pinned down by gunfire tonight." The *Times* also noted that "contrary to initial news reports, Mr. Hudson said the six deputies who were on Ruby Ridge today had not gone there to arrest Mr. Weaver."

The *Spokesman-Review* printed a variation: "Degan, a father of two, was one of the five federal marshals conducting surveillance near Weaver's stronghold. He was shot through the sternum and apparently died instantly. Two marshals with him escaped, but two were pinned down near Degan's body by repeated sniper fire from the cabin." Was it two people pinned down by this sniper fire and forced to remain with Degan's body or five people still pinned down by late Friday afternoon? Were there five marshals in on the operation, or five left after Degan was killed?

Certain allowances can and should be made for the possibility that people, including agency officials and those who had recently come upon the scene, were a little confused themselves about what had actually happened. But from the outset of the assault and siege, despite some variations as to details, a reasonably consistent pattern emerges in the story released by authorities on the scene. Randy Weaver was immediately identified to media people as a "white supremacist" and a "federal fugitive," and his close association with the Aryan Nations was either stated or implied. The charge against him was always described as a "federal weapons charge," but the details—the fact that it was selling a couple of cheap sawed-off shotguns, or that the buyer was a federal undercover informant engaged in an undercover operation—were not described in full.

Federal and law enforcement officials spoke of the marshals either being ambushed or pinned down by sniper fire—sometimes from the cabin, sometimes with the source of the sniper fire left a little more vague. The impression created of the Weaver family was that they were desperate, ruthless, and well prepared for a battle that they had precipitated themselves by firing first "apparently without warning."

By Friday evening, the first television crew with satellite dishes and other electronic paraphernalia arrived. On Saturday morning, more television, radio, and print reporters arrived, and the little bridge across Deep Creek became something of a media "happening." At any given time, dozens of reporters drifted around, interviewing people who might or might not know anything reliable, sometimes mixing with and sometimes standing apart from the growing crowd of Weaver supporters and curiosity seekers who also assembled.

That crowd of Weaver supporters surprised Mike McLean. He had never seen that kind of support for a federal fugitive or other criminal. His second-day lead in the *Bonner County Daily Bee* reflects this: "What authorities fear most is happening. Randy Weaver is becoming something of a folk hero in northern Idaho."

The FBI would usually bring somebody, usually special agent-in-charge Eugene Glenn from the Salt Lake City office, to the roadblock once a day to deliver a statement about what kind of progress, if any, was being made in resolving the standoff. But there was no set time for the government to show up at the bridge, so that made it difficult for reporters to drift too far from the bridge, lest they miss the briefing that provided the closest approximation of real news likely to come from the scene. Nonetheless, Mike McLean noticed that although the road into the Ruby Creek area was blocked, there was another road that led by a circuitous route to a point closer to the Weaver cabin. He drove on that road Friday evening, parked his car and slept in it overnight, and tried to hike in to the standoff scene. But he hadn't brought enough water with him and the terrain was rougher than he had thought. He was unable to get close enough to the scene to see anything significant, so he hiked back to his car and drove back out. When he got to where the dirt road intersected the highway, he discovered that it had now been blocked off with crime-scene tape. He was arrested and spent a couple of hours in the local jail before his editor was able to bail him out. Charges were later dropped.

By Sunday, August 23, the *Idaho Statesman* had more details from official spokespeople on this dramatic story:

> *Ruby Ridge, about 40 miles south of the Canadian border in the northern Idaho panhandle, has been turned into an armed camp after six deputy marshals came under semiautomatic weapons fire Friday while conducting surveillance on Randy Weaver's fortresslike home. . . .*

Weaver, 44, has lived in self-imposed exile with his family since February 1991 when he failed to appear on a federal weapons charge. Authorities say he has ties to white supremacist groups.

Weaver once vowed never to be taken alive, and officers appeared reluctant to immediately storm the home for fear of harming others inside, including his four children, ranging in age from 1 to 14 years.

Nevertheless, at least two armored military troop carriers drove past a blockade staffed by deputy U.S. marshals toting assault rifles. Trucks, jeeps, and rescue vehicles bore license plates from Idaho, Washington, Montana, Oregon, and Washington, D.C. About 30 people living near Ruby Ridge were evacuated Friday.

The shooting began about noon Friday, and three agents unable to escape remained pinned down on the mountainside for nearly 14 hours before they were rescued about 2:00 A.M. Saturday. They were taken to a hospital, treated for exposure, and released.

The *New York Times* printed it a little differently on August 23: "After the shooting, continuing gunshots from the cabin pinned down three other deputies who remained with the body until nightfall, when they were rescued by an Idaho State Police crisis response team."

The *Washington Post* printed it a bit differently yet, again on August 23: "Six marshals were fired on Friday at the fortresslike cabin of Randy Weaver, who has lived there with his wife and four children since February 1991, when he failed to appear on weapons charges."

The familiar elements are there, however. We might not know whether there were two, three, or five marshals "pinned down" for nine or fourteen hours or overnight. The *Post* includes the interesting word "at" the cabin rather than talking of gunfire "from" the cabin. But the clear impression to the casual reader of a newspaper story is that bad people fired repeatedly, probably from an ambush, at federal officers merely trying to do their jobs, and killed one officer, and pinned others down for several hours.

The *Post* story got an interesting fact wrong. The Weaver family by 1992 had lived at the cabin not since 1991, but (except for brief periods of time, especially during some winters) for about eight years. They didn't go to this remote spot to hide out, as one might suppose from the way some reports are worded. They chose to stay in the home they had been inhabiting for several years. But the newspaper reporters had to rely on what the federal officials told them, and presumably it sounded more sinister for the family to have retreated to this "compound" after the federal firearms indictment had been brought.

Perhaps it is only a curiosity just how quickly the small team from the Special Operations Group of the U.S. Marshals Service grew. The *Spokesman-Review*, in its August 22 story, notes, "By late Friday, the assault team included 60 members of the Marshals Service Special Operations Group, an elite SWAT team that specializes in arrest and hostage rescues." Eventually, people would be flown into northern Idaho from all over the country. But how did a response team get there so quickly Friday, after an unexpected encounter leading to a shooting that occurred around noon? Early on, according to interviews done by author Kirby Ferris for *A Mountain of Lies*, local people working in motels in the Naples and Bonners Ferry area told of "dozens" of federal agents checking into rooms the Wednesday and Thursday before the shooting on August 21. There has also been quiet testimony from locals that the FBI was quite directly telling local people to keep quiet about such matters.

There are also discrepancies in the stories told in the first couple of days about how Marshal Degan was shot. In Saturday's story, written Friday, the *Spokesman-Review* says: "Degan, a father of two, was one of five federal marshals conducting a surveillance near Weaver's stronghold. He was shot through the sternum and apparently died instantly." The *Bonner County Daily Bee* on Sunday, August 23, phrased it a little differently: "U.S. Marshal William F. Degan, 42, who was wearing a bullet-proof vest, was hit in the throat area and most likely died instantly."

Even after the trial and all the investigation that has occurred, some questions remain about William Degan's death. Was he wearing a bullet-proof vest? Apparently, he was not. Ordinarily, you would expect a federal agent in an elite SWAT-like team going into a potentially dangerous situation to be required to wear a bullet-proof vest on pain of serious disciplinary action. But the prosecution did not produce a bullet-proof vest worn by Marshal Degan. One early report states he was hit in the sternum (the breastbone), another states he was hit in the throat. His body was flown out of state, to Spokane, for an autopsy. Kevin Harris reported that he thought he had hit somebody, presumably Degan, when he fired into the stand of trees. What caliber of bullet killed Degan, and where did it come from?

For a Monday, August 24 Associated Press story with a Naples, Idaho, dateline (probably written Sunday, the day after Vicki Weaver was killed), the reporter had to rely on spokespeople almost three thousand miles away for information about something that might have happened on Saturday:

> *Scores of federal agents and police officers continued their siege Sunday of a fugitive's mountaintop cabin where a deputy U.S. marshal was killed, and disclosed that shots were exchanged Saturday night.*
>
> *"We do know there was . . . some gunfire between law enforcement officers and the people in the compound," said Joyce McDonald, a spokesperson at the U.S. Marshals Service headquarters in Washington, D.C.*
>
> *She said the shooting erupted about 11:30 P.M. and that she understood nobody was hit.*
>
> *Dan McCarron, a spokesperson at FBI headquarters in Washington, D.C., declined to divulge details of the shooting.*
>
> *"It is a very tough position for us, because we already lost one marshal. These people seem to be very serious about what they are trying to do, so we are proceeding very cautiously," McCarron said.*

The *Washington Post* printed a similar story on August 24: "Law officers exchanged gunfire with people in the compound over the weekend, but the standoff that began after a U.S. marshal was killed continued. No one was injured in the shooting Saturday, the U.S. Marshals Service said."

Note the insistence that it was an "exchange" of gunfire. And that no one was injured.

The Monday, August 24 edition of the *New York Times* didn't have anything written about shots on Saturday: "Officers have kept the cabin under surveillance on and off for about a year. They have not disclosed details of Friday's shooting, except to say shots came from the cabin without warning. Deputy United States Marshal William F. Degan, 42 of Quincy, Massachusetts, was killed and others were wounded."

The *USA Today* story for August 24 includes interviews with protesters and local residents who had become a visible presence at the roadblock by Saturday. It also notes: "More shots were fired late Saturday, and agents Sunday were attempting to negotiate with Weaver." Bill Licatovich, a spokesperson from the U.S. Marshals Service headquarters in Washington, D.C. provided the background: "Friday, six deputies arrived for 'another attempt to gather information about who was in the cabin.' Killed was U.S. Marshal William F. Degan, 42, of Boston. Two deputies fled, but three others couldn't escape until late that night and were treated for exposure."

Thus, the day after the shooting that killed Vicki Weaver had occurred, when authorities on the scene had to know that at the very least one or more of the inhabitants of the cabin had been wounded, authorities were still insisting that the marshals had been pinned down or trapped that first day, and not mentioning that anybody in the cabin might be hurt.

The *Bonner County Daily Bee* printed a similar story, but again with curious variations: "Johnson [a U.S. Marshal spokesperson] said the five marshals who were with Degan on the surveillance operation are being interviewed to determine 'exactly what went wrong.' Two of the marshals, along with Degan's body, were extracted from the line of fire after being pinned down for nine hours near Weaver's residence. In a conspicuous nondenial, Johnson refused to comment on reports of gunfire Saturday and Sunday. He said he couldn't discuss the reports while agents were still establishing their positions around the Weaver residence."

So there's just a hint here of gunfire on Sunday, although later court testimony made it clear that no gunfire occurred on Sunday.

The *Spokesman-Review* printed the following in its August 24 story: "There were reports of shots fired from the armed camp at agents and a helicopter. Glenn [FBI agent Eugene Glenn] refused to confirm the gunfire exchange, but U.S. Marshals Service spokesperson Joyce McDonald said shots were exchanged about 11:30 P.M. Saturday, apparently without injury."

Several things stand out in these reports. Two and three days after Marshal Degan's death federal spokespeople continued to say the marshals were fired upon—sometimes from the cabin, sometimes not—without warning, that the marshals were ambushed. The story that the marshals were "pinned down" or "trapped" by sniper fire from the cabin and thus unable to escape continues to be promulgated. Spokespeople are careful to call the plywood cabin a "compound," a "fortress," or "fortresslike." The gunfire on Saturday is either not denied or called an exchange of gunfire. But the spokespeople are very clear that nobody was hurt.

A good deal of the confusion to be found in the early reports might reflect more confusion than cover-up. A gun battle or violent encounter, whether it's expected or a surprise, is seldom an affair that can be wrapped up in a neat little package with a red ribbon. Accounts from different people who participated in exactly the same action may be radically different, as people who have been or are under a great deal of stress find their memories playing tricks, or emphasizing different aspects of a situation. And if the natural confusion surrounding a violent encounter is compounded by the conviction that things have gone badly and could get worse, the result could be even more confusion, which could well lead to inaccurate and even conflicting explanations about just what happened. These were highly trained, experienced federal officers who had been in other encounters, but they were also imperfect human beings.

In a motion to dismiss the first grand jury indictment, Randy Weaver's defense team wrote the following:

After the smoke cleared, the U.S. marshals realized they were in serious trouble. William Degan, their colleague, was shot through the chest and had died. A child was dead along with the child's dog. Both child and dog were shot in the back (8/25/92 Autopsy Report on Samuel Weaver; 8/24/92 Dr. Rolland Houston Hall 302), although this information has still not been released to the press. The marshals must have realized that these deaths were, in fact, totally attributable to their violation of orders against confrontation and the admonition not to injure any of the Weaver children under any circumstances.

Moreover, Degan's death occurred under circumstances that are still in serious doubt, for although Harris thought he killed Degan in the melee attempting to defend Sammy and himself, the officers must have known that the circumstances surrounding Degan's death would soon be fully investigated, and that the results would establish that the officers themselves, not Harris, had killed Degan during their wild and irresponsible gunfire.

As to the boy, no one could mistake him for an adult. This thirteen-year-old was no larger than the average ten-year-old. (70–80 lbs. per 8/25/92 Autopsy Report.) His voice, when he hollered out that the man had shot his dog, was the voice of a child. The child was shot by the officers running home. They had no warrant to arrest either Harris or the boy. The officers, now responsible for the death of two people, while Weaver himself had escaped, began to consider how to explain their conduct.

That brief did not lead to a dismissal of the indictments against Randy Weaver and Kevin Harris; the judge who read it decided that a trial was in order. But the bare facts, putting aside the lawyerly and sometimes argumentative imputations about what motivated the officers to act as they did, are described fairly accurately, as was finally borne out at the trial.

As soon as the standoff was over and outsiders were allowed to look at the cabin and the surrounding area, it became clear to many reporters that it was virtually impossible for the marshals to have been pinned down from the cabin at the site of the first shootout. The distance is more than a quarter of a mile, and the terrain is steep and heavily wooded. It is impossible to see the Y from the cabin, let alone pin anybody down with gunfire. Did the federal authorities think nobody would ever see the area and notice the discrepancy?

On August 24 FBI agents found Sammy Weaver's body in the birthing shed, the eight–by–fourteen–feet shed about fifty feet from the main cabin. One or two news stories had FBI spokes people registering shock at this discovery.

Other news stories were more low–key, but showed significant differences from earlier versions of earlier incidents. The Tuesday, August 25 edition of *USA Today*, for example, printed it this way: "Six marshals were conducting routine surveillance Friday when they unexpectedly came upon Weaver, one of his children, and longtime friend Kevin Harris outside the cabin, authorities said. They said Weaver and Harris, with a dog, chased the marshals and opened fire, and a shot from Harris, 24, killed U.S. marshal William Degan. Harris has been charged with murder. They didn't say who killed Weaver's son."

There's no mention here of shots "from the cabin." But the story is that Weaver and Harris unexpectedly came upon a group of men dressed in camouflage and armed with fully automatic weapons, chased them, and opened fire on them instead of turning and running for the house.

The *Washington Post* story for August 25 says that "at least 100 federal agents, state police, and sheriff's deputies were posted around the cabin where Randy Weaver, 44, and his family live. Police surrounded it immediately after the marshal was fatally shot Friday." What happened to the nine hours or overnight when the remaining marshals were pinned down by gunfire from the cabin?

The *New York Times* story for the same day notes that "the boy's body was found Sunday night by agents searching an outbuilding 100 yards from Randy Weaver's home, said Gene Glenn, the special agent-in-charge of the Salt Lake City bureau of the Federal Bureau of Investigation." The *Idaho Statesman* story also quoted Glenn as describing the outbuilding as one hundred yards from the cabin. There's a significant difference between one hundred yards and fifty feet. Did federal officials not want to let the media know just how close they were able to get to the Weaver cabin?

The August 25 edition of the *New York Times* also says: "Officials disclosed Sunday that shots had been exchanged Saturday night. Nobody was hurt, a U.S. Marshals Service spokesperson said." Again, although the shooting had taken place around noon, officials said it had happened "Saturday night." And they insisted that nobody had been hurt, when it seems most unlikely that they did not know otherwise.

The Tuesday story in the *Seattle Post-Intelligencer* has a different version yet of Saturday's events: "Authorities also disclosed that Kevin Harris, the man accused of killing Marshal William Degan, was wounded Saturday by gunshots fired by federal agents from a helicopter. . . . Harris, 24, was shot when he emerged from the house, said Stephen Boyle, a spokesperson for the U.S. Marshal's office in Washington, D.C. His condition is not known, Boyle said."

Here we have the introduction of a helicopter into the action, and even the assertion that the shots that wounded Kevin Harris were fired from a helicopter. While authorities say they know that Kevin Harris was wounded, however, they do not disclose that Vicki Weaver had been killed. Could they not have known this? There is also no mention of Randy Weaver having been wounded. Note also that Harris is said to have been shot when he emerged from the cabin, whereas later testimony said he was shot as he was entering the cabin, fleeing into it after Randy Weaver was shot. To be sure, Harris had to "emerge" from the house before he later ran back into the house. But the chronology here is somewhat confusing. Note also that reporters are forced to rely on a spokesperson in Washington, D.C., a continent away, to get official information about something happening a couple of miles away from their outpost, yet out of their range of vision.

An article printed in the August 25 edition of the *Spokesman-Review* says, "Federal agents surrounding the cabin of mountaintop fugitive Randy Weaver found his 13–year–old son shot to death and lying next to the boy's rifle in a shed." Why would Randy Weaver have left a rifle next to his son's body? If there was a rifle, how did federal agents know it was Sammy's?

The *Spokesman-Review* article for Tuesday also says: ". . . even though Vicki Weaver and the children have said they will fight by Weaver's side, agents are treating them as hostages." The *Bonner County Daily Bee* for the same day reports: "He [FBI agent Gene Glenn] said agents are taking a cautious approach because Weaver's wife Vicky [sic] and her remaining three children are also inside the building." The clear implication is that Vicki Weaver was still alive and that the FBI was being especially careful to see to it that no harm came to her. At the time this briefing was given, Vicki Weaver had been lying dead on the kitchen floor of the cabin for two days.

The *Daily Bee* story for Tuesday also says: "Glenn said he has personally been to forward perimeter where the terrain is rugged and any approach would be dangerous, 'especially in light of information that Weaver is heavily armed and his house is well fortified.'" The house was not fortified at all. And since the ground drops off precipitously from the small piece of level terrain on which the house is built, and the whole area is thickly wooded, approach from almost any direction would be relatively easy.

A story in the *New York Times* printed Wednesday, August 26 suggests that federal agents had, in fact, been able to approach the cabin closely. "The agents have used armored personnel carriers and helicopters to get close to the cabin. They said they are using a listening device that allows them to hear conversations, and even the baby's cries, in the cabin." That same story has authorities continuing to talk about agents pinned down by gunfire on the first day of the encounter: "On Friday, the authorities said, six agents approached the cabin and were met by Mr. Weaver and family members. Gunfire erupted, and Mr. Degan was shot dead.

The other agents were pinned down for several hours before they could retreat."

Wednesday's stories also introduce a new scenario. A *Seattle Post-Intelligencer* story on August 26 says: "A U.S. marshal said last night 'it is a possibility' that federal fugitive Kevin Harris accidentally shot Randy Weaver's 13-year-old son during last Friday's shootout with deputy U.S. marshals. At a news conference, Idaho marshal Mike Johnson said an autopsy on Samuel Weaver was completed yesterday afternoon, and indicated the youth 'died instantly' from a bullet wound in the stomach."

The *Idaho Statesman* story for the same day reports: "Also Tuesday, a Spokane, Washington, television station reported that a Boundary County autopsy revealed that the boy, Samuel Weaver, died from a gunshot wound fired by Harris. Federal officials said Tuesday that Samuel was hit twice by bullets, possibly fired by either his father or Harris. They also said the boy's body had been moved to an outbuilding after he was shot."

The *Bonner County Daily Bee* on Wednesday ran the story this way: "The body of the Weaver boy was discovered Sunday night by deputies searching an outbuilding on the property. Marshals spokesperson Mike Johnson said it was possible the youngster was shot by Harris, based on the number of shots fired at the scene. Johnson declined to elaborate. An autopsy on the body of Sam Weaver, conducted Tuesday afternoon, shows he died from a fatal gunshot wound to the torso. He also suffered a gunshot wound to his right arm, Johnson said."

The *Spokesman-Review* noted some details not given: "Johnson revealed some details of the boy's death at a press conference Tuesday night. He would not say what caliber of bullet killed Weaver or if the boy was shot in the front or the back." By that time, the autopsy had been done, and it clearly showed that Sammy Weaver had been killed by a gunshot wound in the back—not in the stomach or the torso—and that the fatal bullet had been a smaller caliber than one likely to come from the .30-06 hunting rifle Kevin Harris was carrying. Why were federal officials so quick to imply—without actually coming right out and saying so—that

Kevin Harris or even Randy Weaver had fired the bullet that killed Sammy Weaver?

Another *Spokesman-Review* article for August 26 offers a story that differs significantly from previous versions:

> John Roche, deputy director of the U.S. Marshal Service, said Friday's gun battle at Randy Weaver's cabin occurred when somebody drove onto the property while federal agents watched the place.
>
> He gave this account to the Boston Globe:
>
> "About noon on Friday, a car drove up to the property, and Weaver, his son, Samuel, and Kevin Harris came outside with semiautomatic rifles and their dogs to check out the visitors.
>
> "At that point, one of the dogs, a yellow Labrador retriever, picked up the scent of the marshals in the gully about 500 yards below the cabin and began running in that direction, followed by Weaver, his son and Harris.
>
> "Marshal William Degan was hiding behind a tree stump when he saw one dog was about to attack a colleague. He jumped up, identified himself as a federal marshal, and ordered the men and the teenager to halt.
>
> " 'The person we believe to be Harris then swung around and shot, striking the deputy in the heart,' Roche said. When the dog tried to attack another deputy, Arthur D. Roderick, Roderick shot and killed the dog.
>
> "Roderick dove for cover in the ravine, just as a bullet believed to have been fired by Weaver grazed his coat. A third marshal—who fired three rounds—thought he hit one of the three as they were retreating. Samuel Weaver's body was found by officers in an outbuilding Sunday night.
>
> "Authorities on Monday would not say why they waited a day to announce the discovery. They would not speculate about why the body was in the shed but said they thought Weaver knew his son had been fatally shot.
>
> "While the gun battle with Degan and his team was going on, the second group of marshals was taking fire from others shooting automatic weapons from the cabin.

"One of the marshals with Degan had been trained as a medic and arrived at his side within 30 seconds. 'He knew he was dead,' Roche said.

"But it wasn't until 10:00 P.M. Friday night that a SWAT team, alerted by two marshals who had managed to escape from the area, could hike up the hill to evacuate Degan's body and three colleagues trapped by sporadic gunfire."

Several elements of this story are fascinating. The action is said to have been precipitated by visitors who drove onto the property in a car. Who were they? They disappear from future accounts. The dog (or dogs?) is said to have picked up a scent from a gully five hundred yards away and to have attacked not just one but two agents. The cabin inhabitants are all said to be carrying "semiautomatic" weapons and "automatic" weapons are said to be fired from the cabin. No mention is made of the fully automatic weapons the marshals were carrying. Sammy Weaver did have a semiautomatic weapon that day, but Randy Weaver and Kevin Harris were both carrying single–shot weapons. No automatic weapons were found when the cabin was searched later. And the elite Special Operations Group of the U.S. Marshals Service is said to have been pinned down for ten hours before being able to evacuate. Note that this version of the story is told to the *Boston Globe*, published in Marshal Degan's home state, with no reporters on the scene. The *Spokesman-Review* had to get this version from another newspaper, probably through scanning the wire services.

Another *Spokesman-Review* article on August 26 offers yet more surprising news:

In Boston, John Roche, deputy director of the U.S. Marshals Service, said Degan, 42, a highly trained, highly decorated deputy, was not wearing a bullet-proof vest when he was shot. But he said a vest would not have stopped the bullet.

"We talked about it before the surveillance operation," said Roche. "Based on the weapons in the house, we decided against it. We knew they had semiautomatic weapons. The weapon Marshal

Degan was killed by was consistent with an AR-15, a semiautomatic weapon. A vest would not have stopped it."

Kevin Harris was carrying a bolt–action .30–06 rifle made in 1917, not a modern semiautomatic AR–15—the civilian semiautomatic version of the M–16 full automatic weapons being carried by the U.S. marshals that day. Why would an experienced agent like William Degan have had such a fatalistic attitude about abandoning standard operating procedure and not wearing a bullet–proof vest? The Weavers did have some weapons that might have pierced a bullet–proof vest, but they also had weapons a vest would have stopped.

Allowances can be made for agency spokespeople, especially people thousands of miles away from Idaho, not being in full possession of all the relevant facts about a confrontation that was confusing and full of tension and uncertainty. And reporters, even experienced reporters, sometimes make errors or fail to understand everything they are told. After all the allowances are made, however, there can be little doubt that the stories given to the media by federal authorities differed significantly from what was said in sworn testimony, subject to cross–examination, in the federal trial of Randy Weaver and Kevin Harris that followed the standoff. Just how fully aware these federal spokespeople were of the wide discrepancies between what they told reporters and what was really happening is difficult to determine, especially after the fact. It is to be hoped that the FBI report or the Department of Justice report on the Ruby Ridge incident will contain some comments about these discrepancies and include some preliminary conclusions about whether FBI or U.S. Marshals Service officials deliberately misled reporters.

To all these federal stories, one more version, somewhat different from any of the other versions and different from what seemed finally to have been accepted by both sides at the trial, is told by Bo Gritz. After Kevin Harris had been removed from the cabin and turned over to the medics, Gritz wrote in a later newsletter: "I returned to examine Randall's wound. It was clear to see that he had been hit by a .223 caliber bullet fired from an M–16 rifle—not a 7.62 millimeter from Horiuchi's Remington 700 sniper rifle. The .223 entered his right upper back and emerged cleanly from the center of his armpit."

Gritz believes that Lon Horiuchi, the FBI sniper, was accompanied by a number-two man, a back-up shooter responsible for communications with the command center, who carried an M-16 rifle with iron sights. Gritz believes that "Horiuchi didn't fire the first round—number two did! Horiuchi was zeroed in on Vicki Weaver, but she would have made a better target standing in the yard. The number-two man aimed his M-16 off-hand with iron sights at Weaver's head, but typically (ask any vet) missed by the margin stated. When Weaver didn't fall and the family ran for the cabin, Horiuchi hit his quarter-inch bulls-eye target—as planned.

That's certainly a provocative version of events. It comes from somebody who, at this point in his life, seems inclined to believe the worst of government agents and agencies. But it comes also from a man with a great deal of military experience, who has seen a lot of wounds.

It is a well-known phenomenon, of course, that different people can watch the same event and have significantly different memories of just what happened. And the tales told by evidence, even properly collected evidence, are not always absolutely clear or unequivocal. But after all allowances are made, there can be little doubt that the stories given to the media during the Ruby Ridge siege and standoff were notably different from the picture that emerged over time in sworn testimony in court. Just how fully aware various spokespersons were of the wide discrepancies between what they were telling reporters and other people at the bridge and what had really happened is difficult to determine.

The distinct possibility emerges, however, that professional spokespersons for federal agencies deliberately misled the media in their reports. If this is determined to be the case, whether through internal reports, congressional investigations, or subsequent court proceedings, will any of these public information specialists be disciplined or reprimanded? Or is deliberately misleading the press not considered something worthy of reprimand in certain federal agencies?

Pretrial Hearings
and Maneuvers

RANDY WEAVER HAD RECEIVED AT LEAST A CONDITIONAL COMMITMENT from Gerry Spence to represent him in the coming trial, and Spence is considered one of the finest trial lawyers in the country. But Kevin Harris didn't have a lawyer yet, and he couldn't afford one. Judge Mikel Williams, who had the assignment to conduct the preliminary hearing to determine if the charges were substantial enough to warrant a trial in the Weaver–Harris case, placed a call to David Nevin, one of the most experienced defense lawyers in Boise, asking if he would serve as court–appointed counsel for Kevin Harris. Nevin had mixed feelings. He had been on vacation during the Ruby Ridge standoff. While he hadn't been able to avoid all knowledge of the events, one of his delights in going on vacation was to ignore the barrage of news as much as possible. So he didn't know much, beyond a general impression that a family with unusual white separatist beliefs had held off government agents for a long time and had finally been captured.

Nevin describes himself as a "yellow–dog Democrat"—a humorous term from Texas politics describing somebody who finds the idea of voting for a Republican so distasteful he would vote even for a yellow dog if that pale canine was the Democratic standard–bearer. Democrats of any kind, let alone stubborn ones, are something of a rarity in Idaho. Nevin had little or no sympathy for what he understood to be Kevin Harris's and Randy Weaver's political beliefs. The compensation for court–appointed attorneys, who represent indigent defendants in cases where it doesn't seem appropriate or practical to have them represented by a public defender, barely covered the fixed overhead costs of his office, and sometimes didn't cover that, and he knew this case would demand his full attention for an extended period of time.

On the other hand, he believed that taking cases as court–appointed counsel was one of his obligations as an attorney. And he would get a chance to work with Gerry Spence, whom he believed would be Randy's private defense attorney.

The words "Gerry Spence" and "flamboyant" seem to go together. From his office in Jackson Hole, Wyoming, Gerry Spence has traveled throughout the country representing increasingly high–profile clients in his shrewd, folksy style, replete with cowboy hat, boots, and fringed leather jacket. Nevin was familiar with Spence's career. Spence had represented the family of Karen Silkwood against the Kerr–McGee Chemical Corporation, and former Philippine first lady Imelda Marcos against the U.S. government. He has not only represented big–name clients, but written several books on the law and larger issues in American life. Beyond the flashy courtroom style, however, he is a shrewd and successful attorney. He has won more million–dollar judgments against corporations than any living attorney, and he hasn't lost a criminal case since 1969. He has a reputation not only as a masterful courtroom performer, but as a lawyer who is always fully prepared, not only quick with a comeback or clever comment, but conversant with every detail of the cases he is working on. David Nevin knew he was a good attorney himself, but he figured he could learn from working alongside Gerry Spence for an extended period of time.

Nevin decided he would at least think about taking the case, and flew to Spokane to meet with his new client the day Randy Weaver himself came off the mountain. Kevin Harris was in a hospital room at the end of a hall guarded by armed federal marshals. After meeting him and spending some time talking together, Nevin had a hard time thinking of Harris as a cold-blooded murderer, and decided to take the case.

When Randy Weaver was taken into custody on Monday, September 1, he was flown to Ada County Jail pending arraignment in federal court on Tuesday. About the same time, Gerry Spence responded in a letter to Alan J. Hirschfeld, a close friend and former chairman of Columbia Pictures and Twentieth Century-Fox who had implored Spence not to take the Weaver case because his representation might give more prominence and encouragement to white racists and anti-Semites:[2]

> I met Randy Weaver in jail on the evening of his surrender. His eyes had no light in them. He was unshaven and dirty. He was naked except for yellow plastic prison coveralls, and he was cold. His small feet were clad in rubber prison sandals. In the stark setting of the prison conference room he seemed diminutive and fragile. He had spent eleven days and nights in a standoff against the government, and he had lost. His wife was dead. His son was dead. His friend was near death. Weaver himself had been wounded. He had lost his freedom. He had lost it all. And now he stood face to face with a stranger who towered over him and whose words were not words of comfort. When I spoke, you, Alan, were on my mind.
>
> "My name is Gerry Spence," I began. "I'm the lawyer you've been told about. Before we begin to talk I want you to understand that I do not share any of your political or religious beliefs. Many of my dearest friends are Jews. My daughter is married to a Jew. My sister is married to a black man. She has adopted a black child. I deplore what the Nazis stand for. If I defend you I will not defend your political beliefs or your religious beliefs, but your right as an American citizen to a fair trial." His quiet answer was, "That is all I ask." Then I motioned him to a red plastic chair and I took a similar one. And as the guards marched by and from time to time peered in, he told his story.

---

2. *The letter is quoted from Gerry Spence's recent book,* From Freedom to Slavery.

Randy Weaver's recollection to a friend later is a little different. According to Randy's memory, Gerry Spence started out by saying, "I want you to know that I can't stand racists," whereupon Randy replied, "I want you to know that I can't stand lawyers." After that, they understood one another and got down to business.

= * =

Court proceedings in the United States are a bit like a long, scripted play or a mini-series. First comes the arraignment, when a judge or magistrate lays out the charges brought by the prosecuting office, takes a plea from the defendant, and sets up a schedule for the preliminary hearing. Randy Weaver and Kevin Harris were accused by the federal government of violating federal laws rather than by a state or local government. So, on Tuesday, September 1, 1992, Randy Weaver, accompanied by Gerry Spence and Boise attorney Chuck Peterson, appeared in federal court in Boise, before Judge Mikel Williams. Weaver pleaded not guilty to the original charges— selling illegal weapons and failure to appear. An additional charge, stemming from the gun battle and standoff, of assault on a federal officer, was filed by the prosecution. Judge Williams ordered a detention hearing and a preliminary hearing for September 10, at which time Weaver would plead on the assault charge. Weaver was returned to custody. Kevin Harris was still in a hospital in Spokane, charged with first-degree murder of a federal officer. David Nevin pleaded not guilty for him.

After the hearing, both Gerry Spence and Randy Weaver presented written statements to the court and to the press. Spence's statement explained why he had agreed to take the case:

> I was told that if I would agree to represent Randy Weaver he would come down off of the mountain and surrender. Hoping that my agreement to represent him would prevent further bloodshed, I have made my appearance on his behalf in federal court today.
> Mr. Weaver and our co-counsel do not see eye to eye on many issues. We do not believe in white separatism.

We do not share Mr. Weaver's religious beliefs.

But our personal beliefs and his are not important to this case. In America, all of our religious and political beliefs are protected by our Constitution. If this were not so, we have lost what is most sacred in America. These freedoms are what makes America the great nation that it is and distinguishes us from all other countries in the world.

We have therefore agreed to represent Mr. Weaver to demonstrate to him and all those who doubt, that the system does work, that citizens will not be killed or prosecuted or convicted because of their beliefs, and that there is justice in this nation for everyone, of every religion and of every political bent, for to the same extent that Mr. Weaver's rights to a fair trial are diminished because of his beliefs, so, too, are the rights of all of the rest of us.

I have been offered the excellent assistance of Chuck Peterson and his partner, Garry Gilman, who will act as local counsel and assist me, along with my son, Kent Spence. These lawyers have authorized me to say that they are offering their services in this important case in order to see that the American system of justice is preserved.

Randy Weaver's statement offered some of his version of events, and an explanation of why he had agreed to surrender:

I decided to come down from the mountain for two reasons: First, I didn't want my children exposed to any further danger. These girls are very brave. They stayed by their dead mother all of those days and took care of Kevin Harris and me and the baby. If it weren't for them we might not have made it at all. In the end, they were afraid, as was I, that if we came out we would all be killed.

I have never believed that I could get a fair trial in a government court. I was assured that Mr. Spence, one of the great lawyers of the country who has spent his life fighting for people and the cause of freedom, will see that I get a fair trial. I believe Mr. Spence will see that my rights are protected. If I did not believe that I would still be up there.

I have authorized Mr. Spence to undertake my defense understanding that he and I see eye to eye on very few political and religious issues. As a matter of fact, we are poles apart in our beliefs. But one thing he and I agree on, and that is people ought not be murdered by their own government.

This case must stand for something. Otherwise my darling Vicki and my dear son Sam have died for nothing. The case must do something for this country that I love. Otherwise Mamma's life and Sam's death were wasted.

The facts in this case are known to everyone. First they killed our dog, a big, friendly yellow Lab. Then they shot Sam, my son. They blew off his arm. Then they shot him in the back. The second day they tried to eliminate all of the witnesses to Sam's murder. They shot me, and then Kevin. Finally they killed my wife as she stood at the doorway of our cabin with our baby daughter in her arms. She fell with her arms still clutching our baby. When I lifted her head, half of her face had been blown away. We did not have enough water to bathe her or prepare her body. We kept her with us eight days.

There is no doubt that she was killed in retaliation for the death of the federal officer. Those officers are all trained and skilled in shooting an identifiable target. They are excellent marksmen. They shot her in the head. This was murder, a horrid premeditated murder. I expect the system to do whatever it can to cover this atrocity, but they know, and I know, that what I say is true.

This is my statement,
Randy Weaver

On that same Tuesday, sixteen–year–old Sara Weaver spoke in the northern Idaho motel room where she and her two sisters were staying with their grandparents with reporter Jess Walter of the *Spokesman-Review*. She told a harrowing tale of cowering on the floor of the cabin for days, always aware of the presence of her dead mother's body, expecting that she would be killed.

"I was praying that if they were going to kill us, they'd take us all at once, because I couldn't stand to see any more of my

Randy and Vicki Weaver at their wedding in 1971.
Provided by Jackie Brown

In 1988, Vicki posed with Sammy, Sara, and Rachel.
Provided by Jackie Brown

Road leading to the Weaver cabin in Naples, Idaho.
Reason/Alan W. Bock

Supporters of the Weaver family during the siege.
Spokesman-Review/Colin Mulvany

Protestors at one of the roadblocks during the siege.
Spokesman-Review/Jesse Tinsley

Local children express their views about Sammy's killing.
Spokesman-Review/*Colin Mulvany*

Weaver supporters are arrested trying to pass roadblocks.
Spokesman-Review/*Colin Mulvany*

Local resident walks by a roadblock with upside down flag.
Spokesman-Review/*Jesse Tinsley*

Government vehicles move up to the staging area.
Spokesman-Review/*Jesse Tinsley*

Hazardous waste officials appear at the scene.
Spokesman-Review/*Jesse Tinsley*

The government's staging area during the siege.
Spokesman-Review/*Colin Mulvany*

A protestor is detained by federal agents and later released.
Spokesman-Review/*Jesse Tinsley*

A federal helicopter flies over the Weaver cabin area.
Spokesman-Review/*Colin Mulvany*

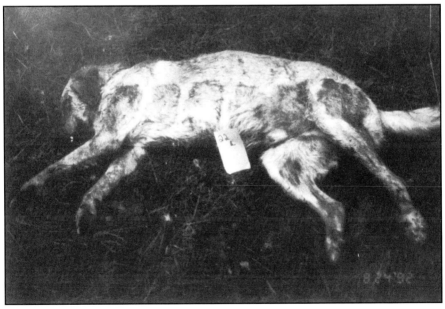

Weaver's dog, Striker, was shot and killed by Marshal Roderick.
He was left in the road and run over repeatedly
by government vehicles.
Government exhibit

Mother and family of Kevin Harris during the siege.
Spokesman-Review/ *Jesse Tinsley*

Flowers displayed after Vicki Weaver had been killed.
Spokesman-Review/*Jesse Tinsley*

Front porch where Vicki Weaver was shot and killed.
Associated Press

Interior of the Weaver cabin sometime after the siege.
Spokesman-Review/*Blair Kooistra*

FBI displays confiscated weapons after the siege. All were legal.
Associated Press

Bo Gritz, who was instrumental in ending the siege, gives a press update.

Spokesman-Review/*Anne Williams*

Randy Weaver being taken to court by a federal marshal.
Idaho Statesman/*Tom Shanahan*

Kevin Harris leaving courthouse after being found innocent.
Idaho Statesman/*Chris Butler*

Weaver attorney, Gerry Spence, talks to press after the trial.
Idaho Statesman/*Chris Butler*

Trash left by the government after the assault.
Reason/*Alan W. Bock*

A side view of the Weaver cabin taken in the fall after the siege.
Spokesman-Review/*Blair Kooistra*

Weaver cabin boarded up sometime after the siege.
Reason/*Alan W. Bock*

Randy Weaver on the day the trial ended in Boise, Idaho.

Spokesman-Review/*Blair Kooistra*

family hurt," she said. "I couldn't watch them pick us off one at a time. I was praying that they would just firebomb us."

She stood by the version of events Randy and Kevin had dictated to her. "They said it was a gun battle," that led to Vicki Weaver's death, she noted. "But no one in my family fired a shot. There were only their snipers trying to kill us. . . . This isn't paranoia. Look what happened to us."

Sara also claimed that on Sunday the family yelled to agents outside the cabin that Vicki Weaver was dead, but the agents responded with taunting:

"They'd come on real late at night and say, 'Come out and talk to us, Mrs. Weaver,' 'How's the baby, Mrs. Weaver?' in a real smart-alecky voice. Or they'd say, 'Good morning, Randall. How'd you sleep? We're having pancakes. What are you having?' It was like psychological warfare. It made me so mad."

Although Sara said she would prefer to stay in northern Idaho, she agreed it was best to return to Iowa with her grandparents for the time being to keep the family together.

Later in the week, federal authorities, not willing to be quoted by name because of the pending court case, disputed the version of events given by Randy and Sara Weaver. "I've heard enough of this talk that we shot a mother with a baby in her arms. That's just not true," one source told the *Spokesman-Review*. "They fired at the FBI helicopter and that's when the FBI guy was given permission to open fire." Two sources said they believed Vicki Weaver was one of those firing at the helicopter, at which point—because agents were in mortal danger—a supervisor gave permission for the sniper to open fire.

The allegation that the Weavers fired at a helicopter before Vicki Weaver was shot would play an important role in the upcoming trial.

Dave Tubbs, assistant to special agent-in-charge Gene Glenn, said he couldn't "officially confirm" that Vicki or other family members fired at a helicopter. "I can tell you, though, that we don't shoot mothers with babies in their arms," Tubbs said. "We can't shoot at fleeing felons. So obviously, if a shooting occurred that resulted in the death of Vicki Weaver, something happened to precipitate that shooting."

On Tuesday, September 8, Judge Williams, in legal skirmishing prior to the preliminary hearing, denied a request from defense lawyers to summon as witnesses three FBI agents, the Boundary County coroner, and four deputy U.S. marshals. The government, represented by Assistant U.S. Attorney Ron Howen, argued against calling federal agents to testify, claiming some had received death threats. "If they want to call witnesses, why don't they call Randy Weaver?" asked Howen. Judge Williams agreed to summon one FBI agent and two marshals. Weaver attorney Chuck Peterson was not satisfied. "They tell Randy Weaver that he has to answer the charges, but when you want to call a witness, they won't tell you where they are," he complained. "The government can't have it both ways."

The preliminary hearing got underway September 10, 1992, as scheduled. Meantime, however, Assistant U.S. Attorney Howen, who was to serve as lead prosecutor in the case—the federal equivalent of the district attorney in local government—convened a federal grand jury to consider an indictment against Weaver and Harris. Early in the day on Wednesday, September 16, the third day of actual court proceedings on the first set of charges, the grand jury delivered an indictment of Weaver and Harris on murder and conspiracy charges.

Gerry Spence asked Judge Williams to quash the grand jury indictment on the grounds that the preliminary hearing would fulfill the need to determine if there was probable cause to hold a trial. Late in the day, however, Judge Williams stopped the preliminary hearing, ruling that the filing of the grand jury indictment ended the need for a preliminary hearing. Announcing that he wanted to reserve the right to appeal this decision, Spence refused to enter a plea on the new charges contained in the indictment. Judge Williams then scheduled a hearing for Thursday at which Weaver would be asked to enter a plea. At that hearing, Weaver and Harris pleaded not guilty.

The actual indictment, consisting of ten counts, including murder, aiding and abetting murder, conspiracy, and assault was released to the public on October 1, 1992, and the trial was scheduled to begin October 26. However, on October 22, after a request from both sides for more time to prepare their cases, the trial was rescheduled to begin in February 1993. On November 19, 1992, an amended indictment was filed by prosecutor Ron Howen.

Count One of the indictment, which took up twelve of the eighteen pages in the document, outlined the alleged conspiracy:

> Beginning at an unknown date in approximately January of 1983 and continuing through August 31, 1992, within the District of Idaho and elsewhere, RANDALL C. WEAVER, Vicky [sic] Weaver, KEVIN L. HARRIS and others known and unknown to the Grand Jury, including some other members of the Weaver family, did knowingly, unlawfully and intentionally conspire, confederate, combine and/or agree together and with each other as follows:
>
> 1. To forcibly resist, oppose, impede, interfere with, intimidate, assault and/or otherwise cause a violent confrontation with law enforcement authorities in the engagement in or on account of the performance of their official duties of enforcing the laws of the United States of America, the individual states, and/or any political subdivision thereof . . .
>
> 2. To purchase, develop and maintain a remote mountain residence/stronghold;
>
> 3. To illegally and otherwise make, possess, sell and/or conceal firearms and ammunition;
>
> 4. To fail to appear for trial on pending federal criminal charges . . .
>
> 5. To hinder or prevent the discovery, apprehension, arrest and trial of federal fugitives from justice;
>
> 6. To steal, conceal, retain and/or convert the personal property of others to their own use;
>
> 7. To intimidate neighbors, as well as law enforcement officers and agents, by the use, display, threat to use and/or discharge of firearms;

8. To use, display, threaten to use, fire and/or discharge firearms at or near human beings, vehicles and/or aircraft; and

9. To assault, shoot, wound, kill and/or murder, or threaten or cause such to occur to, other human beings by means of the use of deadly weapons; all in violation of Sections 2, 3, 111, 115, 641, 922(g), 1071, 1111, 1114, 3146(a)(1) and 3147 of Title 18, and Sections 5861(d) and (f) of Title 26, United States Code and State law.

The count went on to describe the manner and means by which this alleged conspiracy was carried out. "It was part of the conspiracy," for example, that the Weavers had left Iowa and moved to Idaho "in their belief and prediction that a violent confrontation would occur with law enforcement involving a 'kill zone' surrounding their property." "It was part of the conspiracy" that they bought the property and built the cabin, that they attempted to form a group opposed to the New World Order, that they isolated themselves, that they sold illegal firearms, that they bought legal firearms, and that they "precipitated a violent confrontation with federal law enforcement officers by refusing the requests, pleas and entreaties of federal, state or local law enforcement agents and officers, relatives and friends to peacefully surrender and appear for trial."

The count named Randy Weaver, "defendant and co-conspirator," as a leader of the group of criminals, Vicki Weaver as an "unindicted co-conspirator," and Kevin Harris as "a member of the conspiracy." About thirty different instances of buying weapons, having meetings with people, sending letters, and writing statements, as well as the shots fired on August 21 and shots allegedly fired August 22, were all deemed part of the conspiracy.

Count Two was the original illegal firearms charge. "Randall C. Weaver did knowingly make, receive and/or possess firearms, to wit: a single shot H&R 12-gauge shotgun having a barrel length of approximately 13 inches . . . and a Remington 12-gauge pump shotgun having a barrel length of 12–3/4 inches . . . in violation of federal law . . ."

Count Three stated that Randall C. Weaver "did knowingly fail to appear for said trial" on the firearms charge.

Count Four stated: "On or about August 21, 1992, near Naples, within the District of Idaho, RANDALL C. WEAVER, KEVIN L. HARRIS, and another did forcibly resist, oppose, impede, interfere with, intimidate, and/or assault deputy United States marshals Arthur Roderick, Larry Cooper, William Degan, and others while engaged in or on account of the performance of their official duties, by the use of deadly weapons, to wit: firearms."

Count Five was the murder charge: "On or about August 21, 1992, . . . the defendant, KEVIN L. HARRIS, as aided, abetted, counseled, induced or procured by RANDALL C. WEAVER, Vicki Weaver and some other members of the Weaver family, did unlawfully, willfully, deliberately, maliciously and with malice aforethought and premeditation, shoot, kill and murder one William F. Degan, a human being, by shooting said William F. Degan in the chest with a high powered rifle, while said William F. Degan was engaged in or on account of the performance of his official duties . . ."

Count Six charged: "On or about August 22, 1992, . . . RANDALL C. WEAVER and KEVIN L. HARRIS did forcibly resist, oppose, interfere with, intimidate, and assault Frank Costanza, Dick Rogers, G. Wayne Smith, and John Haynes, employees of the Federal Bureau of Investigation or the United States Marshals Service, while engaged in or on account of the performance of their official duties, by the use of deadly weapons, to wit: firearms. . . ."

Count Seven charged: "Vicki Weaver, KEVIN L. HARRIS and some other members of the Weaver family, did harbor, conceal, receive, comfort and/or assist a person, namely RANDALL C. WEAVER, for whose arrest a warrant had been issued" between January 1991 and August 31, 1992.

Count Eight stated: "On or about and between January 18, 1991, and August 31, 1992, . . . RANDALL C. WEAVER, as aided, abetted, counseled, induced, or procured by Vicki Weaver, KEVIN L. HARRIS, and some other members of the Weaver family, did knowingly possess or receive approximately fourteen (14) firearms and thousands of rounds of ammunition . . . well knowing that RANDALL C. WEAVER was a fugitive from justice. . . ."

Count Nine stated: "On or about and between January 18, 1991, and August 31, 1992, near Naples, within the District of Idaho, RANDALL C. WEAVER did commit one or more offenses as alleged herein in Counts Three, Four, Five, Six, and Eight after having been released by federal magistrate Stephen Ayers on January 18, 1991, pursuant to Title 18, United States Code, Sections 3241(b) and (c); all in violation of Section 3147(1) of Title 18, United States Code.

Count Ten charged that Randy Weaver and Kevin Harris "did knowingly carry or use certain firearms and ammunition described herein in Count Eight during and in relation to the commission of violent crimes as described herein. . . ."

Gerry Spence charged that "many things in the indictment have nothing to do with the case and have only to do with laying a foundation for the prosecution to introduce evidence that's prejudicial in the case and that the prosecution knows is improper and prejudicial. They charge him with being a part of the Aryan Nations movement and that raises the specter that this man is being prosecuted for what are allegedly his beliefs rather than for the crimes that he allegedly committed." Spence pointed out that the search warrant issued after the standoff had ended called for the seizure of "correspondence, publications, literature, and other writings, both printed and handwritten, originals and copies, relating to white supremacy, white separatism, neo–Nazi groups, including emblems and slogans of such groups, writings relating to 'zionist occupational government' that revealed thoughts, motivations, threats, plans, or theories involving the use of violence toward other human beings, including but not limited to federal, state, and local law enforcement officers and/or elected public officials."

In January 1993, Gerry Spence and Chuck Peterson filed a motion to dismiss the indictment and to remove Ron Howen from the case on the grounds that he had been present during the siege and standoff and could be a candidate to be called as a witness. The memorandum in support of the motion included the Weaver family's version of what had happened, and made the case that the U.S. marshals, not the Weavers, provoked the confrontation that led to the deaths of Sammy Weaver and William Degan. It said, for example, that the team of marshals, "in preparation for this alleged 'reconnaissance mission' went to a shooting range where they spent several hours sighting–in their guns. Moreover, the marshals brought with them a medic and medical equipment in obvious anticipation that someone would be injured."

From their months of surveillance, claimed the memorandum, the marshals knew that the Weavers usually carried weapons but had confronted people on their property nonviolently. "In face of this history, the marshals' apparent strategy was to engage the Weavers while they were armed which, even in the face of their alleged orders not to engage the Weavers, would provide the marshals cause to use deadly force against the Weavers."

Said the memorandum:

> Roderick now admits that his team was throwing rocks toward the Weaver house (Roderick Grand Jury Testimony, pg. 40) thus taunting the dogs. Later, contrary to these admissions by Roderick, Marshal Jack Cluff of Moscow, Idaho, told the press that the Weavers had loosed their dogs on an approaching vehicle. The dogs were disturbed by the marshals' rock throwing, and the prelude to the forbidden confrontation began.
>
> The marshals ran, and, as must have been fully anticipated, the family golden Labrador started to follow the trail. But having already anticipated that the Lab would follow, the marshals had prearmed Marshal Cooper with a 9 millimeter submachine gun equipped with a silencer for the confessed purpose of shooting the dog. (Roderick Grand Jury Testimony, pg. 49).

So the dog started chasing the marshals, and Kevin and Sammy started chasing the dog, hoping it was on the trail of a large game animal. As the dog began getting closer:

The marshals took hiding places in the heavy trees and undergrowth along the road and waited for the dog and the two boys to come running by. They undoubtedly expected Randy Weaver to be with them. . . . The dog passed Cooper, but the boys were close behind the dog, so Cooper elected not to shoot the dog because, as he admitted, if he killed the dog 'I believed it would precipitate a firefight' (Preliminary Hearing, Cooper, p. 240, 9-11-92) . . . Since Cooper had not shot the dog as planned, Roderick now fired (Roderick 9-15-92 Grand Jury Testimony, p. 54). The bullet shattered the dog's spine and the dog let out a yelp. Since it was shot through the spine, it likely cried out in great pain, pulling itself about on its front legs for some time before it died, during all of which time the dog was in plain view of the boys (Roderick 9-15-92 Grand Jury Testimony, pg. 56). Thus a confrontation, <u>contrary to the marshals' orders</u>, was fully assured—indeed, <u>a forbidden confrontation with one of the Weaver children</u>." [Emphasis in original.]

The defense memorandum was using the evidence available to make the case that the marshals had purposely provoked the confrontation on August 21. It continued:

To the horror of thirteen-year-old Sammy Weaver, he saw a man in a full camouflage suit brutally shoot his dog. Roderick testified that up to that point no one he could identify had fired at the officers. Hence, by Roderick's admission, the first shot was fired by Roderick when he shot the family pet. When Sammy saw his dog, he yelled . . . and fired his gun, a .223 caliber mini-14 in Roderick's direction. There is no allegation or suggestion in this case that the boy hit anyone.

In the meantime, the officers opened fire with their fully automatic weapons and submachine gun. . . . Harris says he saw Sammy running toward home with his back to the officers. The child was crying out in pain, having been hit in the arm by the marshals' fire. Harris says he heard Randy Weaver, who was out of sight of the shooting, call his son to come home. Then Harris heard the boy call back, "I'm coming Dad." Those were the last words Sammy ever spoke. There was a lull in the shooting. Then there was another shot and Sammy cried out and then there was silence.

Seeing that Sammy had been shot and fearing for his own life, Harris opened fire in the direction of those who had been shooting from the bushes. He believed he shot the officer who had been firing at Sammy.

The memorandum went on to describe Randy's trip back to the cabin, including firing a few shots in the air and hearing Sammy say he was coming, and Kevin's trip to the cabin after checking to be certain Sammy Weaver was really dead. Then it zeroed in on the marshals:

After the smoke cleared, the U.S. marshals realized they were in serious trouble. William Degan, their colleague, was shot through the chest and had died. A child was dead along with the child's dog. Both child and dog were shot in the back (8/25/92 Autopsy Report of Samuel Weaver), although this information has still not been released to the press. The marshals must have realized that these deaths were, in fact, totally attributable to their violation of orders against confrontation and the admonition not to injure any of the Weaver children under any circumstances. . . .

As to the boy, no one could mistake him for an adult. This thirteen-year-old was no larger than the average ten-year-old (70–80 lbs. per 8/25/92 Autopsy Report). His voice, when he hollered out that the man had shot his dog, was the voice of a child. The child was shot by the officers running home. They had no warrant to arrest either Harris or the boy. The officers, now responsible for the death of two people, while Weaver himself had escaped, began to consider how to explain their conduct.

The memorandum noted that by the time the exchange of shots was over, Kevin and Randy were back at the cabin, more than a quarter–mile form the marshals, completely out of sight of the Y. There was no way the marshals could have been "pinned down." Nonetheless, the memorandum continued:

> The marshals began to spread a false story concerning the incident, a story that would result in the infamous standoff at Ruby Ridge, the death of Vicki Weaver and the wounding of Randy Weaver and Kevin Harris.

And it detailed several of the early stories the marshals or their press spokespeople had told, and related the tragic events of the following day, describing the rules of engagement as "illegal."

After Vicki Weaver was killed, the memorandum contended:

> The FBI now faced a serious problem. They had killed an unarmed mother standing at the door with a baby in her arms. They had no warrant for Vicki and were not likely to get one (9/30/92 Rogers Grand Jury Testimony, p. 30). Moreover, the FBI had discovered that Vicki had not been involved in the shooting at the "Y." It appears, therefore, that after Vicki was shot, the officers realized they had no legal or moral justification for having killed Vicki. . . . Since they had no right to shoot her, the FBI had no alternative but to later claim her death was an <u>accident</u>. In the meantime the federal officers pretended they did not know they had killed a second member of the Weaver family.

After discussing conflicting evidence regarding sniper Lon Horiuchi's story about shooting to protect a helicopter, and noting that the press had been told that Kevin Harris actually did fire at a helicopter when in fact he had not done so, the memorandum noted a curious fact:

> It is informative to note at this juncture that [Lon] Horiuchi, an expert marksman and team leader, armed with a precision sniping weapon with a ten-power scope now claims that <u>both</u> of his shots hit persons he did not intend to hit. Vicki's death was now supposedly accidental and Randy Weaver was supposedly shot when Horiuchi accidentally mistook Weaver for Harris. Harris, too, was supposedly hit with fragments of the bullet that went through Vicki's head and struck Harris in the arm and lungs. Sammy's death was also attributable to accident. By the time the officers were called to the grand jury <u>every person shot or killed had been shot by accident</u>. [Emphasis in original.]

The memorandum also contended that by being at the federal command post and by assisting in the search for evidence, Ron Howen (whose presence was referred to seven times in the FBI logs) had made himself a witness in this case, and that his testimony before the grand jury also made him a witness. As a potential witness, the defense motion sought to have Howen barred from acting as the prosecutor in the impending case. The memorandum claimed that the "group" alleged to have engaged in the conspiracy described in the indictment was none other than the Weaver family. And by his concentration on white supremacist beliefs and description of dangerous white supremacist groups to which Randy Weaver and his family did not belong, Ron Howen was said to have unfairly and unethically manipulated the grand jury. "Irrespective of what their beliefs may have been, it is the obvious contrivance of the government, as conceived by Mr. Howen, to *take fully protected, but unpopular religious beliefs, and to convert them, by allegation, into an active conspiracy, so that what was once protected under the Constitution is now the foundation for admissible and prejudicial evidence against the defendants."* (Emphasis in original.) All in all, claimed the defense memorandum, "It leaves jurors in the obvious position to reason: 'So the government killed a couple of Nazis who were trying to set up another "Bruderschweigen 1"—so what? They had it coming.' It creates a sort of 'good–riddance' attitude in jurors by which the unlawful killing of three human beings and the wounding of two others can be excused."

This was a defense memorandum, written so as to put the defense's spin on the facts of the case in a sufficiently persuasive manner as to get the judge to dismiss the indictment before the case ever came to trial. It is argumentative and subjective. But while the interpretation of the facts and events might still be subject to dispute, the basic facts used in the memorandum, as later testimony would bring out, were accurately portrayed.

As news media representatives sought to get more background information relevant to the defense motion, courthouse employees released hundreds of pages of transcripts from the grand jury proceedings. Several newspaper stories were written featuring extensive quotes from these transcripts. This upset U.S. District Judge Edward J. Lodge, scheduled to preside over the trial. Judge Lodge was concerned about the privacy of grand jury witnesses, and said that the release of these documents had been a mistake. When the prosecution filed a ninety–seven–page response to the defense motion, which quoted extensively from the grand jury proceedings, the judge refused to release that document and further documents in the case to the media.

Judge Lodge did not accept the defense motion to dismiss the indictment, although some of the language in the indictments relating to Randy Weaver's and Kevin Harris's alleged political and religious beliefs was removed. The judge also allowed Ron Howen to be the lead prosecutor. This motion and other preliminary legal wrangling kept pushing back the opening of the trial from the original February date, however. The trial did not finally begin until Monday, April 12, 1993. The headline on the front page of the April 11 issue of the *Spokesman-Review* turned out to be an accurate prediction: Feds to Face Tribulations in Weaver, Harris Trial.

The Trial Begins

THE FEDERAL COURTHOUSE IN BOISE, IDAHO, IS AN EIGHT-STORY, MODERN, marble structure built in a parklike setting a few blocks from downtown. Anticipating large crowds and possible trouble during the Weaver trial, authorities set up two airport-like metal detectors and X-ray machines, one at the main entrance to the building and one outside the entrance to the courtroom on the sixth floor, to examine bags. Federal agents from the Federal Protective Service and other agents were called in from all around the country to provide extra security. FBI agents and U.S. marshals wearing sunglasses blanketed the main entrance and conspicuously took photographs of the crowd of Weaver supporters, some carrying signs, that gathered outside the courthouse. Throughout the trial, more spectators than would fit into the courtroom, most of them Weaver supporters or critics of the government's action in the case, showed up.

The parking lot outside the courthouse was packed with television news trucks, bristling with antennas and other electronic gadgets. The O.J. Simpson trial has set a new standard for media attention, but at a local level the Weaver trial was something of a precursor in terms of public interest and media attention. The newspapers and television stations in Boise, Spokane, Seattle, and

Portland all had reporting teams assigned full-time to the trial, and most media outlets led their news coverage with the latest developments in the Weaver case throughout the trial. Local radio talk shows featured little else, with callers and invited experts dissecting every detail as new developments or information emerged from the court proceedings.

Monday, April 12, 1993, featured mostly preliminary skirmishing. Gerry Spence and Chuck Peterson, representing Randy Weaver, and David Nevin, representing Kevin Harris, presented arguments against allowing extensive testimony about their clients' religious and political beliefs, stating that this was merely an effort to "demonize" the defendants. Prosecutor Ron Howen argued that information about those beliefs was relevant not only to the state of mind of the defendants, but to the state of mind of federal officers as they tried to assess how much of a threat Randy Weaver posed once he had become a fugitive. Judge Lodge finally ruled that testimony about the defendants' racial and religious beliefs would be permitted in the impending trial.

On April 13 the jury was selected. Judge Lodge asked the original thirty-six-member jury pool if they or their families owned any guns, and almost all raised their hands to indicate that they did. An all-white jury of seven women and five men, along with six alternates, was selected. Judge Lodge told the jury, "This will probably be one of the most interesting cases you could be asked to sit on as jurors." That proved to be almost an understatement.

Wednesday, April 14: Day One

Attorneys for the two sides presented their opening statements to the jury. In his four-hour opening statement, Ron Howen, acting as lead prosecutor, along with his assistant Kim Lindquist, outlined the conspiracy theory contained in the indictment. "We need to go back to Iowa 1982, when the Weavers began believing in Christian Identity," said Howen. Weaving together information about various racialist and conspiracy theory buffs, from people who believe the world is secretly run by the Bavarian Illuminati to people who have taken violent action against Jews, the prosecution contended that the standoff at the Weaver "compound" was the direct result of the Weavers' "hate-filled belief" and their determination to provoke a confrontation with government agents to validate those beliefs. All of their actions, especially the move to Idaho and the decision not to show up for trial, were interpreted as inevitable steps in the formation of a hate group or a new "Order" like the violent Order organizations of the mid–1980s. Kevin Harris was portrayed as a willing dupe of the Weavers, who was led into a plan to "wage war" against the government by this conspiratorial group.

In his opening statement, Gerry Spence argued that it wasn't Randy Weaver who provoked the confrontation at all, but the government. Randy Weaver had broken no laws, claimed the defense attorney, until he was entrapped into sawing off shotguns by an undercover agent. As he warmed up, Spence pointed his finger directly at Ron Howen and angrily accused him of pushing hard for the arrest of Weaver even though he (Howen) knew that the initial firearms charge would probably not stand up in court. "The evidence in this case will be that Mr. Howen knew that it wasn't a good case," Spence thundered. "He told the marshal 'I'll probably have to dismiss it.' " Yet Howen insisted on the surveillance and on stepping up the pressure on Weaver. David Nevin argued that his client, Kevin Harris, shot Marshal Degan in self-defense after having been ambushed and provoked into a response by the killing of Sam Weaver.

The attorneys presented contrasting styles and personalities that would become more marked as the trial progressed. Both Howen and Spence are expert big-game hunters who don't use rifles when they hunt. Gerry Spence takes the field with a camera, while Ron Howen hunts with a beautifully crafted longbow that takes great strength and expertise to use properly. Beyond sharing the patience, the single-minded ability to concentrate unflinchingly on a target, and the timing of the skilled hunter, however, they had little in common.

Gerry Spence wears his grey hair in a mane that flows well over his shirt collar. He favors fringed suede jackets, cowboy boots, and nondescript tan pants. When outside—and sometimes when inside—he almost always wears a cowboy hat. A big-boned man, he stands about six feet two.

Ron Howen's thinning grey hair is cut short. He wears dark suits, brown wingtip shoes, and polyester neckties. He wouldn't reveal his age, but looked to be about a decade younger than Spence, who was sixty-five. Of medium height, he is notably muscular, tightly wound, and intense.

Their courtroom styles were a study in contrasts. Ron Howen was intensely focused and sometimes impatient, even with his own witnesses, when they didn't appear to understand a question or to respond properly. He smiled or grinned only rarely and, as has been his policy for years, refused almost all comment to reporters outside the courtroom. His voice is creaky and dry, sometimes cracking. He doggedly and mercilessly pursues facts, eschewing the opportunity to let emotions peek through. On the first day of testimony, a husky U.S. marshal was on the verge of crying as he described the death of his comrade, Marshal William Degan. Howen abruptly cut the testimony off, ending what promised to be an emotional moment—which might well have been effective for the prosecution side—before it had a chance to get started.

Gerry Spence seldom missed a chance to pull a little extra emotion from a witness, especially from witnesses who were friends or acquaintances of the Weaver family and seemed ready to demonstrate their pain over the loss of Vicki and Sammy. His voice has the range of a trained actor, from soft and quiet sweetness to thundering denunciation. He worked hard at making the jury like him, sometimes lampooning or making fun of himself, even as he skewered government witnesses with pointed questions delivered with large gestures or melodramatic grimaces.

David Nevin provided yet another contrast. Although he is among the most experienced murder defense attorneys in Idaho, he still looks like a young man. He is as quiet and unassuming as Spence is flamboyant and boisterous. As most of the testimony would center around Randy Weaver instead of Kevin Harris, Nevin would seldom be the center of attention in this case. When he did do cross-examinations, he would quietly but persistently probe the weaknesses in a witness's initial statements, relying on logic and gentle persuasion rather than the grand gesture to plant doubts about Kevin Harris's guilt.

Chuck Peterson, the Boise attorney who was Gerry Spence's co-counsel for Weaver, conducted cross-examinations by riddling hostile witnesses with barrages of questions, often telegraphing his message to the jurors with smirks or rolling eyes.

Thursday, April 15: Day Two

The prosecution presented its first witness, U.S. Marshal Larry Cooper, who was to stay on the witness stand two days. At the request of the defense, agreed to by the prosecution, Cooper appeared in the full camouflage outfit, including black ski mask, he had worn the previous August 21, when the killings of Marshal Degan and Sammy Weaver had occurred. He also carried the 9 millimeter M–16 AZ automatic weapon, with silencer, that he had taken onto the mountain that day.

During direct examination by the prosecution, Cooper testified that the six members of the U.S. Marshals Special Operations Group arrived at the Weaver property at 4:30 A.M. strictly for surveillance, to scout out possible sniper and observer locations for a later ambush. The plan, he said, part of what had been dubbed Operation Northern Exposure, was for an undercover agent to pose as a new neighbor and take Randy Weaver to double-check on the exact location of property lines, at which point he would be captured or ambushed. All six marshals, Cooper testified, were dressed pretty much as he was that day, with full camouflage, night-vision goggles, and camouflage jungle hats. Asked why he carried a silenced weapon, Cooper said, "There was no specific reason we carried it; it was just there."

Moving on to the confrontation with Kevin Harris and Sammy Weaver, Cooper said he feared being shot in the back and began looking for cover. He said the yellow dog came up to him, sniffed him and walked around him, but did not attack him, as some versions of the story had it. He also said that Harris and Sammy were not running toward him, which contradicted the account of the incident given in prosecutor Howen's opening statement. Cooper testified that upon being accosted by the marshals, who identified themselves as federal agents, Harris shot first and immediately, killing Marshal Degan. He said Harris and Sammy were standing side by side when he (Cooper) fired a three-shot burst from his weapon, whereupon Kevin "dropped like a sack of potatoes." He testified that he did not shoot at Sammy because he could see he was a kid.

Friday, April 16: Day Three

On cross-examination, Cooper was forced to admit that FBI special agent Greg Rampton had revealed during the grand jury hearing that Cooper was carrying a silenced weapon because Cooper had orders to lure the dogs and shoot them so the marshals could sneak up on the Weaver cabin without worrying about the dogs. He was unable to explain how, if Kevin Harris had fired the first shot of the battle and killed Marshal Degan immediately, there were seven spent shell casings from Degan's gun next to Degan's body. He offered no explanation of how, if he shot Kevin Harris and didn't shoot at Sam Weaver, Harris was in the courtroom and Sam was dead. In the grand jury hearing, Cooper had testified that he had heard hundreds of rounds being fired, but Gerry Spence pointed out that after the evidence had been collected, only fourteen to twenty rounds had been fired, seven by Marshal Degan.

During Gerry Spence's cross-examination of Marshal Cooper, prosecutor Howen repeatedly objected to questions as being repetitive, leading, misleading about the evidence, and a waste of the jury's time. Finally, Gerry Spence approached the bench impatiently, saying, "It's my belief at this time that we have been denied our right to a confrontation with the witness under the Sixth Amendment of the Constitution." He argued that the constant interruptions in his cross-examination had already had the effect of discrediting him in the eyes of the jury, and called for a mistrial. Judge Lodge became angry with both attorneys, denied the motion for a mistrial, and admonished both Spence and Howen to start acting like professionals.

David Nevin stressed the fact that Cooper constantly referred to the Weaver cabin as a "compound," asking for a definition. He asked Cooper about a trip by members of the Special Operations Group to a target range two days before to sight-in their weapons; Cooper said it was a routine procedure after weapons had been transported. Nevin then quoted Cooper's statement to the FBI after the incident, saying his position in the foxhole was a "low one, causing him to fire rounds over his head." Cooper said the FBI report was incorrect, that he was looking through the sights when he fired. Nevin also asked Cooper how many meetings he had had with the FBI, his superiors, and prosecutor Howen to prepare for his testimony. Cooper admitted that there were many meetings, and that before the preliminary hearing he had been taken on a "walk-through" at the shooting site by FBI agents and Howen.

The next witness was FBI special agent Greg Rampton, one of the first FBI agents on the scene after the initial shootout. Under cross-examination, he reaffirmed what he had said in earlier testimony about a plan for Cooper to lure the dogs toward him and shoot them. He also testified that after the dog Striker was shot, he was left lying in the road and that he was run over repeatedly by various vehicles. The defense made sure that the jury saw photographs of the dog's body with tire tracks and tracks from other vehicles on it.

Monday, April 19: Day Four

Cross-examination continued of Agent Rampton, one of the first FBI agents on the shooting scene on August 21, 1992. Rampton had to admit that between August 21, when the initial shootout occurred, and August 24, when the FBI began collecting evidence, that dozens of agents and several vehicles had been all over the area where the first shootout occurred. He also admitted that after the standoff, when all the weapons were confiscated from the Weaver cabin, that one of the pistols was misplaced and sent to Salt Lake City instead of to Boise, where all the other weapons were sent. He also testified that in his previous testimony, on Friday, he had made a mistake about the brand of pistol and the number of bullets in it.

The next witness was Herb Byerly, the special agent for the Bureau of Alcohol, Tobacco and Firearms who had hired an undercover informant to infiltrate the Aryan Nations and to convert Randy Weaver into an informant. He described how he told the informant, Kenneth Fadeley, to use a false name and to swear an oath that it was his real name when dealing with Weaver. The prosecution asked that several audio tapes secretly made of conversations between Fadeley and Weaver be entered as evidence. The defense objected because much of the tape was incomprehensible, and Spence questioned whether the transcript provided by the government was accurate. The judge allowed the evidence.

At the end of the day, Judge Lodge instructed the jury not to watch, listen to, or read news coverage about the burning of the home (or compound) of the Branch Davidians in Waco, Texas, that left more than eighty people dead, which had occurred that day. The home had been surrounded by federal agents since February, and as it turned out, several of the federal officers who had been at Ruby Ridge were also at Waco.

Back in Iowa, the family of Keith Brown, Vicki Weaver's brother-in-law, with whom the Weaver daughters were staying that day, did watch the televised coverage of the burning of the Branch Davidian complex. Brown later told a friend of the family that as the residence burst into flames and burned to the ground, Sara got the same hard look on her face that she had when the children first came down off the mountain, but which had faded and almost disappeared during months of almost normal existence.

Tuesday, April 20: Day Five

Kenneth Fadeley, who had told Randy Weaver that his name was Gus Magisono, and that he was a biker who trafficked in illegal weapons, was the first witness. The prosecution asked him detailed questions about the racist beliefs of the Aryan Nations organization, and about the Ku Klux Klan and other organizations.

Under cross-examination, Fadeley testified that it had been difficult to get Randy Weaver to consider the idea of doing anything illegal, that it had taken a good deal of time and effort to get him to agree to sell two sawed-off shotguns at a time when Randy was strapped for cash. He also said that he had received only $445 in expenses between 1986 and 1989, but that he had been promised a bonus if Randy was convicted. Gerry Spence immediately objected that this made Fadeley a "contingency witness" and that two Supreme Court rulings had prohibited the use of contingency witnesses, because they have an obvious personal interest in the outcome of a case. Judge Lodge said he would consider the objection.

Gerry Spence twice moved on April 20 for a mistrial, arguing that the extensive questions the prosecution had asked most of its witnesses about Randy Weaver's political and religious beliefs—or about their impressions or understanding of his beliefs—made this a political or religious trial rather than a trial about alleged wrongful acts committed by the defendants. Judge Lodge denied the motions and urged attorneys for both sides to keep the trial moving.

Wednesday, April 21, Thursday, April 22, Friday, April 23: Days Six, Seven, and Eight

The prosecution brought back Herb Byerly to contradict Fadeley's testimony that Fadeley had been promised a bonus if Weaver was convicted. But under close cross-examination, he had to admit that prosecutor Ron Howen had indirectly referred to a bonus in conversations with Fadeley. He also admitted that the government's transcript of the tape recordings of conversations between Fadeley and Weaver omitted a section where Randy had said, "You approached me and offered me a deal." Spence said this was proof of entrapment, which was why the government had omitted it, but Byerly said the omission was an inadvertent mistake.

During the next several days, the prosecution presented evidence about Randy Weaver's initial arrest and witnesses to testify that Randy Weaver had failed to appear in court after being released on bail for the original firearms charge. But even this testimony to something that had clearly happened created trouble for the prosecution. Boundary County probation officer Karl Richins admitted to being confused about the date of the trial, said he had told prosecutor Ron Howen that Weaver had been sent a notification with an erroneous date, and that Howen had told him to forget about it. The court clerk also testified that Randy had not previously had any problems with any law enforcement agency, and that the initial arraignment took place with no attorney present, although a court-appointed attorney was later provided.

During testimony from Marshal Ron Mays, who had prepared the threat assessment, Gerry Spence tried to get him to clarify what he meant when he said Randy Weaver was associated with the Aryan Nations. Randy had been to a conference sponsored by the group, but hadn't joined the organization, said Spence. "Let's see, if that means Randy Weaver was associated with the Aryan Nations, I guess that means I'm also associated with the Aryan Nations, since I'm defending Randy Weaver—even though I do not believe a damn thing they say or believe in."

During this first week of the trial, the courtroom was usually filled with interested spectators from several western states, and the trial was covered intensively by local news media. An indication of how the first stages of the trial were going was that the defense attorneys were always friendly and confident when speaking with the media after each day's events, while the prosecution attorneys generally avoided much contact with the media. Staying away from the media, however, had been Ron Howen's pattern during previous cases. After Friday, April 23, the trial was recessed for a week, to resume on Monday, May 3.

Monday, May 3, Tuesday, May 4, Wednesday, May 5: Days Nine, Ten, and Eleven

The next major witness was U.S. marshal Dave Hunt, who was given the Weaver case by Agent Byerly of the BATF after Randy Weaver failed to appear in court. Hunt was led by the prosecution through the thirteen-month surveillance and then the escalation of efforts to apprehend Weaver which he supervised for the U.S. Marshals Service. He told how he interviewed almost everybody who visited the Weaver cabin, set up and paid the Rau family to provide information on who visited the cabin, and dealt with various friends of the Weaver family in an effort to get them to persuade Randy to surrender.

When asked about the threat profile he compiled on the Weavers, he was led through the entire array of racist, right-wing organizations, including the Aryan Nations, the Order, and the killers of Denver radio talk show host Alan Berg. Although Judge Lodge, in pretrial arguments, had ruled that he would allow testimony about the Weavers' religious and political beliefs, Gerry Spence still objected to this testimony, arguing that Randy Weaver was not a member of any group and had not been shown to be a member, and that all this information on supposedly interlocking racist groups was an effort to demonize his client. But Judge Lodge admitted the testimony on the grounds that it was relevant to the state of mind of the federal agents seeking to apprehend Randy Weaver, and that state of mind was important even though it might not reflect the "truth of the matter."

On Monday, May 3, Judge Lodge delivered what newspaper reports referred to as a setback to the prosecution when he ruled that the prosecution had not yet shown that a conspiracy existed among the Weavers or their friends. He said that evidence of the role of Kevin Harris in the alleged conspiracy was particularly slim. The conspiracy charge was considered a keystone of the ten-count indictment, the main reason Ron Howen had gone to the trouble of securing a grand jury indictment rather than settling for the original charges of murder and assault on a federal officer that had been filed during the standoff.

Also on May 3, Randy Weaver's father, Clarence Weaver, seventy-five, was in Boise to see part of the trial. After that day's testimony, he talked with reporters and demanded to know when a federal agent would be charged with the murder of his daughter-in-law and grandson. "I don't think they should have bothered him [Randy] to start with," said Clarence. "Randall, my boy, and Kevin are in jail and as far as I'm concerned there is no charge against them at all. But where are the government men that killed our boy and daughter-in-law?" Weaver did say his son had been treated well since being arrested and that he had a good relationship with the jail personnel. "I've never seen him look any better in his life," said Randy's father, who had come from Iowa with one of his daughters, Colleen Labertew.

Thursday, May 6: Day Twelve

The next witnesses to be called were friends of Randy Weaver who had taken the family food during the eighteen-month period of surveillance, some of whom had been approached by Hunt to act as intermediaries or negotiators. George Torrence, who owned land near the Weavers, testified that he had received $2,700 for appearing to sell some land to a federal agent who would move in and then be in a position to arrest Randy. But he also testified that the Weavers were always friendly in their dealings with him and with legitimate potential property buyers, that the dog Striker was friendly, the house was kept spotless, and the children were well behaved and respectful. He also said, under cross-examination, that Randy had told him he hadn't joined the Aryan Nations because he didn't see eye to eye with them, and that he had gone to Aryan Nations meetings mainly at the urging of Kenneth Fadeley (aka "Gus Magisono"), the BATF undercover informant.

Rodney Willey, a friend of the Weavers and a member of the Aryan Nations, was questioned extensively about his beliefs in a Jewish conspiracy, but after some objections from Gerry Spence, this testimony was cut short. The jury was sent home and the opposing attorneys continued to argue about just how relevant Willey's personal beliefs were to the case at hand.

Friday, May 7: Day Thirteen

Under cross-examination, Rodney Willey testified that Randy had refused to come down off the mountain because he was afraid he couldn't get a fair trial because of his religious beliefs. He also testified that he had never met such a close-knit, loving, and religious family. He described Vicki Weaver as a very strong, intelligent, and lovable person, and that Randy and Vicki's relationship was like an ideal love story; they were always holding hands and embracing. He said the family never expressed any hatred in his presence, only fear. He described Sara as strong and very religious, always looking out for the younger children, and a talented poet. Sammy, he said, was more serious. He loved being on the mountain and was especially fond of reading. He could discuss history from the Roman era to the present, quote the U.S. Constitution, and had memorized extensive passages from the Bible.

This was a prosecution witness.

Next was William Grider, whom Dave Hunt had worked with extensively as a possible go-between. Hunt had testified that he had offered Grider $5,000 to help arrest Randy, and said that Grider would not help arrest Randy but would kill him and tell Hunt where the body was. Grider denied this. He said Hunt had kept raising the amount offered to $20,000, but that he had told Hunt he would never kill anyone except in defense of his home and family. He also said that he had never known Randy Weaver to point a gun at anyone, even though he often carried a gun. And under cross-examination, he said he didn't know a closer family than the Weavers and that he knew several bachelors living alone who had more guns than the Weaver family did.

When the prosecutors asked Grider about his dealings with Randy when the marshals asked what it would take for Randy to surrender, Gerry Spence objected. He was not representing the witness, he said, but he pointed out that during the time Randy Weaver was a fugitive, Marshal Hunt had told Grider several times that he could conceivably be prosecuted as an accessory and fined $5,000 and given five years in jail for each of the fourteen times the federal agents knew he had visited Randy Weaver. After sending the jury and the witness from the room, the judge then worked out a deal with the prosecution under which Grider would not be prosecuted for anything he might say in court.

Monday, May 10: Day Fourteen

The prosecution brought in Marshal Art Roderick, the team leader on August 21, 1992. He provided more details about the surveillance operation on the Weaver family, including photographs of the video surveillance cameras. Afterward, the jury was dismissed while the prosecution and defense lawyers argued about how much of the video material garnered from the surveillance should be presented to the jury. The prosecution wanted to present videotaped material the next day, but Gerry Spence argued that he wasn't prepared, after a full day in court, to spend the night reviewing hours of videotape. The issue was delayed.

Tuesday, May 11, Wednesday, May 12, Thursday, May 13: Days Fifteen, Sixteen, and Seventeen

Marshal Art Roderick was on the witness stand again, offering more details about the surveillance. He detailed the various aircraft that had been borrowed or rented for aerial surveillance or photography, and described various scenarios, including the use of an XR-5000 stun gun, to capture Randy. During cross-examination, Spence elicited the information that among the fifteen top-echelon people who attended meetings at the U.S. Marshals Service headquarters, at which the Weaver situation was declared a major case, was a public relations man. He asked whether the meeting wasn't really held because the case had become such an embarrassment to the marshals, but Roderick was noncommittal.

During his testimony, Roderick kept referring to the Weaver "compound." David Nevin asked him what he meant by this, and Roderick replied that to him it meant a defensible place. Later, Gerry Spence produced a dictionary that defined a compound as a group of buildings with a fence or barricade around it. Roderick admitted that the house had no fence or barricade, but stated that the way the guns were hung inside the cabin constituted a barricade. Gerry Spence then asked, "If I had ten guns in my house, would that make it a barricade?" Roderick replied that it would not.

On May 12, before Marshal Roderick took the stand again, Spence stated that the first order of business was to inform the court that this was an important day in his life. He was wearing his first pair of suspenders. He explained that his son, Kent, had told him that he shouldn't be spending so much time pulling up or adjusting his pants. Things will be different now, he said. He then went on to complain that a defense request for the files of all the agents involved in the standoff was still being resisted by the prosecution, even though the request had been made the previous November and the judge had ordered the prosecution to produce them. "Since November, I have been filing interrogatories about some of the material in those files," he said, "but the defense still hasn't been allowed to see them. Was November too early and is now too late? I'm renewing my request to have access to the full files. From the fire in the eyes of the prosecution whenever I bring this subject up, I've got to figure there's something damaging in those files."

When Roderick was brought back to the stand, Spence asked him about his training. He asked if it was true that trained snipers could hit a quarter-inch target at two hundred yards, and if Roderick himself was that good. Then he asked if the training included being taught how to conduct peaceful negotiations as one human being to another. Spence then asked Roderick if he considered himself a normal human being. Roderick did not answer. Spence asked if he had ever made an attempt to talk to Randy. Roderick replied that he had not. Spence asked if it had ever occurred to him that if he used 1 percent of the effort he was using for trickery simply to talk as one human being to another, he might accomplish something useful. The prosecution objected to the question, and the judge sustained the objection.

The next witness was Jose Antonio Perez, number-three man in the U.S. Marshals Service. The prosecution took him through the steps that led to the Weaver situation being declared a major case. The defense elicited little from him except an admission that the reason Larry Cooper had carried a silenced rifle on August 21 was that there was a plan to lure the dogs from the cabin and shoot them.

Friday, May 14: Day Eighteen

The prosecution brought in several witnesses who had known Randy Weaver when he lived in Iowa, to bolster the contention that the Weavers had been planning a confrontation with government agents from an early date in their lives. Vaughn Trueman, the gunsmith who had attended Bible study sessions with Randy, testified mainly that the Weavers were a very loving and religious family.

The main government witness of this day was Iowa reporter Dan Dundon, who had interviewed Randy Weaver for a story in 1983. His story included the statement that Randy planned to move his family to the west and build a home with a "three-hundred-yard kill zone" around it. This statement was a key part of the prosecution's contention that the Weavers had been planning a violent confrontation with federal officers for years. But under cross-examination, Dundon said that in the context of Randy Weaver's comments, the remark couldn't be viewed as provocative. "It was strictly for defensive purposes," said Dundon. "He never indicated he had any desire to kill officers."

Monday, May 17: Day Nineteen

The main witness of the day was Michael Weland, the reporter for the *Bonner County Daily Bee* who had been the only media representative to interview the Weaver family prior to the siege and standoff. An older couple who were friends of the Weavers and of Weland had arranged the interview, which took place in May 1992, and lasted about six and a half hours. During that time, he said, Randy and Vicki Weaver had freely discussed their political and religious beliefs. Randy had said then that he thought he was being persecuted by the government, which was controlled by Freemasons and Jews. Randy gave him a slightly different account of the first arrest on the firearms charge, and claimed during this interview that the shotguns he had sold to Magisono–Fadeley were not shortened when he turned them over to the BATF undercover operative. It was mainly his family that was keeping him on the mountain, Randy had told him. If he surrendered then, it would upset his family and he would feel as if he were abandoning them.

To open his cross–examination, Gerry Spence asked Weland if he thought the First Amendment was important to his job. Weland responded that it was not only important to his job, but he was convinced that if we didn't have a free press, we wouldn't long have a free country. Spence then asked if the Weavers' First Amendment right to freedom of religion was as important as his own right to freedom of the press. Weland agreed that it was.

Spence then asked him in detail for his impressions of the family members. The dog Striker, Weland said, had sniffed him out when he first arrived, wagged his tail, and then Weland petted him. He described Vicki as "very beautiful, very intelligent, the strength of the family, plainly but nicely dressed, dark hair." He had been told that the house was everything from a shack to a fortress, he said, but it seemed to him very cozy, very much like a home. Sammy, said Weland, was very proud of having trained Striker to pull a sled and haul water for the family. The house had a library that included many children's classics, and the children were all well read and well informed on history and current events. During most of the time he was there, he said, Sammy was happily playing with Elisheba, who was six months old at the time.

It was often Vicki, Weland noted, who came out with the stronger statements during the interview. "We moved up here to remove our children from being taught trash in school, and to practice our religion," Vicki told him. "There is nowhere left to escape our lawless rulers. It is impossible to control law–abiding citizens, so they make laws to control everyone."

After the interview, Weland said, he had contacted the psychological profile division of the FBI and informed them that in his judgment Vicki was a primary reason Randy would continue to refuse to come down, and that if they ever wanted Randy to come in, they would have to separate him from Vicki. "Did you ever think they would kill her to do that?" asked Gerry Spence quickly. Objection. Sustained.

Next came testimony from three people who had gone to look at the property near the Weaver place, to the effect that the Weavers were always armed when they talked with anybody, but were polite. Then Terry Kinnison, who had been involved in a civil dispute and civil suit back in 1984, and who Randy and Vicki had accused of spreading false stories that the Weavers were threatening to assassinate President Reagan, took the stand. He had just begun his testimony when court was adjourned.

Tuesday, May 18: Day Twenty

Gerry Spence had said that he wasn't quite finished with his cross-examination of reporter Mike Weland, and wanted to recall him while he was still in Boise. The prosecution objected, and the judge agreed, saying Spence could recall Weland at a later date. Then Spence objected to the prosecution plan to bring Terry Kinnison back to the stand. "There's bad blood between Terry Kinnison and Randy Weaver, and everyone knows it," said Spence. All Kinnison will do it bad–mouth my client."

"I don't know why you're objecting," said Judge Lodge. "As far as I can see, at least 75 percent of the prosecution witnesses so far have helped the defense in this case." Kinnison and the jury were brought in, and sure enough, the defense had come up with enough information to question his credibility. Kinnison said that Randy had sued him frivolously and cost him a lot of money. The defense produced the suit, which had been filed by Kinnison. Kinnison had not shown up for the trial, and the judge had found in favor of the Weavers, called the suit frivolous, and ordered Kinnison to pay the Weavers $1,000 plus attorney's fees and court costs.

Wednesday, May 19, Thursday, May 20:
Days Twenty-One and Twenty-Two

The prosecution presented the fourteen guns that had been seized from the Weaver cabin. Before the jury was brought in, Gerry Spence argued first that only the weapons known to have been used on August 21, 1992, should be presented, but the judge ruled that all could be shown. Spence then argued against showing all the guns together on a "trophy board," saying that if all the guns he owned were shown together, it would make him look like a warmonger. The judge agreed, ruling that the guns should be brought into the courtroom one at a time. FBI agent Greg Rampton, who had been in charge of the search, acted as witness, bringing in the guns one at a time and showing photographs of where they had been found. About four thousand rounds of ammunition, most of it .22 caliber, was also brought in. Rampton testified that all the guns and ammunition were legal and readily available. Gerry Spence then asked Rampton if, while searching for the guns, he had noticed all the food stored under the cabin. Rampton said he hadn't paid attention, that the warrant only specified guns and ammunition. Spence then listed all the food—60 five-gallon cans of red wheat, a large galvanized bin of dried peas, 800 tins of dried food, 10 five-gallon buckets of salt, 150 gallons of honey, 500 pounds of flour, and 1,200 tins of canned food—emphasizing that this family had accumulated large quantities of supplies of all kinds, and that a large supply of ammunition was consistent with the pattern.

Friday, May 21: Day Twenty-Three

New evidence and witnesses emerged in a way that enraged the defense team and caused Judge Lodge to suspend the trial. The defense lawyers, the night before, had learned for the first time about Idaho State Police captain David Neal, the leader of the state Crisis Response Team who had arrived on the scene after the initial shootout and brought Cooper, Roderick, and Degan's body off Ruby Ridge. In a preliminary interview, he said he was prepared to testify that when he interviewed Roderick at that time, Roderick told him that he (Roderick) had fired the first shot, not Kevin Harris, as Larry Cooper and Art Roderick had testified in court.

Ron Howen also told the judge that a set of notes of FBI agent George Calley's August 25 interview with Larry Cooper had been missing, but had been found three weeks before in an FBI agent's desk drawer. When they were found, said Howen, he put them on his desk and forgot about them until that Friday, when he gave a copy to the defense lawyers. In those notes, Calley had written, "Next Cooper fired his second three–round burst during which time he saw Kevin Harris going up the trail toward the Weaver residence." That contradicted Cooper's testimony in court that Harris had dropped "like a sack of potatoes."

Spence and David Nevin said that the question of who fired the first shot is "the watershed question in the case" and accused the prosecution of purposely hiding evidence that would bolster the defense version of the case. Judge Lodge flushed red as the evidence was described, and then delivered a stern lecture from the bench. "I'm very disturbed by what has happened here, by what appears to have happened here," he said.

Assistant prosecutor Kim Lindquist admitted that he and Howen should have told the defense earlier about Captain Neal's information and about the FBI notes. But he downplayed the significance of the mistake, saying Neal was not clear in his own mind about the sequence of the shooting. He accused Spence and Nevin of "pure cynicism" in their complaints. That caused the normally soft–spoken Nevin to explode.

"They knew about this three weeks ago," thundered Nevin in his rebuttal. "You call me up and say, 'David, there's something you better know.' You don't wait three weeks and then come and tell me and then want to dress me down for being cynical. Judge, this is what makes people cynical."

Judge Lodge agreed to suspend the trial until the following Monday to allow the defense to review the new evidence. Gerry Spence complained, "We are being ambushed. We may have further motions to dismiss based on prosecutorial misconduct."

Monday, May 24: Day Twenty-Four

Gerry Spence thanked Judge Lodge for the recess the previous Friday and said the defense attorneys had talked to Captain Neal. He argued that since Marshal Cooper's notes about the shooting incident had turned up five weeks after Cooper had testified, that he should be allowed to recall Cooper. David Nevin emphasized that Cooper should address the contents of his notes, and discuss how they apparently differed from his testimony. Judge Lodge agreed to look at the notes and take the request under advisement. The defense did not make a motion to dismiss, but were willing to get on with the testimony of Marshal Roderick.

Kim Lindquist led Roderick through a detailed retelling of the events of August 21. Roderick insisted that Kevin Harris shot first, killing Marshal Degan, and said that it was after Kevin Harris killed Degan that he (Roderick) had shot the dog. "There was a possibility it would come after me," he said. "I was afraid that if we did get into the woods, that dog would alert on us and keep leading them to us." On cross-examination, he admitted that he had shot the dog "in the butt end." Gerry Spence showed Roderick pictures of the dog with tire marks over him and asked if he did not know that it took him more than two hours to lie there with his back broken and die. Roderick denied knowing that. When David Nevin confronted Roderick with the fact that Captain Neal was expected to say that right after the incident, Roderick had said that he had killed the dog first, Roderick stuck with his story: "Captain Neal was not conducting an interview," he said. "I told him that Mr. Harris had shot Mr. Degan. That's the first thing I told him. I didn't tell him I shot the dog first. We had a discussion about the dog, but that wasn't a major concern for us."

The defense attorneys did bring out the fact that the weapons carried by the marshals on that first day were viewed as "special weapons" by the U.S. Marshals Service, and that marshals were required to have special permission from the director or deputy director of the U.S. Marshals Service to carry them. But Roderick insisted that the plan on August 21 had been strictly surveillance.

Tuesday, May 25: Day Twenty-Five

Before the jury was brought in, Ron Howen asked for an order permitting the shirt Sammy Weaver had been wearing when he was shot to be sent to an expert for testing. The judge agreed. Then the prosecution announced that it had just found 150 photographs taken during evidence–gathering, which had taken place in the days after August 21, and said those photos would be turned over to the defense. Then the jury was brought in, along with Marshal Roderick, who was still on the witness stand.

Gerry Spence then confronted Roderick with a couple of seventy–five cent transparencies the defense had made Monday night at a copy store, of the sketches agents Cooper and Roderick had made of the shooting scene. The two agents were supposed to have made the sketches independently and without consulting one another, yet when the transparencies were placed over each other, they matched perfectly, with the minor exception of the length of a couple of arrows. How could the agents account for that coincidence?

"It must have been magic," said Spence when he showed the sketches and the transparency overlay to Roderick.

"The truth is the truth," retorted Roderick.

"Yes, it is," said Spence, fixing him with a long stare.

Under stiff cross–examination, Roderick maintained that he didn't know Sammy Weaver had been shot until several days later. How could that be, demanded Spence, when the body was lying there on the road in broad daylight. Roderick replied that he hadn't seen the body.

Spence then pointed out that at the grand jury hearing, Roderick had said that the dog had been running toward him when he shot it, but that during the trial he said the dog's rear end was toward him when he shot it, which the autopsy had confirmed. Roderick had no explanation for this discrepancy. Spence accused Roderick of purposely shooting the dog in the hope that Randy would react so he would have an excuse to shoot Randy. Roderick denied it.

Spence also asked Roderick thirteen questions that Captain Neal had supposedly asked him the night of the shootout. Roderick said he couldn't recall being asked twelve of them. Then Spence quickly asked:

"You had a dead boy and a dead officer and you had been told not to have a confrontation, and you and Cooper had twelve hours to develop an excuse for killing a little boy, isn't that so?"

Objection. Sustained.

"Can you tell me one good reason to shoot a thirteen-year-old boy in the back?"

Objection. Sustained.

The next witness was Mark Thundercloud, a five-year FBI veteran who had been brought to the shooting site to locate and gather evidence. He said that he had been sent to the staging area the day after the shooting, but had not been taken to the shooting site until three days later. He said that he mapped the evidence as he collected it by borrowing a three-hundred-foot measuring tape from the Idaho State Police and measuring the distance from a burnt stump in the woods to each item. He then marked the places on a hand-drawn sketch of the area that was not drawn to scale.

As Spence pointed out upon cross-examination, he did not use the technique known as "triangulation"—taking a second measurement from a second reference point, as police and high school geometry students are taught to do. Spence then used a pair of electrical extension cords as ropes to demonstrate that when only one measurement was taken, inaccuracies and mistakes could result. The witness agreed that this was possible, but said that his superiors had told him not to bother with triangulation and that the rough terrain and thick trees would have made it impossible anyway.

"So nobody knows precisely today where anything was?" asked Spence.

"Generally," replied Thundercloud. "This is the way it was."

After lunch, before the jury was seated, Spence brought up some questions related to the photographs the defense had been handed that morning. One bullet, which had been found August 31, the day Randy Weaver came down from the cabin, was virtually unmarked although it had been fired. Spence had been referring to it as the "magic bullet," and comparing it to the "magic bullet" in the Kennedy assassination. In the photographs, it was shown facing one way in one photograph and the other way in another photograph. Ron Howen—who had been at the federal staging area during most of the standoff—then said that for some of the evidence (he wasn't sure exactly which), it had been removed, then brought back at a later time and dropped in the approximate locations where it had been found, and photographed. Spence exploded. In forty years of criminal practice, he said, he had never seen a case handled like this.

"I have been raising all kinds of unappreciated Cain in this case about the magic bullet. Today we are told that the photos we were given were reconstructed photos." Spence demanded that prosecutor Howen be called as a witness himself, as he had requested several times before, since he was apparently there at the time the evidence was gathered. Not to do so, he said, would be tampering with due process. Ron Howen said he had shared the photographs with the defense as soon as he had them himself, and had told the defense about the problems, and had no intention of showing staged photographs to the jury. The judge again denied the request.

The next witness was Joseph Venkus, a thirty–one–year FBI veteran who had been in overall charge of gathering evidence at the shooting site. He showed videos that the FBI and the Boundary County sheriff had made, one three days and the other seven days after the shooting. Both videos showed the body of Striker, the dog, with tracks on his body. Venkus said the tracks looked like those of an armored personnel carrier, not of a vehicle with tires.

After the afternoon recess, Spence had more complaints. He had just found out, he said, that it wasn't just the magic bullet but all the evidence that had been gathered up before a photographer was available, then placed back later as if to appear in the original locations and photographed. He reminded the judge that he had learned about Captain Neal and Marshal Cooper's notes only the previous Friday. The FBI is a principal party in all this, he said, and there's enough to warrant at least the suspicion that it's been withholding evidence. The jury should be told about all this, and Ron Howen should be put on the witness stand. The judge said he would take under advisement what the jury should be told, but that Mr. Howen would not be called as a witness.

After that ruling, the prosecution began to go through photographs of evidence that it wanted to admit. Spence suggested that the court could save about two days of trial time if the defense and prosecution could get together and stipulate to much of the material—to agree, after both sides had a chance to look it over, that certain evidence was relevant and should be admitted. Judge Lodge agreed, and recessed court at 4:10 so the prosecution and defense could get to work on the process.

Wednesday, May 26: Day Twenty-Six

Ron Howen began the day by saying he had known previously about some of the evidence being reconstructed, but he reassured the court that it had never been his intention to introduce that material as evidence. The prosecution and defense then stipulated to the introduction of almost all the small evidence the prosecution had begun to introduce the previous afternoon, with the exception of the magic bullet found August 31.

The jury and witness, FBI agent Joseph Venkus, were then brought in, and Venkus discussed the small evidence—shell casings, shells, bullet fragments, and the like—found near the scene of the August 21 gun battle. He testified that some small mistakes had been made in the gathering of evidence, which had begun August 24—three days after the battle, after numerous people and vehicles had been through the area. When he received Marshal Degan's gun, for example, he signed for twenty rounds of ammunition with it, but when he counted them several months later, there were only nineteen rounds. When he received the gun belonging to Larry Thomas, he didn't receive a magazine or ammunition. When the guns were turned over to him the day after the shooting, one was missing. The agents then explained that they had left it at the Rau house, and had to go back to get it. When he received it, it came with a bag of ammunition containing nineteen rounds, but later there were twenty rounds in the bag.

Venkus testified that he had gone back to the shooting site in April 1993, and that all the stakes he had put in the ground to mark places where evidence had been found had been removed. But, he said, he vividly recalled the area.

None of the sidearms belonging to the six U.S. marshals were collected for evidence. The marshals said that none of the handguns were fired. But the defense suggested that some of them were 9 millimeter handguns, which might account for some of the shell casings that had been found but not positively identified.

Venkus testified that when he interviewed Marshal Cooper the day after the shooting, Cooper told him that Marshal Degan had not fired any shots that day. But his gun had been fired, and seven bullet casings were found by his body. Venkus said he didn't have enough information to draw definitive conclusions from this, that he was only reporting what he and the team had found.

Just before adjournment, Gerry Spence had an enlarged photo of the dog, Striker, with tracks from various vehicles clearly on the body, passed from one juror to another so they could get a close look.

Thursday, May 27: Day Twenty-Seven

The prosecution continued to flesh out the story told by the physical evidence about the first shootout, August 21, but this day was to center around the magic bullet, about which the jury learned for the first time. The day began with FBI agent Greg Rampton back on the stand. He stated that he had gone back to the Weaver cabin and to the Y where the shootout took place, on March 22 and 23. He took with him a former FBI agent who was now a private investigator specializing in the use of metal detectors. On March 22, they didn't find anything new. But on March 23, Rampton testified, while he was away from the site for two hours, the others found five pieces of new evidence, including the butt–plate of Sammy Weaver's gun, buried two inches deep in the ground. The group had also made new measurements, as a result of which the prosecution had changed the diagrams it had been using to describe the scene for the jury. This was the first the defense had been informed of this new evidence.

Gerry Spence wondered why Rampton went back seven months after the shooting, and elicited the information that the site had not been secured—not even with crime-scene tape or rope—during the intervening seven months. But, Rampton said, it was thought some new evidence might be found. As Spence drew him out, he said the visit had proved useful because, as he had been sitting in court listening to testimony a few weeks before, he had realized that the diagram the prosecution was using was inaccurate. Based on his notes, he had helped the prosecution lawyers redo the diagram in late April, two weeks after the trial had begun. Spence found this simply incredible. Rampton also said he couldn't recall talking to Agent Venkus about the mysterious bullet that had been found August 31—the day Randy Weaver left the cabin, and a week after the initial FBI searches of the shooting site. It was his memory that Larry Wages, another FBI agent, had found the bullet in the berm of the road, and testified that he had informed the prosecution lawyers about it in January.

FBI special agent Larry Wages, who had led several of the searches on August 24 and thereafter, was the next witness. He had taken the dog, Striker, to a veterinarian for an autopsy, and had observed the procedure. He testified that no bullet fragments had been found in the body, suggesting that the bullet had entered three inches from the dog's rectum, traveled parallel to the spine, and through the dog.

Wages was also the one who found the magic bullet on August 31. He testified that the area had already been searched by hand and with a metal detector on several occasions, but that on that day he saw it by the side of the dirt road. Just then, he was ordered out of the area as Randy and the girls were leaving the cabin, and he didn't have a photographer with him. So he picked up the bullet, put it in an evidence bag, and carried it in his pocket for several hours. Then he returned to the scene, dropped it in the approximate location where it had been found, and had it photographed. But, he said, he could not remember which way it had been facing, so he had it photographed both ways. He said he had told the prosecutors that the photograph was a recreation before the trial started. Prosecutor Ron Howen had to acknowledge that he hadn't told the defense about this when he had turned over the photographs.

On cross-examination, Gerry Spence made much of the fact that BATF agent Herb Byerly, who had supervised undercover agent Kenneth Fadeley during the operation to set Randy Weaver up on a firearms charge and as an informant, had been one of the searchers two days before this bullet was found. Wages said he did not know why Byerly was the only non-FBI person involved in the searching, since the FBI had taken charge of all aspects of the case by that time. Spence wondered how the bullet could be so pristine, despite apparently having been fired. Wages, who had some ballistics training, suggested a bullet might look this way after being pushed through a rifle barrel with a rod of some kind.

Spence then asked that the photographs of the bullet be shown to the jury, but the prosecution objected. Spence asked that the X-rays of Striker be shown to the jury, and the prosecution objected. Spence started to complain that he had had all he could take of the prosecution hiding evidence, at which point the jury was sent out of the courtroom. Spence told Judge Lodge that in forty years in the courtroom, he had never seen a prosecutor work so hard to try to hide evidence from a jury. It wasn't just the bullet or the X-rays, he said. The prosecution had furnished various evidence and documents to the defense with the implicit understanding that it was good evidence properly collected, then objected to showing it to the jury on the grounds that it wasn't genuine. They just wanted to cover up the fact that they had known about the staged photos and other problems months before and wanted to keep the fact hidden from the jury.

Judge Lodge took action on only a few of Spence's complaints, then went on to say he was concerned about the trial. Two of the jurors didn't feel up to night court, and one of them had paid for a summer school course that he didn't want to miss. Several jurors had complained that their time was being wasted by technical arguments over inconsequential matters. He urged all the attorneys to keep things moving as quickly as possible, then ordered that the attorneys be ready at 8:00 A.M. the next morning with any issues that should be handled without the jury present, prepared to deal with them before the jury was called in at 9:00. That would be the schedule for the rest of the trial, he said. He wanted the jury to spend all of each day on the case, rather than being sent in and out all the time. He ruled that when the jury returned now, it wouldn't be shown the X–rays of the dog, but that the magic bullet could be passed around the jury box.

In another matter, David Nevin convinced the judge not to allow the prosecution to call a witness who was apparently prepared to testify that Kevin Harris had prowled around the neighboring Rau cabin, sometimes harassing the family, and that he had stolen some gasoline from the Raus. "It all boils down to nothing more than throwing some mud on him to make him look bad in this case," said Nevin, arguing that what he might have done at the Raus' house didn't prove anything about the charges against him. Ron Howen argued that the testimony would show Harris was involved in a conspiracy to break the law, but Judge Lodge rejected the argument, saying such testimony would be a "waste of time."

Then Ruth Rau, herself, the Weavers' nearest neighbor who had cooperated with the marshals and with the FBI for many months before the shootout and siege, took the stand. She said that what had begun as a friendly, neighborly relationship with the Weavers went sour after the Weavers began harassing the Raus. She said the first thing she noticed about Randy Weaver was his "paranoid" belief system and his odd interpretation of the Old Testament. "They wanted to find a remote mountaintop where they were going to eventually have a confrontation with the federal government," she said, echoing almost word for word the charge in the grand jury indictment.

"It seemed to be Randy's favorite subject. He seemed obsessed with the idea," she said, adding that she remembered him saying "It's gonna happen and, personally, I can't wait."

Mrs. Rau also accused the Weavers of stealing her back–up water tank and some water pipes and related equipment.

Friday, May 28: Day Twenty-Eight

Although Ruth Rau hadn't finished her testimony, she was postponed until Tuesday so that Duke Smith, associate director of the U.S. Marshals Service—the number-two man in the organization—could testify and return to Washington, D.C. for the Memorial Day holiday weekend. The testimony centered around the "rules of engagement" for August 22, the day Vicki Weaver was shot, and the whereabouts of a helicopter in which Smith had been a passenger on that same day.

Smith testified that he and Richard Rogers had jointly drawn up the rules of engagement during their flight to Idaho from Washington, D.C., after a brief telephone report from a deputy who had not actually witnessed the August 21 encounter. "We decided jointly at that point that the rules of engagement would be that any adult who was seen with a weapon would be considered subject to deadly force," said Smith. "They had already demonstrated a willingness to kill one of our people."

Under cross-examination by Ellison Matthews, Kevin Harris's co-counsel, Smith said that when he and Rogers wrote the shoot-to-kill order, he did not know Sam Weaver had been shot, nor had he talked to any of the marshals actually involved in the shootout. Matthews pointed out that the eighteen-month surveillance revealed that the Weavers responded to noises by running, almost always with a weapon, from the cabin to the big lookout rock in the yard. He asked Smith if the rules were written in order to assure that the Weavers would be killed.

"Weren't you aware that your actions virtually guaranteed your snipers shooting somebody on that hill? Wasn't it part of your plan, because you had a dead marshal, to in fact draw them out of the cabin?" asked Matthews. Smith disagreed with this analysis of the intent or result of the rules, saying the rules of engagement permitted but did not require the use of deadly force. In response to further cross-examination by Gerry Spence, who read the deadly force passage from the U.S. Marshals Service manual, Smith said his understanding at the time was that his deputies had attempted to arrest Randy Weaver peacefully on August 21, but they had been chased and one of them killed by the Weaver family.

When he arrived at the federal staging area around midnight August 21, he testified, there were about seventy marshals from the Special Operations Group there and perhaps eighty other federal agents. He said he learned that Vicki Weaver had not been at the initial shootout and it was unlikely they could get a warrant for her arrest. So they changed the rules of engagement to read that any adult male outside the house with a weapon could be subject to deadly force. The rules also stated that agents were not to shoot into the house because of the danger of injuring the children. He also said that at this time, he and Rogers still didn't know that the U.S. marshals involved in the initial confrontation had fired any shots at all.

On August 22, he then testified, he and three FBI agents got into a helicopter, flew up, and circled near the Raus' home in order to familiarize themselves with the area. The story in the next day's issue of the *Spokesman-Review* explained that this testimony "contradicted what an FBI sharpshooter told a federal grand jury last fall to justify his shooting of Vicki Weaver."

During the grand jury hearings, Lon Horiuchi, the FBI sniper who had fired the shots that killed Vicki Weaver and wounded Randy Weaver and Kevin Harris, had said that he fired to protect the helicopter in which Smith was riding. His sniper's nest was on a mountainside two hundred yards north of the cabin. He had told the grand jury that the helicopter "was not in front of me. . . . I'm assuming it was somewhere behind me, either to my right or left." He later testified, "The helicopter . . . seemed to be behind my location or above me." That would have placed the helicopter north of the Weaver cabin.

But according to Duke Smith's testimony, the helicopter followed a path that never took it to the north of the Weaver cabin. As *Spokesman-Review* reporter Dean Miller put it: "Standing at a scale model of Ruby Ridge, he waved a pointer in a circle, indicating the pilot guided the chopper in a tight loop above the property of Wayne and Ruth Rau, who live downhill from the Weavers. To be in the position described by Horiuchi, Smith's helicopter would have had to fly from the Raus' property over or around Weaver's property."

═ * ═

The Memorial Day weekend offered a convenient opportunity for
the newspaper reporters who had been covering the entire trial to
assess the Weaver case up to that point. The *Spokesman-Review*'s
Dean Miller, in a Sunday story headlined So Far, Weaver–Harris
Trial Is Filled with Errors, put it bluntly:

> *Federal prosecutors in the Randy Weaver-Kevin Harris trial
> limped into the Memorial Day recess with their case crumbling at
> the edges.*
>
> *Hobbled by sloppy investigative work, balky witnesses and
> nuggets of contradiction mined from mountains of official
> documents, Assistant U.S. Attorney Ron Howen had lost some of
> his steeliness.*
>
> *On three of the six days before the break, Howen was forced to
> make contrite retractions in court, admitting he misled defense
> lawyers about evidence. . . .*
>
> *Howen's problems accelerated in the last two weeks.*
>
> *Three FBI agents testified they either mishandled or lost key
> pieces of evidence. . . .*
>
> *Lost FBI documents that Howen found and turned over to
> defense attorneys contradicted the testimony of the deputy U.S.
> marshals involved in the shootout.*
>
> *The last witness to take the stand Friday—a top U.S. Marshals
> Service official—contradicted the account of an FBI sniper who shot
> and killed Vicki Weaver, saying his helicopter never flew over the
> Weaver cabin as the sniper indicated.*
>
> *Prosecutors have not had much better luck with civilian
> witnesses.*
>
> *Neighbors and acquaintances called by Howen to describe
> Weaver's racist and doomsday beliefs have done so, but on cross-
> examination portrayed the Weavers as an ideal family of respectful
> children and loving parents and federal investigators as
> "destructive" people.*

Tuesday, June 1: Day Twenty-Nine

After the long weekend, Randy Weaver's neighbor, Ruth Rau, was on the stand again. She talked about her family's relationship with the Weavers, which had been good for five years (Mrs. Rau's daughter and Sara Weaver had gotten jobs together at the local cafe) until the two families began feuding. Rau attributed it to Randy's obsession with having a shootout with federal agents and his increasingly radical, Nazi–like beliefs. On cross–examination, she acknowledged that she had disagreements with other neighbors as well, and that in fact her husband had shot another neighbor's goat on one occasion. But she stressed that she had come to believe that Randy was a serious threat to society. Gerry Spence asked her if Randy had ever gone so far as to shoot a neighbor's goat. She said he hadn't, but that Marshal Dave Hunt, who was supervising the surveillance of the Weavers before the shootout, told her that Vicki and the girls were shooting at her and her house.

Marshal Hunt was next on the witness stand, and after some discussion of the events of August 21, denied telling Ruth Rau that Vicki had shot at her—although he did say that he had reason to believe somebody in the Weaver family had fired shots over the Rau house, in a way that didn't threaten direct bodily harm but was ultimately quite threatening.

The next witness was Larry Thomas, who had been part of the marshals' back–up team on August 21. His account of the day's events were similar to what marshals Cooper and Roderick had said.

Wednesday, June 2: Day Thirty

Marshal Thomas began the day, continuing testimony that hadn't been completed from the previous day. He said he had fired neither his rifle nor his handgun on August 21. He said he couldn't recall any conversation at the shooting scene after the shootout of August 21. He did say that after the first shootout, he heard, from his back-up position down the road, shouts, wailing, and crying, but he wasn't sure from whom it came.

The next witness was Frank Norris, also on the marshals' back-up team on August 21, and a tactical emergency medical technician (EMT). He testified that the first three shots he heard "sounded like a .223 rather than the bigger and louder report that would have come from Kevin Harris's .30-06 hunting rifle. That contradicted what both Larry Cooper and Art Roderick had said, when they had testified that Kevin Harris had shot first. Norris also testified that the second burst of shots he heard also sounded like a .223. David Nevin drew him out, noting that Norris's testimony squared with what he (Nevin) had been contending all along—that Art Roderick shot first, killing the dog and provoking Sammy Weaver to fire a couple of shots in the general direction of the marshals. After that, in Nevin's version, Degan, Cooper, and Roderick shot back, at first wounding Sammy and then killing him with a shot in the back. Only after Sammy had been killed, Nevin contended, had Kevin Harris fired his hunting rifle at the deputies, apparently killing Marshal Degan.

Frank Norris also testified, during cross-examination, that he had heard that before going onto the mountain on August 21, Marshal Art Roderick had been expecting violence that day.

The next witness was Richard Rogers, the commander of the FBI Hostage Rescue Team, a special agent with over twenty-two years' service in the FBI. He explained that the Hostage Rescue Team consists of fifty-one full-time agents plus support staff. All are volunteers—the cream of the crop in the FBI. All receive continuous special training. The snipers are expected to be able to hit a person with iron sights at one thousand yards, and to hit a person in the head every time with their sniper rifles at two hundred yards. They use Remington Model 700 rifles, with the barrels replaced by a special stainless steel match-shooting barrel (designed to be used in competitive shooting matches rather than in ordinary, day-to-day plinking), with special .308 caliber match ammunition.

Gerry Spence asked him if this caliber rifle wasn't also used to hunt deer and elk. Rogers replied that he didn't hunt. "You mean animals," retorted Spence. Kim Lindquist quickly objected to the remark, and it was stricken.

Rogers testified, as Marshal Smith had testified the previous Friday, that Smith had briefed him on the situation during their plane ride from Washington, D.C., to Idaho, and that together they had developed the rules of engagement for the crisis to come. He said also that he had not talked with anybody who had actually been involved in the first day's shooting before writing the rules of engagement, but that he had operated on a couple of assumptions: that Randy Weaver had joined Kevin Harris in chasing the marshals through the woods, and that after the first confrontation there had been a continuous firefight, perhaps extending for several hours. As the *Spokesman-Review* story pointed out, however, "No marshals involved in the shooting have testified that Randy Weaver chased them through the woods."

Jurors were shown the text of Rogers's rules of engagement: "If any adult in the compound is observed with a weapon after the surrender announcement is made, deadly force can and should be employed to neutralize the individual. If any adult male is observed with a weapon prior to the announcement, deadly force can and should be used if the shot can be taken without endangering the children." He testified that one of his snipers, Lon Horiuchi, shot before a team of FBI negotiators could travel inside an armored vehicle into Weaver's yard to make the initial announcement demanding the family's surrender.

Rogers also testified that he had been in the helicopter when it took off from the staging area on August 22, just before Vicki Weaver was shot. His version of the helicopter ride more closely resembled what Lon Horiuchi had said—that the helicopter was to the north of the cabin, where those in the cabin or in the yard might conceivably have shot at it—and differed from the testimony of Marshal Smith, who had testified that the helicopter never went near the cabin.

Rogers's first response to Gerry Spence when cross-examination began was smart-alecky, disrespectful, and not responsive. Spence looked at the judge and said, "We're going to be here a long time," whereupon Judge Lodge instructed Rogers to answer the questions directly, without comment.

Rogers said that Lon Horiuchi had fired while Rogers and Smith were in the helicopter, that he had been the only sniper who fired. When he was debriefed, Horiuchi said that he had fired two shots but didn't know for sure if he had hit anybody. Rogers said he was shocked, considering his proficiency level, that Horiuchi didn't know if he had hit anyone. "But you eventually found out," said Spence, "that he had done pretty good, that he had hit three people with two shots."

After that encounter, Rogers testified, a hostage negotiator with a bullhorn approached the house and said, "We're the FBI with arrest warrants. We're not here to harm you. There's a phone on that device in the yard, just send out a child to pick up the phone."

"Of course," said Spence. "After Sammy had been shot in the back and his arm almost blown off, Striker shot in the back, Randy shot, Kevin shot, Vicki killed, did you really think he was going to believe that?"

Rogers testified that FBI agents had found Sammy Weaver's body in the shed near the cabin, and that they had been shocked to find it. He said that they unwrapped the body and took pictures, then took the body down the hill and turned it over to the county coroner. Spence asked him if, at any time in the next few days, they informed Randy of what had been done with his son's body. He said nobody had done so.

The prosecution wanted to show the photographs of Sammy's body in open court, but Spence objected. Finally, Judge Lodge consented to having photographs taken with only jockey shorts shown to the jury. As the photographs were handed around, several of the female members of the jury could be seen weeping openly.

During cross–examination Rogers said that the FBI team had put electronic experts under the house to hook up special microphones so they could hear everything inside the cabin, but that the microphones didn't work. Consequently, he said, they didn't hear the baby crying "Mama." Spence then produced logs from various members of the snipers team that indicated that they had heard the baby crying without any special microphones. Rogers acknowledged that they might have heard the baby crying, but still denied that the siege team had heard the family calling out that Vicki was dead. Spence accused them of knowing Vicki was dead almost from the first moment. He brought out that some people had seen signs at the federal staging area saying Base Camp Vicki. Rogers denied having seen such signs. Spence accused the hostage team of purposely mocking the family by calling for Vicki when they knew she was dead. Rogers denied it. Rogers did acknowledge that the feds bathed the cabin and the immediate vicinity in the brightest lights possible all night, but said he couldn't recall whether they had played loud music or not.

Thursday, June 3: Day Thirty-One

The day began with Richard Rogers, still on the stand under cross-examination by Gerry Spence. Rogers said the hostage negotiator was Fred Lancely, who was also a behavioral scientist who worked up a profile on Randy Weaver. Lancely told Rogers that Randy was paranoid and very dangerous, perhaps even to his own children. If he was so dangerous, asked Spence, why was Bo Gritz able to walk right up to the cabin door unarmed? Rogers spoke about Gritz being with Jackie Brown, whom Randy knew and trusted, and with a minister. "Could the reason Randy talked to Bo Gritz have been," asked Spence, "that Gritz was the only person since the confrontation began who had treated him like a human being?"

The questions then turned to the rules of engagement. Rogers acknowledged that in the three years he had been head of the Hostage Rescue Team, this was the first time such rules had been used. He said, however, that it was his belief that this was the most dangerous situation the team had ever faced, that they were facing a desperate and skilled man who had already shown his willingness to kill a federal officer. Spence then asked Rogers if he had used those rules at Waco. Rogers became angry, told Spence that no shots at all had been fired by federal agents on the last day of the Waco standoff. Judge Lodge admonished both of them, and ruled that Waco was not to be discussed again.

Spence then asked Rogers whether he was concerned that the rules of engagement he had written for the Ruby Ridge standoff violated Idaho state law as well as the standard FBI procedure. Rogers said he was operating under the federal codes, which preempted state law, and that his actions were covered "in the U.S. codes." Spence asked him: "Just which U.S. code is it that authorizes you to take the law into your own hands?" Rogers said he really didn't know. Spence repeated the question, a little more forcefully and a little more sarcastically, and Rogers angrily shot back, "The entire federal code!"

The next witness was Lon Horiuchi. When he was to be called, court was recessed for ten minutes, while the marshals retrieved him from wherever he was, in some other part of the courthouse, and brought him in under heavy guard. He was, as *Spokesman-Review* reporter Dean Miller later said, "a real piece of work"—cold, unemotional, his expression never changing no matter what the nature of the testimony. He explained that he was a West Point graduate, that he had served eight years in the U.S. Army, then joined the FBI, that he had been on the Hostage Rescue Team for eight years and had volunteered to be a sniper four years before. He explained the requirements—accuracy within a quarter–inch at two hundred yards, and thousands of practice rounds (and some in live confrontations) fired at moving targets. He said he enjoyed his work.

He testified that the rules of engagement for the Weaver siege were unique in his eight years of experience, but that he accepted them. "The decision that we were in danger had already been made for us, prior to going up the hill," he said. He explained how he had crawled and hiked to a position two hundred yards from the Weaver cabin and settled in to watch the Weaver yard for activity. About the time he heard an FBI helicopter in the air, he saw a girl in the yard. She went back into the cabin and reemerged with two men, one of them armed with a rifle. He said the armed man circled the outbuilding while peering at the sky. "Sir, he seemed to be looking for the helicopter," he told Kim Lindquist. "He seemed to be moving, trying to get back on the other side of the house. By being behind the house, he could take a shot."

Horiuchi testified—although he had photos of the occupants of the cabin, Randy Weaver is almost a foot shorter than Kevin Harris, and he was observing through a ten-power scope—that he thought this person was Kevin Harris. "Sir, I perceived he may be getting ready to take a shot at the individuals in the helicopter," he said. "It appeared that just before I pulled the trigger, the individual made a sudden move I wasn't expecting." Although he was shooting to kill, because of that sudden movement he hadn't done so. He thought he had wounded the target but wasn't sure. A few seconds later, he saw the girl and the two men running for the house. He said he tracked the armed man—who really was Kevin Harris this time—bringing up the rear, and he hoped to keep him from reaching the house. "I didn't want him back in the house. He would have been more protected in the house. He could have shot back at me," testified Horiuchi.

So he led Kevin Harris by about nine inches—the appropriate lead at two hundred yards—and squeezed the trigger just as the man crossed the front porch of the house. He acknowledged that snipers were not supposed to shoot into the cabin, but he said that at the angle he was, he figured a shot across the porch would just go off into the woods if it missed.

"He was reaching with his left hand, trying to open the door or move someone out of the way when I took the shot," Horiuchi said. "He appeared to flinch as soon as I pulled the trigger and then he disappeared inside the doorway. Immediately after that, I heard a female screaming for approximately thirty seconds, maybe longer . . . I was assuming she was screaming because Mr. Harris was hit." Horiuchi said that at the time he didn't know that he had shot wide of Harris and hit the door instead, or that Vicki Weaver was standing behind the door and had taken the bullet.

During cross-examination, Spence was unable to shake Horiuchi from his contention that he had intended to shoot Kevin Harris and didn't know he had killed Vicki Weaver. At one point, Spence asked Horiuchi to point out Kevin in the courtroom. "You wanted to kill him, didn't you?" asked Spence. "Yes, sir," replied Horiuchi. At another point, after asking questions about the thirty seconds of screaming, Spence said, "Let's just take thirty seconds and pretend in our mind's eye we hear screaming." The courtroom was silent for thirty seconds—a long time, especially if one is concentrating—except for a few chairs scraping.

Friday, June 4: Day Thirty-Two

Lon Horiuchi was on the stand again in the morning. He testified that he did not shoot the first armed adult he saw because his sniper team planned to wait until all the adults were out of the house. "We wanted them all outside if we were going to shoot the two subjects," he said. "We were intending to take 'em all at one time," which he said was standard FBI sniper procedure. "Anytime you have more than one subject, you try and shoot 'em all at one time."

When Horiuchi finished testifying, he was again taken away under heavy guard—armed guards also lined the hallways during the two days he was on the stand—and whisked away. Within a few minutes of Horiuchi's leaving, the prosecution turned over to the defense an inch–thick stack of documents. This turned out to be background material on Horiuchi, some of his service and FBI records, and the notes he had made and notes about his debriefings after the shooting of Vicki Weaver and Kevin Harris. The judge had ordered the prosecution to find this material and share it with the defense a month before. It turned out that the material had been gathered at FBI headquarters, but that agents at the headquarters in the nation's capital had sent it by fourth–class mail instead of by overnight mail or even first class. "I have no explanation why these were not overnighted," a chagrined Ron Howen told Judge Lodge.

Gerry Spence was at his most theatrically angry. "If this were an isolated instance of this kind of conduct in this case, we would not make so much of it. But we've been prejudiced, your Honor, throughout this case by this kind of conduct." He reminded Judge

Lodge of the recreated photographs, of evidence found and provided to the prosecution and later to the defense when the trial was almost half over. Judge Lodge agreed that the FBI's response to his court order to produce the Horiuchi file was "totally inexcusable and extremely poor judgment. The court is very upset about these things happening. It does appear it is somewhat of a pattern on the part of agencies outside the district of Idaho." He explained that he had several available sanctions available to him—from dismissing the case for prosecutorial misconduct, as Spence had suggested, to forcing the Justice Department to pay for a certain portion of the Weaver defense team, to striking the testimony of some key government witnesses, to calling Lon Horiuchi back to the stand. He said he would rule on Monday, and court was recessed.

Monday, June 7: Day Thirty-Three

Court started thirty-five minutes late because the attorneys had been in a meeting to stipulate to the report of the government's ballistics expert to save the time that would have been involved in having him testify. The lawyers agreed that a bullet fragment found in Kevin Harris had come from sniper Lon Horiuchi's .308 rifle. A bullet fragment in Marshal Degan had come from Kevin Harris's .30-06 hunting rifle. Since the bullets that hit Vicki Weaver, Sammy Weaver, and Striker had gone all the way through, no positive identification was possible.

After the morning recess, Judge Lodge said an emergency had come up and court would recess until the next morning. But at 3:00, without the jury or most of the media present, the lawyers held arguments before the judge about the evidence that the FBI had apparently been holding back until the previous Friday. Gerry Spence offered a proposed set of instructions stipulating that the jury should be told that the government had been withholding evidence. Judge Lodge said he was not inclined to tell the jury about it, but said he would reserve his rulings on other issues until the next day.

One of the pieces of evidence was a sketch Horiuchi had made of the door of the Weaver house right after the shooting. It showed two semicircular objects in the window that, given the roughness of the sketch, appeared to be heads.

Tuesday, June 8: Day Thirty-Four

The day began with a highly unusual move, one that attorneys said hadn't happened in federal courts in the state of Idaho for a decade. As a formal punishment for the tardy background information on the sniper, Lon Horiuchi, the court required the government to pay an amount equal to the cost of the Weaver and Harris defense attorneys for one day. At sixty dollars an hour, the amount paid to court-appointed attorneys, that would amount to about $3,000, plus whatever costs the court would award for work done outside the courtroom during the lost day.

Judge Lodge also ordered Horiuchi to return to the stand for further cross-examination concerning those documents. He was angered anew when he discovered that the prosecution had allowed Horiuchi to return to Washington, D.C., even though he (Lodge) had indicated earlier that further cross-examination might be required.

The next government witness was Dr. Martin Fackler, a surgeon who had spent thirty-one years in the military and was now a professional expert witness on wound ballistics. He testified that it would not have been at all unlikely that Marshal Degan, even after being hit by the bullet from Kevin Harris's rifle that killed him, could have lived for as long as three minutes and could have had sufficient control of his right arm and other faculties to have fired the seven bullets whose empty casings were found next to his body. The autopsy on Degan had shown that he was shot through the lung, cutting one of his main veins, breaking four ribs and the left collarbone, rendering his left arm useless. Fackler also testified that, in his opinion, Sammy Weaver was hit in the arm with a .223 slug (which would match the rifle Degan had carried) and in the back with a 9 millimeter slug (which would match the rifle carried by Marshal Larry Cooper).

On cross-examination, Randy Weaver's co-counsel, Chuck Peterson, asked how much he was paid for his expert testimony. He responded that he charged $2,000 per day plus $250 an hour for time spent in preparation, plus travel and other expenses. He estimated that this day of testimony would cost the government about $4,500. He said he had been recommended by Lucien Haag, a ballistics expert scheduled to testify later. He acknowledged that he and Haag often recommended one another as expert witnesses.

Peterson got Fackler to acknowledge that many of his opinions were "rough estimates" or "reasonable approximations." Peterson then produced a paper Fackler had written in 1988, in which he stated that forensic physicians too often rely on untrustworthy "war stories" about what people can do after being hit by a bullet rather than on controlled laboratory observations of the ability of humans to continue functioning after being shot.

Wednesday, June 9: Day Thirty-Five

The day began, before the jury and witness were brought in, with a plea from prosecutor Ron Howen not to waste further time on cross-examination of Dr. Martin Fackler, the wound ballistics expert. Chuck Peterson responded that he had now sat through seven weeks of prosecution, and that he would probably have finished his cross-examination the day before if the prosecution had not interrupted with so many objections. The judge admonished both sides to behave professionally, and brought in Dr. Fackler and the jury.

Dr. Fackler, under cross-examination by Peterson, said he didn't know about Degan's backpack nor had he examined it. The prosecution had pointed out that the pack had holes in it which it contended were bullet holes from Kevin Harris's rifle. Dr. Fackler said he had not talked to the forensic pathologist who had done Marshal Degan's autopsy, nor had he interviewed Marshal Cooper, the eyewitness to Degan's death. The autopsy showed that Degan's main artery had been closed 75 percent due to stenosis, which Peterson contended would have made him go into shock faster than a healthier person. Fackler disagreed. He said that it was likely, considering his high level of training, that if Degan had fired at Sammy Weaver before he had been shot, he would have hit him with all seven rounds rather than only one. Peterson got him to acknowledge, however, that he had no idea what or whom Degan was aiming at.

Next, Lon Horiuchi was back on the stand, again closely guarded, under cross-examination. The defense concentrated on the drawing that showed what were apparently two heads in the window. They insisted that the drawing suggested strongly that Horiuchi could see two people crouching behind the window and that he shot in full knowledge that two people were there, even though the enhanced rules of engagement had called for not shooting into the cabin. Horiuchi insisted that he could not see through the window because the curtain was drawn, but he had drawn the two heads where he thought they might be as an illustration for one of the shooting review officers. The judge disallowed many of the questions the defense wanted to ask, and the entire testimony lasted only about thirty minutes.

The next witness was Lucien "Luke" Haag, a ballistics expert. He focused on the fatal wound to Marshal William Degan, and offered an explanation sharply at odds with what Marshal Larry Cooper had said about Degan's death. Cooper had testified that he was just to Degan's right when Degan, kneeling behind a stump, aimed his rifle at Kevin Harris's back and ordered him to stop. Cooper said that Harris then spun and shot his rifle from the hip, hitting Degan and knocking him off his knees.

Haag testified that the wound that killed Degan had to have been fired from about 90 degrees to Degan's right if he had been kneeling in a shooting position. The bullet had taken a downsloping right-to-left trajectory through Degan's left breast. "It does not square at all with Bill Degan being in a shooting configuration," said Haag. Instead, he contended, it was more likely that at the moment he was shot, Degan was either holding his gun in an at-rest position across his chest or was diving or rolling for cover to his left.

Lucien Haag was scheduled to be the last prosecution witness, with cross-examination slated for the next day.

Thursday, June 10: Day Thirty-Six

The morning began with Lucien Haag on the stand for cross-examination. He repeated that the ballistics evidence could support the government's version of events. But as the defense took him through the evidence step by step again, he finally acknowledged that there was no physical evidence available to dispute the defense's contention that Marshal Art Roderick had fired the first shot. The ballistics evidence was simply not conclusive, he said, on the all-important question of who had fired first.

Haag's testimony went until late afternoon, and Ron Howen announced that the government's case was complete. Then the defense attorneys huddled briefly at the judge's bench. The first announcement came from David Nevin: "In view of the evidence that has been presented, Mr. Harris waives his right to present evidence," said Nevin. One of the juror's jaws dropped in surprise.

Then Gerry Spence stood and paused a moment: "In view of the evidence that has been presented and the evidence that has not been presented, the defendant Mr. Weaver also waives his right to present any evidence and rests at this time." In the spectators' gallery, an excited buzz began. Kevin Harris's mother and girlfriend began to cry.

In an interview later, Gerry Spence simply said: "It's occasionally done when there seems to be a gross absence of proof." He reminded reporters that he had called no defense witnesses the previous year in his successful defense of former Philippine first lady Imelda Marcos against fraud charges. David Nevin said he had felt for weeks that the government was failing to prove its case beyond a reasonable doubt.

Judge Lodge dismissed the jury for the time being, announcing that closing statements would begin on Monday. The stage was set for Friday, when attorneys for the defense said they would move to have all charges dismissed, and attorneys would present arguments to the judge over the precise wording of the judge's instructions to the jury.

The Lawyers Close,
The Jury Decides

Friday, June 11, 1993, began with a defense motion to dismiss all charges—or to order a directed verdict of acquittal on all charges. Both Gerry Spence and David Nevin argued, for their respective clients, that the prosecution had failed to prove any aspect of the case against Randy Weaver and Kevin Harris.

Ron Howen rose to argue against the dismissal of charges. About fifteen minutes into his response, as reporter Dean Miller wrote in the *Spokesman-Review*, "he appeared to lose his train of thought. Up to that time, his left hand was shaking violently and his delivery lacked its characteristic vigor. After a long pause, he sighed loudly, shuffled through his notes and looked over at co-prosecutor Kim Lindquist, who smiled encouragingly back, raising his eyebrows. Howen turned back to his notes and then stopped."

" 'I'm sorry, judge, I can't continue,' he said, his voice unsteady, and sat down. Marshals and FBI agents moved forward to pat his shoulder as he sat with his hands between his knees and his face averted. Howen left the courtroom after Judge Lodge called a recess and did not return. The U.S. Attorney's office declined repeated requests for an explanation of Howen's behavior."

After the recess, co-prosecutor Kim Lindquist declined to finish Mr. Howen's argument. Judge Lodge then announced his rulings. He dismissed Counts Six and Eight, saying the evidence was such that they simply could not be proven. Count Six said that Kevin Harris and Randy Weaver "did forcibly resist, oppose, impede, interfere with, intimidate, and assault Frank Costanza, Dick Rogers, G. Wayne Smith, and John Haynes," which referred to shooting or threatening to shoot at the FBI helicopter the day Vicki Weaver was killed. Judge Lodge ruled there was no evidence of a threat to the helicopter. That alleged threat to the helicopter had been the justification FBI sniper Lon Horiuchi had given for opening fire that day.

Count Eight charged that Randy Weaver, "as aided, abetted, counseled, induced, or procured by Vicki Weaver, Kevin L. Harris, and some other members of the Weaver family, did knowingly possess or receive approximately fourteen firearms and thousands of round of ammunition" while a federal fugitive. Judge Lodge noted that the evidence suggested that he had possessed these firearms before he became a federal fugitive, that they certainly hadn't been shipped in interstate commerce during the time he was a fugitive, and that the charge was superfluous to the main complaint.

Judge Lodge also reserved the option of dismissing a third charge, one that charged Kevin Harris with harboring and concealing Randy Weaver while Weaver was a fugitive (Count Seven). The remaining seven counts, he ruled, would be presented to the jury.

Judge Lodge then announced that the schedule for the remainder of the case would be changed slightly. Instructions on the law would be read to the jury on Monday afternoon. That gave the opposing attorneys the weekend to draft proposed instructions, and Monday morning to argue for their positions before the judge. Closing arguments would take place on Tuesday.

As is often the case with highly publicized trials, several incidents during the trial were known to the general public but not to the jury, because they had occurred during times Judge Lodge had sent the jury out of the courtroom, either because he doubted the relevance of the material to be discussed, or he wanted to peruse the information with the jury gone, so he could decide whether it was directly relevant to the central question of guilt or innocence on the specific charges brought by the prosecution. Sometimes the jury was not allowed to hear comments the judge felt were inflammatory. At least one witness's testimony had been edited to exclude potentially inflammatory comments.

Thus the jury had not heard that Kevin Harris might have stolen gas from the Raus, the Weavers' closest neighbors, nor that Randy Weaver was at the home of a member of the Aryan Nations the night the man was arrested on charges of conspiring to bomb a gay bar in Seattle. Nor were the jurors told that the prosecution had been fined for what appeared to be FBI efforts to delay the release of background files about Lon Horiuchi. The jurors were not present on the several occasions when Ron Howen had to apologize to the judge when it turned out that some of the evidence had been reconstructed or when files or investigative reports that had been missing a long time suddenly turned up. The jurors had not been in court when Howen appeared to lose his train of thought and sat down without finishing his argument on Friday. And they were not to be in court while the attorneys argued over the nature of the instructions they were to receive.

On Monday, June 14, those arguments took place. Ron Howen was still not present in the court, and no explanation was offered for his absence. So the prosecution's case was carried by Kim Lindquist.

As it had been throughout the trial, the courtroom was full. The public section held some familiar faces who had not been permitted to attend other sessions because they were on the list of possible defense witnesses. Bo Gritz's associate Jack McLamb, the former Phoenix police officer, was there. Randy Weaver's two older daughters, Sara and Rachel, were in the courtroom, as were his Naples neighbors, Bill and Judy Grider. Herb Byerly, the BATF agent who had hired Kenneth Fadeley as an undercover agent to persuade Randy Weaver to sell illegal weapons, was also present.

The first issue raised by the defense was over the question of whether the jury was to assume that the U.S. marshals were acting in their official capacity on August 21, 1992, the day of the first shootout. The prosecution had proposed instructions that the jury had to assume that. But Gerry Spence argued that no evidence had been presented to the effect that they were in possession of a warrant for Randy Weaver's arrest on that day, so the issue of "official capacity" was open to interpretation. If the jury members were instructed to assume they were there in their official capacity, he argued, Judge Lodge would himself be deciding in advance for the jury one of the central issues of the trial.

Kim Lindquist argued that since the prosecution had the burden of proving guilt beyond a reasonable doubt, it was necessary and reasonable for the government to have a slight advantage. Spence expressed sympathy, saying that in this case that was a very large burden, indeed. But, he continued, "I think we should also make some small effort to make it clear as far as the possibility of acquittal of the defendant is concerned." Judge Lodge struck the portion of the proposed instructions, leaving it to the jury to decide whether the marshals were there in their official capacity.

Next, the defense wanted to add an instruction that the jury should be aware that a federal officer was not authorized to violate Idaho state law. This proposed instruction was related to the defense contention that the FBI Hostage Rescue Team's rules of engagement for August 22 had been illegal under Idaho law. David Nevin led off the argument, claiming the proposed instruction had "evidentiary significance" in that it showed the state of mind of the federal officials in charge of the scene after the fiasco on August 21. Kim Lindquist objected, accusing the defense of merely seeking this instruction as the basis for a future lawsuit against the government. Nevin denied it and stated even more forcefully his contention that the rules of engagement were designed to eliminate the surviving witnesses after the marshals had bungled things August 21. "That's how desperate they were," he argued. "That's how much they perceived other law enforcement officers to be in the wrong. That's why this instruction needs to be in there."

Gerry Spence then jumped in, reminding Judge Lodge of the testimony and attitude of Hostage Rescue Team chief Richard Rogers, saying Rogers came "bouncing into the state of Idaho and manufacturing rules of engagement that, to him, supersede the laws of the state of Idaho. . . . Can you see [U.S. Supreme Court Chief] Justice Rehnquist," asked Spence, "being told that states no longer have any right to decide what is and is not proper conduct for officers enforcing a warrant? . . . That the states no longer have any states' rights?" Spence then recalled Rogers's responses when Spence had pushed him to cite what section of the U.S. Code gave Rogers authority to superseded Idaho state laws, and Rogers had snapped back: "The entire federal code."

"And he said it vehemently," Spence reminded Judge Lodge.

Spence then brought up Idaho Code Section 18–4011, arguing that it prohibited the use of deadly force in the way the rules of engagement for Ruby Ridge had been written. "If you don't give it [the instruction that federal agents don't have authority to violate state law]," said Spence to Judge Lodge, "then we might as well let Mr. Rogers write the instructions to the jury!" Kim Lindquist then argued that since this was a federal warrant, that federal rather than state laws should apply. Under the Fourth Amendment (which protects people from search and seizure without a warrant), he argued, rules and procedures have evolved in federal courts, and these should govern the serving of a federal warrant rather than state law.

David Nevin then argued that there was a difference between August 21 (when the marshals came onto the property and the shootout occurred) and August 22. You could make an argument that federal rules should prevail on August 21, he said, when the issue was serving a federal warrant. But once the standoff had begun, state law should have prevailed. Apparently sensing that there was one more argument to be made, Gerry Spence then moved back into the verbal fray, arguing that the jury needed to consider more than the Fourth Amendment, because that amendment "doesn't deal with rules of engagement and officers who set aside the law and go out and kill people." Turning directly to Judge Lodge, he completed his point: "Now, are the rules of engagement the law of this case or not?"

Judge Lodge then ruled that although the instruction might not be directly relevant, he would include an instruction to the jury that Idaho law could not be violated or superseded by federal agents.

The defense also carried the day regarding a First Amendment issue. Judge Lodge agreed to include an instruction that the religious beliefs of Randy Weaver and Kevin Harris could not be held against them, that jury members were to set aside their own attitudes about those beliefs and reach a verdict based on their understanding of what had happened, not what the defendants believed.

By the time all these arguments had been made, it was midafternoon. The jury was then brought in and given a complex list of fifty-five instructions, and dismissed until the next day, when closing arguments would be held.

After the jury was dismissed, the defense had a couple more issues to raise. Gerry Spence told the judge he had a "serious problem to adequately represent my client." He then suggested that since there were two defendants in this case, and the jury instructions were that each defendant was to be considered separately, that each defendant should have the same amount of time as the prosecution during closing arguments. Each side was scheduled to have three and a half hours. He told Judge Lodge how he and Harris defense attorney David Nevin "had looked at each other with tears in our eyes," neither wanting to ask the other to relinquish any time, but both convinced they really needed more time to present an adequate defense. He implied that by limiting an argument that really warranted five or six hours to three and a half hours, he was already making a sacrifice. Limiting his time to one and a half to two hours would place him in a position where he couldn't help the jury to analyze the case as he would like.

Prosecuting attorney Lindquist, obviously not wanting to have the jury listen to Gerry Spence for any longer than was absolutely necessary, argued against the proposal, pointing out that during jury selection prior to the trial, the defense was given no more peremptory challenges than the prosecution, despite the fact that there were two defendants. Judge Lodge gave a little. Spence had asked for an additional hour for the defense. Judge Lodge allowed an extra thirty minutes.

Finally, Gerry Spence said that there was "one last thing, your Honor." Throughout the trial, both prosecution and defense had been required to speak from a podium between the defense and prosecution tables, across the room from both the witness stand and the jury box. During closing arguments, Spence wanted to be able to get closer to the jury.

"During this trial," he said, "I've learned to live with a rule that I haven't been under in forty years. . . . I've been married, shackled, and in a spastic embrace with this podium for two months when I'm trying to fight for the rights and life of my client." He pointed out that the distance between the lawyers and the people in the back row of the jury box was thirty or thirty-five feet. "I thought about bringing in binoculars to look at the jurors' faces," he continued. "But I was told the judge wouldn't approve. It's been very hard on me. I don't think very well like that. Let me move a little bit. . . . Let me talk to my jury."

Kim Lindquist immediately objected. He noted that both sides were operating under the same rules. He pointed out that even with these local rules (which were not applied in every federal court), Spence and the other attorneys had much more freedom than in the more rigid English system. He accused the defense attorney of wanting to indulge in courtroom theatrics and lacking proper courtroom decorum.

Spence retorted scornfully: "I am really disturbed when I hear about people trying to emulate the English. I'm not interested in trying to emulate the English. . . . We're not in England, we're in Idaho!" Pounding his fist on the podium for emphasis, he addressed Judge Lodge directly: "This is about the most important single set of facts that will probably ever be heard in an Idaho court. This is a watershed case. . . . This [the rule about podiums] is not the federal system. I've argued cases in countless federal courts around the nation, and never been required to be married or shackled to a podium."

Judge Lodge remarked, on behalf of the jury, that "it is difficult to think when people are right on top of you." But he did rule that the podium could be moved to a position eight to ten feet from the jury and directly in front of the jury box. He also agreed that lawyers would be able to move a reasonable distance away from the podium if necessary to retrieve a piece of evidence or for some other valid or logical reason.

The Boise Federal Courthouse was buzzing with activity early on Tuesday morning, June 15. By 7:00 A.M. a long line had already formed outside the security area on the first floor. It snaked around a line of chairs and back again, and before long the line of people wanting to get into the courtroom to see the closing arguments stretched out the front door. Among those waiting were some who hadn't been able to attend most of the trial because they were potential witnesses, including Bo Gritz with his wife Claudia, Vicki Weaver's friend Jackie Brown with her husband Tony, and Jack McLamb. Sara and Rachel Weaver were in attendance again, with Vicki's sister Julie Brown and her husband Keith. Of course, the media were there. The parking lot was almost full of TV remote vans, bristling with satellite dishes and antennas, with reporters and camera operators swarming through the crowd in search of familiar faces or interesting spectators to interview.

The courthouse guards started letting people in shortly before 8:00 A.M., when court was scheduled to start. The main courtroom was soon filled, so a nearby courtroom equipped with a closed-circuit television hookup was opened as well. Soon this courtroom was filled, and still more than one hundred people had to be turned away.

Ron Howen was still not present, and the U.S. Attorney's office had no explanation for his absence or news about his whereabouts. So the task of presenting the prosecution case fell to co-prosecutor Kim Lindquist. He started by saying that Randy Weaver was nothing more than an illegal gun dealer who had been plotting for more than a decade to get into a confrontation with the government.

When it finally happened, he wanted to be viewed as a victim. In a methodical, businesslike fashion, he took the jury step by step through the government's conspiracy theory, beginning with the evolution of the Weavers' religious beliefs back in Iowa. "Somehow, Mr. and Mrs. Weaver developed a particular philosophy for a religion—beliefs, if you will—and those beliefs play a vital role in the understanding of this case."

Lindquist knew he had to walk a fine line. "It's been suggested that the United States government is prosecuting—nay, persecuting—Mr. Weaver because of his beliefs," he told the jury. "That is utterly not true." He explained that as far as the government is concerned, it is perfectly all right to have weapons (at least legal weapons), to store food, and to have beliefs about a battle called Armageddon. But the Weavers went too far with this latter belief. "Their beliefs about Armageddon included the fact that government is satanic, and by being satanic, is evil. Those beliefs were beginning to strain the parameters of reasonableness and common sense. They believed government persecutes—not in the future, but now." Eventually they "believed they were dealing with Satan himself, and that became the center of their lives."

"This is a case of resolve on the part of Weaver and Harris," said Lindquist, "to defy laws to the point of using violence. . . . This whole thing is a tragedy . . . but the cause of the tragedy was the resolve of the Weaver family, and that translates into murder." Everything Randy Weaver had done—selling illegal weapons, failing to appear in court, holding out in his cabin—was the direct result of beliefs that led him to a resolve to provoke a confrontation with the government. "And as Kevin Harris joined the family and became a son, he joined the conspiracy."

Lindquist then showed slides—one each of the fourteen weapons confiscated from the Weaver home, and argued that this was "a quantity of weapons and ammunition that reflected a resolve to defy government, to defy laws, and be prepared to resist [the government] in a very significant way."

According to Lindquist, it wasn't a coincidence that the Weavers chose Idaho as their new home. Idaho is known to have a lot of people with radical right–wing beliefs and Christians with an apocalyptic bent. It is also known as the home of the Aryan Nations group, a racist organization that preaches Jews are the spawn of the devil. It wasn't a coincidence that Randy and Vicki Weaver "became associated" with the Aryan Nations. All this reflected their determination to provoke a confrontation with the U.S. government.

Once Randy Weaver had made his decision to defy the government by not appearing in court, Lindquist argued, the government showed remarkable restraint and reasonableness. It bent over backward to avoid a confrontation for eighteen months. It tried not to give Randy and Kevin any excuse or justification for the confrontation they desired. When the conflict finally came, he said, it was not the government's doing. The conflict came because of Randy Weaver's resolve to defy a government he viewed as satanic.

Lindquist also addressed the issue of the undercover agent who had approached Randy Weaver to persuade him to sell illegal weapons. Undercover work is honorable, said Lindquist. Without people willing to risk their lives in often dangerous undercover work, many crimes would never be uncovered and the laws could never be enforced adequately.

David Nevin led off for the defense. He began with a famous quote: "Government is not reason, it is not eloquence; it is force. Like fire, it is a dangerous servant and a fearful master." He asked the jury how many of them realized that it was George Washington who had said those words. Then he began a methodical exposition of his case: "I want to begin my remarks by telling you why I made the decision not to call any witnesses." Leaning toward the jury, he said, "It's because the government's case against Kevin Harris is false." Point by point, he chipped away at the government's version of events, often using the testimony of the government witnesses.

He reminded the jury that U.S. Marshals Service medic Frank Norris had testified that the first shots he heard August 21 were from a .223 caliber weapon, not the distinctly different sound that would have been made by Kevin Harris's .30–06 hunting rifle. He talked about the testimony of another witness, who said that while

Randy and Sammy Weaver and Kevin Harris were following the dogs, Vicki remained calmly outside the cabin "kicking the dirt." Did that sound like somebody expecting or looking forward to a violent confrontation? And he reminded jurors that prosecutor Lindquist, in his opening statement, had admitted that the reason Marshal Larry Cooper was carrying a silenced weapon was that the marshals planned to shoot one or all of the Weavers' dogs that day.

David Nevin asked jurors to think about how incredible a coincidence it was that only members of the U.S. Marshals Special Operations Group were at the Y on August 21, while "non–SOGs" were placed at observation points some distance away. Was this really just a surveillance mission or was it an action mission? And he reminded the jurors of the testimony of the prosecution's wound ballistics expert, Dr. Martin Fackler, who stated that "my job was to confirm the government's theory of the case." "Guess that must have been a Freudian slip," said Nevin.

Then Nevin moved further, raising serious questions as to whether the government contention that Kevin Harris had killed Marshal William Degan was true. He noted that it wasn't until the second test of bullet fragments in Degan's body that an expert had said that the fragments were consistent with a factory load in a factory .30–06 casing. But, he pointed out, it was commonplace to reload .30–06 shells, and Kevin and Randy had gone out of their way to save money when buying ammunition. The shells in Kevin's rifle, he said, could have been reloaded any number of times, with bullets and loads considerably different from a standard factory load. He also asked the jury to consider how likely it was that Kevin turned around, and with one shot, hit a man dressed in full camouflage to blend in with the woods with such deadly accuracy.

Then Nevin brought out the backpack Degan had been carrying that day and showed it to the jury. He showed the jury one hole an FBI lab had found and identified as an exit hole of a bullet. But a few days before, Nevin explained to an increasingly fascinated jury, Gerry Spence's son Kent had been taking another look at the backpack and noticed a second hole that the FBI lab seemed to have missed. Could this possibly be the entry hole of a bullet? If so, he said, showing the relationship of the two holes, and if the FBI was right about this first hole being an exit hole, then the round that went through the pack, probably without hitting Degan, could only have come from behind him and must have been fired by Marshal Larry Cooper.

Then this quiet, scholarly attorney, who had been logical and sometimes relentless but low-key throughout the trial, did something that seemed out of character. He was explaining that William Degan, a highly trained, highly decorated member of the Special Operations Group, might have been trying not to kill Sammy Weaver, but to wound him or just to knock the rifle out of his arms. As a skilled sharpshooter, this might not seem out of the question to him. But he would want to be sure he had a clear view of his target, which might mean he would have to move as Sammy moved and the target thus moved. Nevin then crouched into a shooting position, as if shooting from behind a tree, as Degan might have done. "Pow!" he exclaimed, then moved a few steps sideways, still crouching as if aiming a gun or playing cops and robbers in a backyard, to get a better view of the moving target. He did this several times, moving to the right—which could have brought him, Nevin contended, dressed in full camouflage and therefore hard to see, right in front of Larry Cooper, who was firing a silenced 9 millimeter weapon, which Degan wouldn't have heard.

Did a round from Cooper's silenced 9 millimeter enter Cooper's backpack from the rear? If so, contended Nevin, it would likely have spun him around at least part way toward Larry Cooper—and he spun himself to demonstrate. If that happened, he contended, the next bullet Cooper fired would have entered Degan from the chest, and with Degan turned around and crouching in a firing position, it would have entered his body at precisely the angle the fatal bullet did, in fact, enter Degan's chest.

Nevin then backed off a little. "I'm not saying that this is what happened for sure," he said. "I'm only saying this is a possible scenario—but one that is at least as consistent with the evidence and as believable as anything the government has proposed about how William Degan died." He then reminded the jury of one of the judge's instructions as to the law—that if the jury can arrive at a verdict of either guilty or innocent with equal plausibility, it must return a verdict of not guilty.

Then it was time for the lunch break.

═ * ═

After lunch came what most of the spectators had come to see, Gerry Spence's closing arguments.

Spence began by going over to the defense table and shaking hands with his client, Randy Weaver, and with his fellow attorneys and their wives. After acknowledging Judge Lodge and Kim Lindquist, he began. "I've been at this for over forty years, and I've never begun a closing argument in any case with what I feel now. I just hope I can be the best lawyer I know how to be for the next two hours and thirty-five minutes, because this case demands the best from all of us."

"You may be the most important jury that's come along for many a decade," he told the jury, explaining that this was a watershed case. "I want you to realize that few of us, me included, ever really know how important we are or where we stand in history." Spence estimated that the average age of the jurors was forty, meaning that the jury taken together had 480 years of experience in life. Then he talked a little about the founding fathers of the United States, the framers of the U.S. Constitution. "Do you think those men were important?" he asked the jury. "They were just local guys doing their job, just like you're doing your job. They did something permanent and magnificent—just as you will do in this case."

"Your purpose here isn't just to find out who wins this case . . . you have a more noble function," said Spence. The jury in this case was destined to be a concrete manifestation of the fact that eternal vigilance is the price of liberty. They would let it be known that the government couldn't hide facts just because it was the government, and couldn't refuse to negotiate just because it had power. The federal government can't just come into Idaho and declare Idaho law null and void, as Dick Rogers had done.

Then Gerry Spence identified Sara and Rachel Weaver, seated near the front of the gallery. He said his purpose was for Randy Weaver to be able to walk out of this courtroom with his two daughters when the jury had done its job.

He talked about how the government had tried to sweep the deaths of Sammy Weaver and Vicki Weaver under the rug, to keep the world from finding out about them. To the government, he said, shooting a boy in the back is "like changing your pants in the morning." Shooting a woman in the head is about the same, "like changing your pants in the morning. Nobody cares."

Then he claimed that virtually the entire government case, the entire government approach amounted to an effort to demonize Randy Weaver. Take those slides of fourteen mostly secondhand, mostly inexpensive guns presented a few hours ago. "I'll bet there are people on this jury who own fourteen guns," Spence commented. "I'd hate to have the BATF come and look in all my closets . . . if they came and brought all my guns in here, you'd distrust me."

How did all this happen? Spence claimed that when the federal agents woke up to the light of the day, they realized they had done something terribly wrong. You can't just shoot a little boy in the back, and the marshals belatedly realized it, Spence contended. They had a U.S. marshal killed under mysterious circumstances. Art Roderick had shot a friendly dog whose most dangerous weapon was a wagging tail, and had shot him in the rump. The next day, Vicki Weaver was murdered when the expert sniper from the FBI put her head in his cross hairs and squeezed the trigger. Thus Spence summarized the defense version of what had happened August 21. After looking at all of that, Spence argued, they knew they had to cover up what they had done. So Ron Howen came up to the federal staging area on August 22, and started writing a script and rehearsing the cast for a cover-up, so the feds could demonize Randy Weaver and take the blame off themselves.

Spence went through some of the means by which, he contended, the government had undertaken to demonize his client.

The prosecution used belt buckles, haircuts, T-shirts, and literature found in his house to tie Randy Weaver to the Aryan Nations, when Randy was never an Aryan Nations member. Spence commented that he himself had literature in his house that the government might not approve of. Then he turned to his wife in one of the spectators' seats, as if to reassure her, saying, "but I'm going to get rid of it as soon as I get home."

The defense attorney pointed out that the government took special care to show the jury the guns and ammunition Randy Weaver had stockpiled in quantity, but not the equally impressive stockpiles of food, clothing, and household supplies taken from the house when evidence was gathered. Was this really evidence of somebody spoiling for a fight, he asked, or was it more likely evidence that this was a family that sought to be independent, to live apart from the world, and had simply taken the steps and obtained the supplies that anybody who was serious about such a decision would naturally take?

Spence then delivered a tribute to Vicki Weaver, Randy's wife. The government demonized her and killed her because she let it be known that she wasn't afraid of the government, he claimed. "If she were standing in this courtroom today, I'd go up to her and give her a big hug—and tell her I'm glad we have people who are no longer afraid of the government," that this nation can only survive as a free people if there are more brave and independent people like Vicki Weaver.

Spence summarized his case so far. He said, we've had killings of innocent people by the government, the demonization of innocent people, all tied together by a pervasive hostility to any sort of accountability on the government's part. "Now somebody has to say no to this," he told the jury, and they were the ones to do it. "You have more power than anybody, and that's the way it's supposed to be. You have more power than the FBI, the BATF, the U.S. Attorney, the U.S. Marshals Service, or anybody in the government. You have more power than his Honor," he continued, good-naturedly walking over and pointing to Judge Lodge, who couldn't help a small smile in response. "And I don't know many people who have more power than his Honor." He stressed that not only did the jury as a body possess this awesome power, but that each and every member individually possessed it and was responsible for how it was used.

Spence then turned his scorn on how the government had behaved in this case. The marshals knew there were no booby traps on Randy Weaver's mountain, but they told the FBI there were, in the hopes that everybody in the cabin would eventually be killed, so no witnesses to their previous crimes would remain. He told the jury that the FBI's Hostage Rescue Team "was a nice euphemism for 'expert killers'. . . . These are the Waco boys."

"This is a murder case," he almost roared. "But the people who committed the murders have not been charged, and the people who committed the murders are not in this courtroom."

Spence then ridiculed the government's charges that the confrontation was the result of a ten-year conspiracy on the part of Randy Weaver and his family. "If you want to know what a conspiracy is, it would be asking you [the jury] to help *them* [pointing at the prosecution table] cover up their crimes by convicting Randy and Kevin of *something*."

To be sure, Spence said, Randy Weaver had shown poor judgment several times in this matter. He had shown poor judgment in not recognizing the government snitch for what he was. Anyone who bought a shotgun could saw the barrel off himself. The fact that Kenneth Fadeley was so insistent that Randy do the sawing off should have alerted him. He said Randy used poor judgment when he didn't show up for the trial. He was guilty of being afraid and having poor judgment sometimes. But he [Spence] had probably used poor judgment just a few minutes ago when he had pointed to his wife and asked her to stand up. "How would you like to be turned over to him," he asked the jury, pointing at the prosecutor, "every time you exercised poor judgment?" The prosecution had called fifty-six witnesses and worked hard to get them to say bad things about Randy Weaver. But they never mentioned—and never would have mentioned if we didn't have a tradition of competent defense in this country—that his wife had lain dead and rotting in his cabin for eight days while Dick Rogers and his professional killers were trying to kill everybody on the mountain.

Then Spence reminded the jury of how much spying and snooping had gone on in this case. The original snitch had tape-recorded Randy's conversations. "I'd hate to have all my conversations tape-recorded and I'll bet you would too," he told the jury. But that was only the beginning. The U.S. marshals spied on the Weavers so extensively that they knew when Sara Weaver's menstrual period was and constructed a plan to snatch her built around this knowledge.

Spence then walked up to and pointed directly at a nonplused Herb Byerly, the BATF agent who had hired Kenneth Fadeley, and who was sitting in the courtroom, just to the left of the jury. "Here's the man who started it all. He started it all by trying to create another snitch." His snitch Fadeley was a contingency witness (due for a bonus if Weaver was convicted) so he shouldn't be believed at all. If anything he was guilty of entrapment for enticing Randy Weaver to commit a crime. "Mr. Byerly represents a new twist in America today, called Big Brother," Spence thundered. Looking right into Byerly's face, he said, "Only in America can I point a finger at this guy and his agency and say this is the new Gestapo here in America!" And it should be remembered, said Spence, that if Randy Weaver had agreed to become a snitch himself, the sawed-off shotgun would have been forgotten immediately; instead, Byerly "would have kissed him on both cheeks."

The judge in Randy Weaver's initial hearing, Spence contended, had made three different mistakes, including sending the wrong court date to Randy Weaver. But those mistakes are to be forgiven and forgotten. But Randy Weaver made the mistake of believing a government snitch, and that made him a criminal as far as the government is concerned. But perhaps that shouldn't be surprising. As the government indictment clearly indicates, it views a family trying to live life independently as a group of co-conspirators.

Spence began his conclusion by going over some of the evidentiary confusion in the case. A magic bullet suddenly appears after Herb Byerly joins the evidence search team. An expert witness says the bullet hole in William Degan's backpack was probably made from behind—and Spence quickly retraced the theory Nevin had more dramatically demonstrated. A paid expert witness confirms that his job is to support the government theory. But another expert witness is finally forced to admit that the defense version—that government agents shot first, not Kevin Harris—is at least as consistent with the physical evidence as is the government version of events.

Finally, Spence closed with a story. There was a smart-aleck bully of a boy, he said, who would catch birds and hold them in his hands. Then he would ask a person whether the bird was dead or alive. If the person said he or she thought the bird was alive, the bully would crush the bird with his hands and kill it, proving the person wrong. Finally, the boy approached a wise man with a bird in his hands and asked the usual question. "Son, the bird is in your hands," the wise man said. "You can kill it or free it."

Spence concluded, "Ladies and gentlemen, Randy and Kevin are in your hands. You can free them or imprison them."

One juror, an elderly gentleman, had been leaning forward eagerly during Gerry Spence's closing arguments, often taking notes. As Kim Lindquist approached the podium to deliver his rebuttal, this gentleman closed his notebook, sat back, and folded his arms. During his rebuttal, after briefly reiterating the government's case, Kim Lindquist reminded the jury that there was another person killed in this tragedy: William Degan. He spoke of the loss to Marshal Degan's family, saying, "There is a wife and two boys who would give anything to get their dad back."

After the closing arguments, Judge Lodge turned the case over to the jury, sequestering them—keeping them insulated from outside influences and access to news about the case—in a nearby hotel. Most of the newspaper stories said the experts they had consulted figured the jury would come to a verdict by the end of the week.

Outside the courtroom, speaking with reporters, Gerry Spence equated the siege at Ruby Ridge with the tragedy at the Branch Davidian complex. There, too, he insisted, the government conducted a botched investigation and went in with undue force, leading to a standoff in which even more excessive force was used.

The jury began its deliberations Wednesday, June 16. Outside the federal courthouse, many of the people who had attended large portions of the trial stayed on—friends and supporters of Randy Weaver and Kevin Harris, a few skinheads, Christian patriots and constitutionalists, and unaffiliated citizens concerned about what seemed to them like an abuse of government power. Some continued to carry signs. The parking lot, meanwhile, continued to be occupied by television news trucks. The jury was brought from the Red Lion Inn each morning in Chevy Suburbans with brown paper over the windows, and driven into a basement garage for the day's deliberations. At the end of the day, they were returned to the hotel the same way. At the hotel, they were not allowed to watch television or read newspapers, and the reading material a few wanted to bring in to pass the time was looked at closely. Tom Clancy's spy novel, *Patriot Games*, for example, was not allowed. The jurors were watched closely, even (or especially) when their families were allowed to visit on weekends, by U.S. marshals who became increasingly edgy as time wore on with no verdict. One juror later said they felt so isolated from the outside world that it was almost like being a prisoner of war.

The Weaver–Harris jury initially consisted of five men and seven women. The youngest was thirty–one, the oldest seventy. Three of the members were retired. Among the others were a junior high school teacher, a pressman, a production worker, a farmer, a bookkeeper, a homemaker, a university education coordinator, an accountant, and a medical lab technician.

On Friday, June 18, with no verdict yet reached, Judge Lodge decided to ask the jury to continue deliberations on Saturday, but not on Sunday. The courthouse was kept closed on Saturday, with the understanding that if a verdict was reached, it would be opened so the media and at least some members of the public could be in the courtroom when the verdict was delivered. On Saturday, with many people not working, the crowd around the courthouse swelled, with many people coming who had not been present at the trial. One was a law enforcement officer, Dan Hite, from Caldwell, Idaho, who had not been able to be present before because of work commitments. But he took his vacation time and canceled a recreational vacation so as be at the courthouse during jury deliberations. He met LeRoy Armstrong, a Weaver supporter from Iowa, who said he had known four generations of Weavers there, and who had been attending the trial from the first day. Hite insisted on giving Armstrong $15.00 to help with expenses, and his eight-year-old daughter emptied her piggy bank to give him $4.38.

The jurors suspended deliberations on Saturday at 2:30 in the afternoon with no verdict reached.

On Monday, Tuesday, and Wednesday, June 21 through 23, the pattern continued. The jury would deliberate for a full day and return to the hotel without having reached a verdict.

On Thursday, June 24, the jury sent word to Judge Lodge that it had reviewed the evidence and would like to go to Ruby Ridge in northern Idaho—some four hundred miles from Boise—to see where all the activity took place for themselves. Judge Lodge held a hearing without the jury present to consider the request. The prosecution argued against allowing the jury to go to Ruby Ridge, arguing that the vegetation would probably be different from the time of year (in August) when the initial shooting took place. The defense argued that the jury should be allowed to do whatever it took to reach an intelligent decision, even if it meant taking the trip to Ruby Ridge. Judge Lodge denied the request for the time being, urging the jury to work diligently toward reaching a verdict with the evidence available to them, but held out the possibility that if a verdict hadn't been reached at some time in the future, and the jury felt that actually seeing the area would make the difference between reaching a verdict and failing to reach a verdict, he might reconsider the decision.

On Friday, June 25, the ninth full day of deliberations, after the jury began work at 7:00 A.M., attorneys Chuck Peterson, Gerry and Kent Spence, and David Nevin came to the courthouse at 9:00 A.M. to visit with their clients. Later, holding court for reporters, Gerry Spence said that visit had taken three hours, because "Randy had a lot on his mind." One of the reporters asked whether Randy was likely to return to Ruby Ridge when the trial was over. Gerry said that because of the tragedies that had occurred there, he doubted if Randy Weaver would ever go back to that particular ridge. Asked about the jury going to Ruby Ridge, he said he could almost guarantee they wouldn't be going. Asked if it might be grounds for an appeal if they weren't allowed to go, he said there was a bridge on his ranch in Wyoming, and just before you get to it is a sign that says, "Don't cross the bridge until you get to it." Asked about some of the evidence he had not been able to get placed before the jury, he said that in his forty-one years of practicing law, he had never seen a prosecutor work as hard as these two had done to keep the truth from a jury.

The jury did not reach a verdict that day. Or the next.

On Tuesday, June 29, the twelfth day of jury deliberation, the jury arrived at 8:00 A.M. Shortly thereafter, the lawyers from both sides were called in to confer with Judge Lodge.

A session of open court was then convened at 1:30 P.M. Lead prosecutor Ron Howen was back, apparently with an escort of four marshals. The newspapers were told simply that he had been sick.

Judge Lodge announced that Cyril Hatfield, a seventy-two-year-old securities salesman who had been elected jury foreman, had been monitored by the court and by a doctor for the past twenty-four hours. The previous day he had asked for a longer than usual lunch break, then walked out of the jury room without saying a word. Close to collapse, he was taken to a hospital. The doctors determined that his chronic mild heart condition would make the stress of the deliberations—now underway for almost two weeks—dangerous or could pose a serious threat to his health. They recommended that he be excused from the jury. One of the two alternates who had been sequestered with the jury, but had not participated in the deliberations, was then brought into court. She told Judge Lodge that she believed she could be a fair and impartial juror, and was sworn. A new foreman—forty-three-year-old pressman John Harris Weaver, no relation to either defendant—was elected. But the jury would have to start almost from the beginning to acquaint the new member, Anita Brewer, with what it had been able to do to date. It would be almost like starting over.

July 1 marked the fourteenth day of deliberations. That established a new record for jury deliberations in a criminal case in the state of Idaho. Media people in the pressroom on the fifth floor started penny pools on when the jury would finally reach a verdict. Some started joking that the jury planned to stay in session long enough to put in for retirement benefits.

On July 5, during the seventeenth day of deliberations, the jury passed a note to Judge Lodge asking for clarification about some of the words in some of the counts. Specifically the jury wanted to know whether one of the defendants has to be found guilty of resisting arrest, murder, and concealing a fugitive for the other to be found guilty of aiding and abetting those crimes. It also wanted clarification of the term "principal" in one of the jury instructions. Judge Lodge elaborated: "To convict one of aiding and abetting another, the principal must first be convicted of the offense; that is, you must find beyond a reasonable doubt that the principal committed the alleged offense."

About three minutes of court time set off several hours of speculation and guessing among the frustrated media people and other observers of the trial. David Nevin cautioned against reading too much into the request: "The fact is, these people have been up there grinding for seventeen days, and, really, any explanation is conceivable. I looked hard for the tea leaves, and I just didn't see any." Pressed a little more, he agreed with reporters that it was possible the jurors had agreed to acquit his client, Kevin Harris, of homicide, but weren't sure if they wanted to let Randy Weaver go. But he cautioned again that this was pure speculation.

Gerry Spence agreed. "Anybody who tries to second-guess what the questions mean and where the jury is, is making a mistake. This jury is working long and hard, and I suspect they're going to work some more." But although he said these were the longest jury deliberations he as an attorney had ever experienced—enough to make him "certifiable"—he cautioned again that "anyone who tells you how long this jury is going to deliberate is by definition a fool."

On Wednesday, July 7, the jury asked to be brought back into court to have read to them transcripts of testimony from BATF agent Herb Byerly and undercover informant Kenneth Fadeley, along with cross-examination by Weaver attorney Chuck Peterson.

Finally, on July 8, 1993, in a verdict the *New York Times'* Timothy Egan called "a strong rebuke of the government's use of force during an armed siege," the jury returned verdicts. Kevin Harris was acquitted of all charges. Randy Weaver was acquitted of all the serious charges—murder, conspiracy, aiding and abetting—arising from the siege and standoff. He was found guilty of two minor charges arising from the original arrest—failure to appear and violating the terms of his bail—but was found not guilty of the original weapons charge. Later interviews with jurors determined that they decided he had been entrapped by BATF undercover agents and should not be held guilty on that charge.

Kevin Harris was released from custody immediately. The charges on which Randy Weaver was found guilty carried a possible sentence of up to fifteen years. But Gerry Spence said he would try to have Randy Weaver released with a sentence based on the time he had already been in jail at his sentencing hearing September 28.

John Weaver, the jury foreman, told reporters that the government's case had raised more questions than it answered during the two-month trial. The central conspiracy charge against Weaver and Harris, he said, was quickly dismissed by the jury. He also noted that many government witnesses had helped the defense more than they had helped the prosecution.

As the verdicts were read, both Kevin Harris and Randy Weaver wept. Asked about Randy Weaver's reaction later, Gerry Spence said: "He thanked me and cried. I asked him if he learned anything. He said, 'If given a chance, the American justice system can work.' "

Gerry Spence urged that federal agents be charged in the murder of Sammy and Vicki Weaver: "A jury today has said that you can't kill somebody just because you wear badges, and then cover up those homicides by prosecuting the innocent," he said. "What are we now going to do about the deaths of Vicki Weaver, a mother who was killed with a baby in her arms, and Sammy Weaver, a boy who was shot in the back? Somebody has to answer for those deaths."

Gerry Spence was careful to say that the verdict should not be seen as a victory for the skinheads or neo-Nazis who had rallied to Randy Weaver's cause. "Those people are idiots," he said. "Randy Weaver wasn't a member of their group, and his cause is no cause of theirs."

Kevin Harris, who walked out of court holding his mother's hand, said, "I just want to thank the jury for everything. I think the right thing happened."

Henry E. Hudson, director of the United States Marshals Service, kept a stiff upper lip as he defended his own: "I believe there was no legal justification for the shooting of Deputy Marshal Degan," he said in a written statement. "The deputy marshals involved in the shooting incident were attempting to find a way to peacefully carry out their lawful responsibility of serving a federal, court-ordered warrant for the arrest of Randall Weaver."

Jackie Brown, Vicki Weaver's best friend, announced that people in Naples and Boundary County were rejoicing. "We're ecstatic," she said. "The message from the jury to the government is very simple: You screwed up. You made a major mistake. And you are responsible for the deaths of three people."

U.S. Attorney for Idaho Maurice Ellsworth, read a statement: "Beyond a reasonable doubt is a very high burden for the government to meet in a case, and in this case it appears we came out one run short. I don't think we got shut out."

The FBI had no comment.

Some law enforcement experts said the verdict in this case should cause federal agencies who shadow "fringe" groups and individuals to question their tactics and philosophies. Tony Cooper, a law enforcement consultant who teaches terrorism, negotiation, and conflict resolution at the University of Texas at Dallas was quoted in the *Los Angeles Times*: "I see the formation of a curious crusading mentality among certain law enforcement agencies to stamp out what they see as a threat to government generally. It's an exaggerated concern that they are facing a nationwide conspiracy and that somehow this will get out of control unless it is stamped out at a very early stage. These acquittals send a message that representatives of authority may not only have exceeded their mandate but have carried out their mission in an irresponsible way."

Jess Walter and Dean Miller of the *Spokesman-Review*, based on interviews with jury members who were willing to speak with them, put together a chronology of the labyrinthine road the jury took to reach its verdicts. Few were ready to judge when the case was dropped in their lap. They had been expecting the defense to spend almost as much time as the prosecution presenting its case, giving the jurors a little more time to crystallize in their own minds just what they believed about the evidence presented. So they recreated the trial, retrying the case on their own, creating models on the floor, and rehashing at length what had been presented in court. Early on, three or four jurors leaned toward guilty verdicts on most counts, believing that Randy and Kevin's obnoxious beliefs had led to Randy's failure to appear, which had precipitated the rest of the tragedy. Some sympathized with Randy and Kevin, seeing them as victims. But in the first few days, confused by the government testimony, they created their own time line and constructed their own model on a courtroom floor showing where everybody had been during key actions. Bookkeeper Mary Flenor became recording secretary. Schoolteacher Dorothy Mitchell kept pushing everybody to get things right. "You don't put a teacher on a jury and expect them not to research everything," she said. John Weaver acted as conciliator, trying to reconcile people with opposing views during sessions which often degenerated into angry shouting matches.

After ten days of study, the jury still hadn't taken a vote on anything.

By the time the first foreman, Cyril Hatfield, had left, the jury had voted on only one charge, murder. When alternate Anita Brewer was placed on the jury, the other jurors spent almost a week reviewing for her what they had done so far. It became clear to John Weaver, the new foreman, that a resolution would not be easy: "I could tell some people felt [Harris and Weaver] were victims right from the start," he said. "Others felt, we got murderers here, and we got to deal with them."

Finally, on July 3, they started voting again, taking up the murder charge again. Foreman John Weaver urged jurors to ignore their emotions and to concentrate on testimony and other evidence. The only question was: Is there reasonable doubt? The result was a 12–0 vote to acquit both Weaver and Harris of murder.

The other counts were handled during the final week of deliberations. The guilty vote on failure to appear and breaking pretrial release conditions came early on. Then the assault, resisting arrest, and conspiracy charges finally got unanimous not guilty votes. Then things bogged down. There was confusion over the charge that Kevin Harris aided and abetted in harboring a fugitive, since nobody else had been charged with harboring. That led to the question to Judge Lodge. His clarification led to a not guilty vote on that charge. The only undecided issue left then was the original gun charge. "A couple of jurors wanted to convict Randy Weaver on that charge, discounting he defense claim that he was entrapped," wrote Walter and Miller. "The jury asked for a replay of testimony in which an agent with the Bureau of Alcohol, Tobacco and Firearms told the informant not to entice Weaver and not to record meetings with the white separatist."

As juror Dorothy Hoffman told the two reporters: "From the beginning, when the BATF did their entrapment job, they didn't keep records and they did selective taping." But after hearing the testimony again, the jury was still undecided. After everybody slept on it, however, a unanimous verdict of not guilty on that count was forthcoming. "At the end, when we finally came out unanimous," said Dorothy Hoffman, "we all ran around crying and hugging. It was just the most emotional thing I've ever been through."

The Aftermath

The Weaver–Harris verdict was delivered July 8, 1993. Feds Lose Big was the banner headline in the *Spokesman-Review*. Although most of the jurors were interviewed by various local media, two jurors in particular, sixty-year-old Dorothy Hoffman, who tutors athletes, and forty-five-year-old Dorothy Mitchell, a junior high school teacher, were particularly outspoken in their criticism of the government's actions at Ruby Ridge. Senator Larry Craig of Idaho, a conservative Republican, called for a federal investigation into the conduct of federal officials.

On July 13, a bit of unfinished business arising from the siege and standoff was concluded. The FBI delivered a check for $23,040 to Chief Gary Gage of the North Bench Volunteer Fire District. The fire company in rural Boundary County had been struggling over this payment since the previous August. A few days after the standoff had begun, federal officials had called upon three local fire districts to lend a hand. Apparently some officers had been using improper fuel mixtures in their diesel heating stoves, and a couple of tents had been set ablaze. Once the fire fighters got that problem under control, they were asked to stay on to water down the dirt roads to keep too much dust from getting into federal fax machines and computers.

When the local fire departments had asked for reimbursement for the expenses involved, the federal government had at first refused. Gary Gage had received a letter from the FBI on February 18, 1993, stating that "Charging the federal agency for fire-fighting services would amount to a tax or a payment in lieu of taxes and would . . . violate the federal government's constitutional immunity from taxation." That had not pleased the local fire companies, and they continued to press their case. Finally, the FBI gave in and paid the bill.

The day of the verdict, Gerry Spence had said he hoped that Boundary County prosecutor Randall Day would bring charges against at least some of the federal officers involved in the deaths of Sammy and Vicki Weaver. He even held out the possibility that he would be willing to serve as a court-appointed prosecutor in such a case. Attention turned to Randall Day—who as of this writing is still conducting an investigation and interviewing witnesses and has not yet decided whether to press charges. Patriot and constitutionalist newspapers and Internet chat rooms published his telephone number, and he soon stopped accepting phone calls. Kevin Harris talked with Day, then returned to Washington State with his mother, Barbara Pierce. His injuries prevented him from finding a job right away, and they still impair his mobility. He is now working as a welder.

Gerry Spence, in a posttrial interview with the *Denver Post*, said he felt "bittersweet" about what many were hailing as his latest legal triumph. "I wanted Randy to walk out of that courtroom," he said, but instead Randy was awaiting sentencing in the Ada County Jail in Boise. He stressed that while he still felt Randy Weaver's beliefs were wrong, it was important for him to have received a fair trial. "I was afraid Randy Weaver was going to be prosecuted and persecuted for what he thought rather than for what he did. For his beliefs rather than his criminality." He also offered some insight into why he had chosen not to put on a defense. Not only did it eliminate the opportunity for the government to counterattack defense witnesses, it forced the jury to focus hard on the prosecution's evidence, to scrutinize it alone. "Then you can become the prosecutor," he said. "You can attack their evidence and you don't have to defend anymore. You can prosecute the prosecution. That's what happened with Weaver."

He also mused about the tendency of prosecutors, not just in this case but in many cases, to overcharge defendants. "I don't mean that people don't commit crimes. But when some woman shoots her husband, she'll be charged with first-degree murder when the prosecutor knows that she's guilty of nothing worse than manslaughter." This "puts the poor woman in the position where either she pleads guilty to a crime she didn't commit or she may go to the electric chair. . . . My experience in criminal law is that prosecutors never . . . charge people with what they're guilty of. They charge them with crimes they're not guilty of."

Having won millions of dollars in judgments from insurance companies, Gerry Spence says he now does about 80 percent of his trial work for free. He says he spent about $100,000 of his own money on the Weaver case. In 1992, Spence formed a public-interest law firm, Lawyers and Advocates for Justice, to pursue what he believes are important cases outside the framework of his own law firm, Spence, Moriarty & Schuster.

The next important event in the Weaver case was Randy Weaver's sentencing hearing. It was postponed from September 28 to October 18, 1993, in the Boise Federal Courthouse. Once again, an overflow crowd showed up, and a second courtroom with closed-circuit television had to be set up to handle it. One of the earliest spectators to arrive was John Harris Weaver, the final jury foreman. He made a point of going over to introduce himself and shake hands with Kevin Harris, who had also come early. Soon Dorothy Hoffman and Dorothy Mitchell, the two jurors who had been particularly outspoken in the weeks after the trial, arrived. Sara and Rachel Weaver were there, with their uncle, Keith Brown, who is married to Julie, Vicki Weaver's sister. The Browns had been taking care of the three Weaver daughters since the standoff had ended more than a year before. Randy Weaver's father, eighty-four-year-old Clarence Weaver, and Randy's three sisters from Iowa were there. They were hoping to take Randy back to Iowa that day.

Randy Weaver had been found guilty on Count Three—failure to appear—and on Count Nine—committing a crime while on release. The prosecution recommended a fairly hefty sentence of forty-one to fifty-one months in prison in its sentencing report presented to Judge Edward Lodge, who presided over this aspect of the trial as well.

At the beginning of the hearing, Judge Lodge announced that in handing down a sentence he would not consider the conviction on Count Nine. In his view, the conviction under Count Nine did not constitute a separate offense from the failure to appear charge. Although this decision was not a surprise, it took a little starch out of Ron Howen, who was once again acting as lead prosecutor. Taking the elimination of the second count into account, he now recommended a sentence of between thirty and thirty-seven months in prison, two to three years of supervised release, and a fine of between $6,000 and $60,000, plus court costs and costs of incarceration. Having modified the sentencing report, Howen stated that he had no objection to it and no witnesses to call. Gerry Spence then said he did wish to present a case for a less stringent sentence. "This case is a case that touches many people," he said, after Judge Lodge granted him the opportunity. "This is also a case that is being closely watched; not only by little children here to take their daddy home, but also by an entire nation."

Gerry Spence first called juror Dorothy Hoffman. He asked what her motivation had been for taking such a strong interest in Randy Weaver after the trial had ended. "I became very concerned by what looked like an injustice that had happened," said Hoffman. "This family had been treated in a very wrong way." She said she was surprised and disappointed that Randy was not already out of jail. When she had heard on television that Randy Weaver might be sentenced to a long jail term, she said she was "devastated." She testified that since the end of the trial she had been to visit Randy Weaver in jail almost every Saturday morning, and had come to believe that he was not only innocent, but a fine man. She said that during these visits, Randy had told her that all he wanted was "to go back to his girls, have a time of mourning together, then a private life."

Ron Howen then had the unenviable task of cross-examining Hoffman. In exchange that soon became tense, he asked her, "Did you not think it important to visit Karen Degan [widow of Marshal William Degan]?" Mrs. Hoffman retorted that "the Degan children still have one parent; Randy's don't have any right now." Howen continued to speak of Marshal Degan's war record, his bereaved family, and the culpability Randy Weaver bore for his death. Gerry Spence objected that Ron Howen was attempting to convict Randy Weaver all over again for the death of Marshal Degan, and the jury had already found him not guilty. Judge Lodge agreed.

After Dorothy Hoffman stepped down, Spence introduced a letter written by Senator Larry Craig to U.S. Attorney General Janet Reno demanding a full-fledged investigation into the circumstances surrounding the Ruby Ridge incident. Senator Craig's letter spoke forcefully of a "powerful, corrupt government attacking citizens and trying to cover up."

Spence then argued against items in the sentencing report that urged that Weaver's sentence be "enhanced"—lengthened—because he had not yet accepted responsibility for his failure to appear in court. Spence argued that, to the contrary, at the very beginning of the trial, as Randy's attorney, he had offered a guilty plea on the failure to appear charge if the other charges were dropped. At several other points in the trial, he had offered sympathy to Ron Howen since the prosecutor "was getting information late; taking responsibility for things," and offered a guilty plea on Count Three in exchange for having the other charges dropped. On each occasion, Ron Howen had refused the deal.

Gerry Spence then called Randy Weaver's father, Clarence Weaver, to the stand. Clarence introduced Randy's daughters, and pleaded for his son to be released that day so his family could start the rebuilding process. "As the family goes, so goes the nation," he said to Judge Lodge. "We have a family here that's torn apart." Then juror Dorothy Mitchell took the stand and reinforced what juror Dorothy Hoffman had said earlier—that as a juror she had not expected their decision to result in a long sentence and that she would be displeased if it did.

Then Keith Brown took the stand, with co-counsel Chuck Peterson handling the questioning. He testified that although he would describe himself as a "flaming liberal" who disagreed profoundly with Randy Weaver's political philosophy, he had viewed Randy and Vicki Weaver as role models. On several occasions, they had helped him and his wife through rough times in their marriage. And the Weaver girls, far from being "radicals" or incipient little "Nazis" as the prosecution and sometimes the media had portrayed them, were normal teenagers—perhaps Sara was more serious than most. He looked toward the prosecution table and recounted how the prosecution, referring to the fact that the girls often carried guns while outside the cabin, had referred to them as "these Annie Oakleys." Some media reports, he said, had the girls giving a Nazi salute to their father as the helicopter carried him away at the end of the standoff. "How can you bash a child's integrity like that? How could you accuse a child in that position of giving a Nazi salute?" he demanded heatedly.

Ron Howen denied that he had anything to do with those media reports. Nonetheless, in his cross-examination, he tried perfunctorily and without success to get Keith Brown to admit that the girls were somehow radical or extreme in their actions.

Then it was time for Gerry Spence to summarize the case for a less stringent sentence. Under federal sentencing guidelines, courts follow a "point system" in determining sentences. After points are established for the "base" offense, points can be added or subtracted for aggravating or mitigating circumstances. Spence argued that there were numerous mitigating circumstances in this case.

He noted that Randy Weaver had no prior criminal record. He spoke of the "homicide" of his wife and son. Because of the government's actions, he said, "this is a single father of three children." He took issue with the government's recommendation of sentence enhancement because of "harm to a law enforcement officer." Under a recent Ninth Circuit Court of Appeals decision, he said, this "acquitted conduct" couldn't be held against Randy Weaver. He also noted that the government argued for enhancements because of Weaver's alleged obstruction of justice and his role in leading others to crime. The jury had decided otherwise, he contended. Finally, he told the judge that in criminal cases it was unusual to find a strong family in which to release a prisoner. "You have a rich and loving and insightful place to send this man," Spence argued. "You can send him back to his family. . . . You have something to work with. You have a support system to deal with."

Ron Howen began his rebuttal with a little swipe at Gerry Spence: "As usual, Mr. Spence has taken his time, my time, and your time for oral argument," he said. Then he blamed himself, sometimes coming close to tears, for losing the case. Speaking sometimes in a whisper, he talked about how he has to "bear his responsibility" that his shortcomings resulted in this verdict. He has to look at himself in the mirror each morning and ask himself what he didn't do right, what he could have done better. He spoke of how personally offensive Vicki Weaver's letters addressed to the "Queen of Babylon" had been to "those of us in government with a strong faith in God . . . especially at a time when people like Marshal Degan were fighting the 'King of Babylon' in Operation Desert Storm." He spoke of how hard it had been to prosecute this case because his ancestors had been German Mennonites who came to this country to escape religious persecution, and in some ways Mennonites were separatists. Nonetheless, he argued, Randy Weaver's failure to appear was a serious offense, and it had led to dire consequences. It should be punished with the maximum sentence possible. The court then broke for lunch, and for Judge Lodge to consider the sentence he would hand down.

"Counsel do their jobs well when they put a lot of pressure on the court," Judge Lodge remarked, when the court returned to session after lunch. "I assure you, they have done that." He then gave Randy Weaver a lecture about how Randy, of all people, having served in the military and having run for sheriff, should have respected the law enough to appear in court. He predicted that the sentence he would pass would not please some people, but that he had weighed the many factors involved carefully. "There are probably very few right answers when people suffer this kind of tragedy," he said.

Judge Lodge then announced that the sentence would be eighteen months in jail, a fine of $10,000, and three years of supervised release, or probation. With the fourteen months already served, plus eligibility for fifty-eight days off for good behavior, that meant Randy Weaver would be released around December 18, 1993. The three years' probation was longer than the prosecution had requested, but Judge Lodge stated that he was doing it for benevolent reasons. Three full years should give Randy a chance to get back on his feet and find a way to pay his fine during the time he was under supervision.

Most of Randy Weaver's friends, family, and supporters in the courtroom were disappointed at first. But after a little reflection, considering what the prosecution had asked for, and especially considering the fact that Judge Lodge had a long-standing reputation as a "hanging judge," most agreed that it was fair. Randy Weaver got permission from Judge Lodge to walk across the courtroom and embrace his two daughters. Then he was returned to his cell in the Ada County Jail.

On December 18, 1993, Randy Weaver was released from jail. He returned to Iowa, where he lived with his parents for awhile. He wears an electronic bracelet so the probation department can monitor his whereabouts. After a few months with his parents, he got a house of his own, where he now lives.

In October 1992, shortly after the end of the Ruby Ridge standoff, some 250 people met in Naples, Idaho, to form the United Citizens for Justice. Among the early organizers were several veterans of the groups that had stood vigil at the Ruby Creek bridge, including Bill and Judy Grider, Randy Trochmann, Chris Temple, Jackie and Tony Brown, Eva Vail of Hayden Lake, and others. The idea was to make sure something like Ruby Ridge would not happen again, through organization, exposing other government abuses of power, and lending support to other people "across this country who have been violated by an overzealous government." The idea was to form chapters in every state, and in every county of every state, with national headquarters providing literature and strategic guidance, and publishing a monthly newsletter. The group met for several months in Naples, then gradually lost steam until it fell apart.

Randy Trochmann moved back to Montana and helped his father, Dave and his uncle, John, to form the Militia of Montana in the tiny town of Noxon in the northwest corner of the state in early 1994. The Trochmanns researched the history of militias in the United States, developing the information that most of this country's founding fathers endorsed the idea of a militia—a reserve or part-time semimilitary organization consisting of all people (or in the early days all able-bodied males) above a certain age—as an alternative to a standing army, which most Americans in the early years of this country feared as an instrument of tyranny. They printed this material in booklets, and distributed booklets containing model organizational documents and organizing tips to like-minded people throughout the country.

The Militia of Montana does not sponsor or participate in weapon-carrying paramilitary maneuvers, as do some organizations also calling themselves militias. MOM, as the organization is known, concentrates on educational activities. It publishes a wide array of booklets on the latest evidence that the government has sold out to New World Order conspirators and is plotting to undermine and subvert traditional American freedom. It sells or distributes booklets, books, and videotapes made by other individuals or groups. MOM, which grew directly from the Ruby Ridge standoff, grew in numbers as more people began to be suspicious of the government's handling of the Branch Davidian standoff in Waco, Texas. It has been a forerunner of the militia movement. Local groups calling themselves militia—of varying degrees of sincerity, sophistication, and organizational ability—were organized in most of the fifty states by 1995.

Concern about the Ruby Ridge incident and other apparent abuses of government power led to the organization or revitalization of a wide array of patriot or constitutionalist groups across the country. Using fax machines and the Internet, some of these groups, or their leaders, are in fairly constant communication with one another.

On October 27, 1993, the director of the Bureau of Alcohol, Tobacco and Firearms, Stephen E. Higgins, fifty-four, resigned. This action came a few days prior to the release of an investigative report by the U.S. Department of the Treasury into the actions of the BATF at the Branch Davidian complex on February 28, 1993. That armed assault for the purpose of arresting Davidian leader David Koresh on suspicion of manufacturing illegal firearms led to four BATF agents and six Davidian members being killed and several wounded on each side, then a fifty-one-day standoff, culminating in a tear-gas attack during which the entire complex burned to the ground. The Department of Treasury (within which the BATF is administratively situated) report was sharply critical of the way the BATF handled the initial raid. The initial raid should have been canceled, it said, when an undercover BATF agent informed commanders that Koresh knew about the raid.

The BATF's associate director Daniel Hartnett and deputy associate director Edward Conroy came in for especially harsh criticism. Along with others in Washington, D.C., the report said, they had failed to take into account the inexperience of the raid commanders, and to recognize the need for less risky contingency plans. They had also, according to the report, made misstatements to the public, or allowed them to be made, and had failed to keep their superiors apprised of the true nature of the situation. Hartnett and Conroy, who were among five BATF officials placed on administrative leave when the report was released, resigned on Saturday, October 2. (They were later reinstated with back pay.) The Treasury report did not delve into the BATF's actions at Ruby Ridge. Nor did it explore whether a January report on CBS's *60 Minutes*, in which female BATF agents alleged that they were ignored or punished after complaining of sexual harassment, or subsequent complaints by black agents that the BATF hierarchy systematically discriminated against them, might have been a motivating factor in the decision to mount a spectacular attack against the Branch Davidians.

John Magaw, former director of the U.S. Secret Service, was appointed the new director of the Bureau of Alcohol, Tobacco and Firearms, and immediately set about trying to restore morale. Vice President Al Gore's "reinventing government" commission, in August 1993, had recommended that the BATF be merged into the FBI, but Attorney General Janet Reno and BATF officials had resisted the idea. Magaw's appointment—accompanied by a two-year extension of his mandatory retirement date—was generally regarded as a signal that no serious move would be made to disband the BATF during the Clinton administration. Although the Treasury Department's assistant secretary Ronald Noble told a House Appropriations subcommittee that the BATF would be revising its tactical policy so that it would be less likely to use "dynamic entries" as at Waco, Magaw assured reporters during several interviews in late October and early November, that the BATF would continue to keep an eye on religious cults. "They're out there," he told Scott Shepard of Cox News Service. "They don't yet have the kind of weaponry that we saw in Waco . . . but they will develop if society allows them to."

In the meantime, however, prodded by a letter from Senator Larry Craig to Attorney General Janet Reno, the U.S. Justice Department's Office of Professional Responsibility was conducting an inquiry into the FBI's conduct at Ruby Ridge. According to a *New York Times* story on November 24, 1993, Deputy Attorney General Philip B. Heyman, who was supervising the inquiry, described the inquiry as a top-to-bottom review of the entire case. People who had been interviewed by the investigators said the questions centered on whether officials misjudged the danger Randy Weaver posed to them and knowingly violated standard limits on the use of deadly force. "The inquiry is also examining whether officials failed to consider less aggressive tactics and later closed ranks to avoid scrutiny of their actions," wrote *Times* reporters David Johnston and Stephen Labaton. The investigators were also reportedly warning top managers, agents, and prosecutors that they faced the possibility of criminal charges, including obstruction of justice and violations of civil rights laws.

According to the *Times* story, "Within the ranks of the hostage rescue unit, the inquiry has stirred deep resentment. Agents who took part in the operation defend their actions and regard the inquiry as second-guessing of those who place themselves at risk to uphold the law. Some, including Richard M. Rogers, its commander, have refused to cooperate with investigators, officials said."

The inquiry came at a delicate time for the FBI. FBI director William Sessions had been nudged out of office by President Bill Clinton in July, and Louis J. Freeh, a former FBI agent who had also served as a federal prosecutor, had been named FBI director in September, 1993. In November, Floyd I. Clarke, the FBI's number-two official, resigned as deputy director to take a position with financier Ronald O. Perelman. Clarke had risen from street agent to be, in effect, acting director during a period of turmoil just before and after the resignation of William Sessions. Although Louis Freeh praised Clarke when Clarke's resignation was announced, most observers believed that Freeh had wanted to put his own top team in place, and Clarke was identified with the old regime at the FBI. Altogether, the inquiry into Ruby Ridge was being held at a time when the FBI was in a period of difficult transition.

In January 1994, an unusual coalition of groups including the American Civil Liberties Union, the National Rifle Association, the Drug Policy Foundation, the National Legal Aid and Defender Association, the National Association of Criminal Defense Lawyers, and the Independence Institute wrote a letter to President Clinton expressing concern over what they viewed as a growing tendency of federal law enforcement agencies to overstep their constitutional and statutory authority, and to use deadly force indiscriminately. The letter asked President Clinton "to appoint a commission to review the policies and practices of all federal law enforcement agencies and to make recommendations regarding steps that must be taken to ensure that such agencies comply with the law." The Ruby Ridge standoff was cited as one of the incidents that troubled all these groups. Some Justice Department officials met with some representatives of the groups that had signed the letter, but no commission was appointed, nor is there evidence that the administration plans to do so.

The Justice Department inquiry was completed in April 1994, but as of this writing has not yet been released to the public. However, both the *New York Times* and the Washington, D.C. *Legal Times* obtained or had leaked to them a copy of the report (or significant excerpts) in December 1994 and March 1995.

In August 1994, Gerry Spence, David Nevin, and Chuck Peterson filed two civil lawsuits on behalf of Randy Weaver and Kevin Harris. One was a civil wrongful death suit against more than a dozen named and unnamed federal agents, seeking civil damages for the deaths of Sammy Weaver and Vicki Weaver. The other was a suit against the federal government itself for violation of the constitutional rights of Randy Weaver, Kevin Harris, and the remaining Weaver family members.

Under the doctrine of sovereign immunity, the government can be sued only if it gives permission for a private party to sue it. But suits against the government for allegedly violating the constitutional rights of citizens have been entertained throughout the nation's history. In the 1960s, in what is called the Bivens case (*Bivens v. Unknown, Unnamed Agents of the Bureau of Narcotics*), the U.S. Supreme Court set up standard procedures for cases that allege that the federal government has violated constitutional rights. After the suit is filed, the government has six months within which to respond and to grant permission to sue. If the government does not respond within six months, the plaintiff is authorized to go ahead with the lawsuit, usually by filing an amended complaint, which will get the ball rolling. Because the federal courts are so crowded, it usually takes years for such lawsuits to work their way through the system to some sort of resolution.

The attorneys for Randy Weaver and Kevin Harris agreed with the attorneys for the federal agents sued in the separate civil complaint that they would not push for a court date or for discovery—looking through relevant records and getting documents under subpoena to determine the basic facts—until the Bivens constitutional rights case against the government went forward. As of this writing, the six months waiting period had expired, and attorneys Spence, Peterson, and Nevin were at work on their amended complaint, but had not yet filed it in federal court.

On December 12, 1994, a story appeared by *New York Times* reporter David Johnston, apparently based on having seen at least part of the 542-page Department of Justice report on Ruby Ridge, prepared by a twenty-four-member investigative team reporting to the department's Office of Professional Responsibility. According to Johnston's story, the report found that senior officials not only violated standard FBI policies but the U.S. Constitution when they promulgated the rules of engagement for Ruby Ridge. Johnston wrote:

> *The 542-page report portrays the operation as a chaotic sequence of events that nearly spun out of control. The FBI hurriedly dispatched officials to Idaho, and their superiors in Washington stumbled through a series of mistakes and misjudgments, at one point changing the rules of engagement for the operation and ordering agents on the scene to shoot at any armed adults if they had clear shots, the report said.*
>
> *Under traditional policies on the use of deadly force, agents do not shoot unless their lives or the lives of others are in jeopardy. The report said one agent involved in the standoff interpreted the rule change as a departure that meant, "If you see them, shoot them."*
>
> *"Certain portions of the rules of engagement not only departed from the FBI's standard deadly force policy, but also contravened the Constitution of the United States," by violating Mrs. Weaver's civil rights, the report said. "In addition, we found these rules to be imprecise and believe that they may have created an atmosphere that encouraged the use of deadly force, thereby having the effect of contributing to an unintentional death."*
>
> *Frederick Lanceley, a hostage negotiator for the bureau during the standoff, told the investigators after the incident that he was "surprised and shocked" by the rules of engagement, the most severe he had seen in handling more than three hundred hostage situations. Two FBI lawyers, interviewed later, said the rules were "too broad" and could be misread.*

That criticism and the official findings of the report contrast sharply with the tepid reaction of the Justice Department, which has decided not to prosecute Lon Horiuchi, the FBI sharpshooter who killed Vicki Weaver, or anybody else for violating Mrs. Weaver's civil rights.

In a still unreleased memorandum dated October 15, Deval Patrick, assistant attorney general for civil rights, said that given the circumstances, Horiuchi had reason to believe that his life or the lives of other agents were in jeopardy and thus was justified in his actions.

According to the *Times* story, the report was based on dozens of interviews with FBI and other law enforcement officials and provided "a wealth of fresh details about the incident. The report concludes that the FBI did not act with malice, but documents show officials misjudged the threat that Weaver posed to federal agents and initially adopted an aggressive assault plan to resolve the standoff without negotiations. One senior bureau official at the scene, not identified in the report, was quoted as saying that the Weaver crisis 'was not going to last long' because it would be 'taken down hard and fast.' "

This story caused Senator Craig to announce that he had lost patience with the Department of Justice and to demand the release of the report on the Weaver incident as soon as the law permits. "Full public disclosure—and nothing less—is what's needed to put an end to the guessing game and restore peoples' trust in federal law enforcement," said Craig. "Selective leaks to select members of the Washington media do not constitute public disclosure, and if they are leaking it to the media, there is no reason the people can't see it too." The Idaho senator said he had been told repeatedly by Justice Department officials that release of the report was imminent, but the *New York Times* story had said the report would not be available until some time next year [1995]. "Going back as far as last year, Department of Justice officials, including Attorney General Janet Reno, have assured me of a speedy release," Craig continued. "So far that hasn't happened, and if the talk is true about the report being released next year, we've got a problem."

During the first week of December, FBI director Louis Freeh announced that he planned to promote Larry Potts, who had been assistant director in charge of criminal investigations during the Ruby Ridge crisis, and had the responsibility of giving final approval to the rules of engagement, to assistant director, the number-two position at the FBI. Attorney General Janet Reno would have final approval over this appointment.

On January 6, 1995, FBI director Louis Freeh disciplined twelve FBI personnel, including Larry Potts (acting assistant director) in connection with the Ruby Ridge standoff. Although he said that the shooting of Vicki Weaver was not intentional, Freeh said that those disciplined had "demonstrated inadequate performance, improper judgment, neglect of duty, and failure to exert proper managerial oversight." The FBI's acting deputy director Larry Potts was given a letter of censure in his personnel file. The special agent-in-charge of the Salt Lake City office (Eugene Glenn) and the Jacksonville, Florida, office, were censured and suspended without pay. Two other FBI employees, including Richard Rogers, former head of the Hostage Rescue Team, were censured and suspended. The suspensions ranged from five to fifteen days.

Although the actions were the most severe discipline Freeh had imposed within the FBI during his seventeen months as director, Gerry Spence and David Nevin denounced the discipline as outrageous, and nothing more than a "hand slapping."

Director Freeh took no action against Lon Horiuchi, the sniper whose shot killed Vicki Weaver. The reason, he said, was because Horiuchi fired in the belief that one of the Weavers had raised a weapon in the direction of an FBI helicopter. "The sniper fired one round to protect the lives of the fellow agents in the helicopter and struck but did not disable the suspect," Freeh said in his announcement. As Randy Weaver, Kevin Harris, and Sara Weaver ran toward the cabin, Freeh continued, the sniper fired a second round "at the person he believed had only seconds before threatened to fire on the helicopter." The second shot, Freeh said, was fired not at or into the cabin, but to prevent the armed suspect from "gaining the tactical advantage of the cabin from which he could have fired on other law enforcement officers on the scene."

Director Freeh's account of the action that day is in contrast to the sworn testimony, during the trial, of Duke Smith, number-two man in the U.S. Marshals Service, who was in the helicopter that day. Smith testified that the helicopter was careful not to go near the cabin. Other snipers on the hillside did not perceive a threat to a helicopter or fire a shot. And during the Weaver–Harris trial, Judge Edward Lodge dismissed the charge of threatening a helicopter because in his opinion no credible evidence to support the charge had been presented.

Thomas Shapley, an editorial writer for the *Seattle Post-Intelligencer*, found the episode troubling for another reason. In a column distributed by the *New York Times* News Service, he wrote:

> *I think that what Freeh was really announcing was the exoneration of Larry Potts. Freeh said that although he was recommending Potts' censure, he was also 'enthusiastically' proposing that Potts' placement in the bureau's no. 2 spot be made permanent.*
>
> *But the premise for Potts' gentle discipline and simultaneous promotion appears at the least to be built on a questionable foundation.*
>
> *Supposedly, what Potts was being censured for was failing to read and correct what Freeh calls potentially unconstitutional rules of engagement given to the FBI's Hostage Rescue Team.*
>
> *Those rules of engagement were implemented by the Hostage Rescue Team leader, assistant special agent-in-charge Richard Rogers, and FBI Salt Lake City special agent-in-charge Eugene F. Glenn. According to Freeh, Potts was to be partly excused for not reading the rules of engagement because he had left FBI headquarters after 36 hours on duty when the hard copy of those rules arrived. Potts' deputy, Danny Coulson, now FBI chief in Dallas, was also censured for not reading the rules of engagement after his tired boss went home.*
>
> *"Had they read those rules, I'm confident both Coulson and Potts would have fixed them," Freeh said.*

According to Shapley, however, a sworn affidavit from Richard Rogers tells a different story. In Shapley's *New York Times* column, he continues:

> *A nine-page sworn statement dated Sept. 11, 1992, signed by Rogers, was obtained from court files by the* Coeur d'Alene Press *last November. [This affidavit was taken around the time the grand jury was being called to bring the first indictment against Randy Weaver and Kevin Harris.] In the statement, Rogers says he discussed the rule change with Potts.*
>
> *"While en route [from Washington, D.C. to Idaho on August 21, 1992] I was in telephonic contact with assistant director Larry A. Potts, and we thoroughly discussed the proposed rules of engagement for this operation. . . . I therefore proposed that the rules of engagement specify that any adult with a weapon who was observed in the vicinity of Randy Weaver's cabin or the firefight area could and should be the subject of deadly force. . . . I proposed to Potts that the rules of engagement be as so stated and he fully concurred. I asked him to make this a matter of record and Potts told me he would do so immediately."*
>
> *This FBI special agent, the leader of the bureau's elite Hostage Rescue Team, says he fully briefed Potts on the revised rules of engagement and Potts "fully concurred." How, then, can Freeh claim he's confident that had Potts "read" those rules Potts "would have fixed them"? According to Rogers, Potts knew about the rules and not only didn't "fix them" but approved them, and agreed to make that approval a matter of record.*

An FBI spokesperson told Shapley that Potts's recollection simply conflicted with what Rogers recollected—that Potts only approved the wording that deadly force "could" be used, not "could and should." But the FBI could not find any written documentation from that time period of Potts's recollection of the conversation with Rogers.

Early in March 1995, the *Legal Times* of Washington, D.C., a weekly newspaper primarily geared to lawyers and others in the legal community, obtained a copy of either the entire Department of Justice report on the Weaver incident or of significant excerpts from it. The newspaper ran a brief story based on the report in its March 6 edition, then lengthy excerpts from the report itself in the March 13 issue. The first story drew the attention of the Associated Press, which based a story on it centering around apparent contradictions between the recollections of FBI deputy director Larry Potts and Eugene Glenn, the Salt Lake City agent-in-charge who was the on-site commander at Ruby Ridge.

"A sworn statement by a senior FBI official in an unreleased Justice Department report contradicts acting deputy FBI director Larry Potts' account of his role in a deadly 1992 FBI shootout, according to a legal newspaper," began the AP story by Michael J. Sniffen. "Eugene Glenn . . . swore to Justice investigators that Potts approved unusual orders that deadly force 'could and should' be used against any armed men in the open," *Legal Times* reports in its Monday edition. "Glenn told Justice investigators he spoke by telephone to Potts, then assistant director in charge of criminal investigations, about the rules on August 22, 1992, a few hours before the shooting of Vicki Weaver," the AP story continued.

" 'I was telephonically advised at the time, I believe by assistant director Larry Potts, that the [rules of engagement] were approved as formulated and could be enacted,' Glenn swore in his statement to Justice investigators."

The more extensive excerpts from the report printed the following week shed more light on the issue of the rules of engagement and the various ways different people in the FBI claimed to understand them. "The three people who discussed the Rules of Engagement that evening, recall the proposed Rules differently. . . ." according to the report as printed in *Legal Times*.

"Potts told this inquiry that he did not realize the Rules had been changed from deadly force 'could' be employed to deadly force 'can and should' be employed until after the crisis was resolved. However, he believes that 'should' does not mean 'must' and that it only served to heighten the awareness of the threatening situation at hand. Danny Coulson, deputy assistant director of the FBI at the time, also recalled the Rules as formulated as using the term 'could' and opposed to 'can and should.' "

The report's next comments, in the context of bureaucratic language, are almost plaintive:

> *A lack of documentation in the FBI files made our review of the approval of the Rules of Engagement very difficult. . . . There are no notes or records of Potts' or Coulson's initial approval of the Rules. Moreover, there is no documented approval thereafter. We find this lack of documentation significant and serious. The FBI prides itself on its attention to detail. We find no such attention given here. . . .*
>
> *No one at FBI headquarters claims to have seen the Rules as written in the proposed plan, and an operation plan was never approved, although a number of plans were submitted throughout the siege.*

After recounting Eugene Glenn's sworn statement about the telephone conversation with FBI headquarters in Washington, D.C., the report goes on:

> *It is our conclusion that Rogers justifiably believed that the Rules of Engagement provided to the HRT and [Marshal Service Special Operations Group] personnel were fully authorized. On the trip to Idaho, Rogers had received oral authorization for the use of special Rules from Potts and Coulson. Finally, before the snipers were briefed on the Rules and deployed, Rogers secured Glenn's acknowledgment that FBI headquarters had approved the final version of the Rules. . . .*
>
> *However, since there is no written record of specifically what version of the Rules that FBI headquarters approved, we cannot confidently say that the word "should" was approved by FBI headquarters at any time. Nevertheless, since those Rules, which contained "should" remained in force at the crisis scene for days after the August 22 shooting, it is inconceivable to us that FBI headquarters remained ignorant of the exact Rules of Engagement during that entire period.*

Those on the scene at Ruby Ridge who were interviewed for the Justice Department report didn't interpret the rules of engagement as simply a reminder of a heightened threat within the framework of the standard FBI policy on deadly force. Here is what the report had to say:

> *Among the FBI SWAT teams deployed to the Ruby Ridge site, there was a wide variety of interpretations of the Rules of Engagement. Denver SWAT team leader Gregory Sexton recalled the Rules as "[i]f you see Weaver or Harris outside with a weapon, you've got the green light." He had never seen such severe Rules of Engagement, and he believed that they were inappropriate because briefings about the subjects, Degan's death, and observation of the terrain would be sufficient to alert tactical personnel to the dramatically increased danger without superseding standard deadly force policy.*
>
> *Another member of the Denver SWAT team characterized the Rules as "strong" and as a departure from the FBI's standard deadly force policy. A third member of Denver SWAT, who was briefed by the Denver SWAT team leaders, remembered the Rules of Engagement as, "if you see 'em, shoot 'em." This agent had never been given such Rules of Engagement before, and he felt they were inappropriate. He said other SWAT members were taken aback by the Rules and that most of them clung to the FBI's standard deadly force policy. A fourth Denver SWAT team member's reaction to the Rules at the time was "You've gotta be kidding." He viewed the Rules as an imperative without clarification and inconsistent with the FBI's deadly force policy. . . .*

The excerpt from the Justice Department inquiry also discussed sniper Lon Horiuchi's second shot, the shot that killed Vicki Weaver, at some length. It took at face value Horiuchi's contention that when he fired the first shot, he "made a judgment of threat and necessity based on his observation that the armed male posed an immediate threat of death or serious harm to the occupants of the helicopter. Horiuchi admitted that, after taking the first shot, he intended to shoot at that man again, given the opportunity, because the threat the subject posed would increase after he returned to the cabin." The inquiry questioned that judgment.

> *This perception must be evaluated in conjunction with the reality that the subjects were retreating to the home and had not returned fire when shot upon. Thus their actions as they ran into the cabin were not aggressive, but rather protective or defensive.*
> *We find Horiuchi's explanation of the threat and necessity of the second shot speculative. Based on the facts known and the actions of the subjects, we do not think that it was reasonable to perceive an immediate threat as they ran back into the cabin. Once the family was back in the cabin, the potential threat to the safety of the helicopter and law enforcement personnel was more remote than when Horiuchi had earlier believed that the armed male was about to position himself to shoot at the helicopter. Although we believe that Harris and the Weavers knew that law enforcement was present, no call out or surrender announcement followed the first shot. The subjects were never given a chance to drop their arms to show that they did not pose a threat. The subjects simply did what any person would do under the circumstances. They ran for cover.*
> *Horiuchi also confused his targets. He erroneously believed that the last man returning to the cabin was the man he had originally tried to shoot. Thus, Horiuchi never saw Harris, the target of the second shot, take any threatening action toward the helicopter. . . .*

If the people in the helicopter at the time are to be believed, of course, the helicopter was never remotely in danger of being fired upon by anybody at the Weaver cabin. As the inquiry excerpt continues, however:

> *In sum, even giving deference to Horiuchi's judgment, we do not find that the second shot was based on a reasonable fear of "an immediate threat to the safety of the officers or others." Moreover,*

we believe that the shot was unnecessarily dangerous and should not have been taken. . . .

We cannot fault Horiuchi alone for these actions. We are persuaded that his judgment to shoot at the armed man again, if given the chance, was influenced by the Rules of Engagement, which he had no role in creating, but which he was instructed to follow. We believe that Horiuchi fired his second shot and [FBI sniper/observer] Edward Wenger prepared to shoot because the Rules of Engagement had a significant effect on the sniper/observers' sense of danger and had encouraged their use of deadly force.

Although we believe that, even under the special Rules, Horiuchi should not have taken a shot into a door with the possibility that persons other than the target could be injured, the responsibility for taking that shot may not rest exclusively with Horiuchi. As we noted above, the special Rules of Engagement were subject to different interpretations as to who was a subject and what conduct was required before a shot could be taken. This inquiry finds that the Rules expanded the use of deadly force beyond the scope of the Constitution and beyond the FBI's own standard deadly force policy. Despite this conclusion, we are convinced that those who prepared the Rules believed that their provisions were within the law.

The excerpts from the Justice Department report printed by *Legal Times* also dealt at some length with the behavior of the FBI during the trial of Randy Weaver and Kevin Harris, concluding that the FBI resisted full disclosure—or discovery, in legal parlance—of all relevant information about the Ruby Ridge incident:

From the beginning of its preparation of the Weaver case, it was always the intent of the U.S. Attorney's office in Boise, Idaho (USAO), to provide discovery to the defense in accordance with a modified open discovery policy. This discovery policy together with the scope and breadth of the indictment created concern among members of the FBI including those at FBI headquarters. Such concern contributed to a resistance by the FBI to produce certain

materials that the USAO deemed pertinent to the case but which
the FBI believed were either irrelevant to what it perceived to be the
real issues or too sensitive to be disclosed.

As the report explains, the U.S. Attorney's office felt that a more open discovery process than usual was appropriate because it knew the trial would be under intense media scrutiny, and that the defense would be pushing the idea that the government had acted unlawfully and then done a cover-up. "[U.S. Attorney Maurice] Ellsworth and Assistant U.S. Attorney Ronald Howen, who was primarily responsible for the discovery matters in the Weaver prosecution, strongly believed that a complete production of relevant materials was critical to defend against the charge of a government cover-up." The report explained how, for most discovery matters, U.S. Attorneys Howen and Lindquist were able to work with special agents Joseph Venkus and Gregory Rampton in the Idaho FBI bureau. But for certain items at the FBI headquarters, supervisory special agent T. Michael Dillon "was required to make frequent phone calls to FBI headquarters in an attempt to assist in the release of discovery materials."

"The first discovery conflict surfaced," the inquiry report said, "on September 23, 1992, when Lindquist traveled with Rampton to Quantico, Virginia, to meet with assistant special agent-in-charge Richard Rogers to discuss the actions of the Hostage Rescue Team. While at Quantico they met with special agent Lester Hazen who showed them a copy of the operations plan drafted for the HRT during the Ruby Ridge crisis. When Lindquist requested a copy of the operations plan, Rogers responded that the operations plan had never been approved and he did not want to produce the document to Lindquist because it contained sensitive information. Finding this position unacceptable, Lindquist is reported to have told Rogers that he would obtain a court order that would permit him to have access to the operations plan. Because it appeared that neither Rogers nor Lindquist were willing to compromise, Rampton suggested that Lindquist be able to review the report but not be given a copy of it. If the court requested the information later,

Rampton proposed that the parties could negotiate further about the release of the information. . . ."

The *Legal Times* excerpt from the report did not include the second prosecution–FBI conflict over discovery, but went on to the third:

> *The third document that the FBI did not want to produce in discovery has been referred to as the "marshals critique." This is a two-page document containing 12 critical observations of the actions of the Marshals Service at Ruby Ridge. These observations are supposed to be based on interviews of members of the Marshals Service and the HRT. Special agent Venkus and Assistant U.S. Attorney Lindquist first learned of this document on December 1, 1992, when they traveled to Washington, D.C., to review the FBI headquarters file and to talk with HRT members. Venkus made a copy of the critique and took it back to the FBI office in Boise where Venkus gave Lindquist access to it under the condition that it be returned.*
>
> *Because of the critical nature of the critique, the Bureau resisted its disclosure. . . . Dillon reportedly told Deputy Marshal Marsaitis that he would rather see a mistrial than produce the marshals critique in discovery. When Lindquist tried to explain to Dillon the serious repercussions that would occur if the government failed to produce the critique in discovery but later produced it in response to a Freedom of Information Act request, Dillon responded that the document had come from someone's desk and was not in any official file that would be searched for a FOIA request. From Dillon's comments, Lindquist was concerned that someone from the Bureau might be contemplating destroying the document so that it would not have to be produced. Lindquist advised strenuously against such action. . . .*

In terms of the discovery issues, the Justice Department report found that the Boise office of the FBI cooperated quite well, and that the FBI headquarters produced most of the requested material in a timely fashion. However, the report continued:

We have found two areas where problems existed. The first involved the problems associated with the actions of the FBI laboratory. . . . The second area concerned the resistance of personnel at FBI headquarters to produce a group of documents that was small in number but significant in importance to the issues in the case.

With regard to the production of this group of documents, it is our conclusion that FBI personnel, predominantly at the headquarters level, imposed unreasonable resistance and applied inappropriate standards to the discovery requests from the USAO, exhibited an unjustified unwillingness to cooperate as a team member in the prosecution, and evidenced a troubling distrust of the USAO. Indeed, we were distressed by the persistent intransigence shown by FBI headquarters personnel.

From the outset, officials at FBI headquarters opposed the prosecutors' theory of the case. They steadfastly adhered to their view that the indictment should be limited to the assault of a federal officer charge and that the conspiracy count was not supported by the evidence. The prosecutors were aware of this view but disagreed with it. Although a free exchange of ideas and information should always occur between the FBI and the USAO, the FBI in this case failed to appreciate that it is the prosecutor not the FBI that controls the direction of the prosecution. The FBI failed to identify the point where healthy debate became destructive resistance.

In addition to the unjustified refusal to produce these materials we are concerned by the bureaucratic resistance of the FBI. Although objections were raised to producing these documents in discovery, no one ever assumed control at the headquarters level in an attempt to resolve the dispute expeditiously. Instead the controversy lingered for months before all of the documents were eventually produced in discovery. During this process, the FBI seemed to lose sight of its role as the investigative arm of the Department of Justice which is supposed to assist, not impede, federal prosecutors in pursuing violators of federal criminal laws. It was not until the Criminal Division of the Department of Justice intervened that the discovery dispute was resolved.

What this inquiry suggests, in language that sometimes goes beyond the usual dry, bureaucratic boilerplate so common in such reports, is that fierce turf wars were being conducted between the FBI and the U.S. Attorney's office, and probably between the FBI and the U.S. Marshals Service and the Bureau of Alcohol, Tobacco and Firearms as well. Whether these turf wars are business as usual, with the symptoms surfacing in an unusually publicized case, or resulted from and were unique to the strains of the high-profile Weaver case is almost impossible for somebody not in a federal law enforcement agency to know for sure. It is worth noting that the Department of Justice has not done—at least not for public consumption—a critical analysis of the conduct of the prosecution in the Weaver case. Such an analysis might be as critical of the U.S. Attorney's office as this inquiry was of the FBI.

Although a comprehensive analysis might not have been done, the U.S. Attorney's office did come in for some criticism in an April 5 memorandum from U.S. Deputy Attorney General Jamie Gorelick, addressed jointly to Louis Freeh of the FBI, Eduardo Gonzalez, director of the U.S. Marshals Service, and Betty H. Richardson, now U.S. attorney for Idaho. Ms. Gorelick noted that she had not only reviewed the Justice Department Office of Professional Responsibility and the FBI reports, but more than one thousand pages of other material that "constitute a comprehensive review of the incident from the first attempts by the Bureau of Alcohol, Tobacco and Firearms to enlist Randy C. Weaver as an informant to the conclusion of the trial. . . ." She reached the following conclusions, and asked the parties addressed to report what remedial actions were being taken to assure such mistakes were not made in the future:

> 1. *The United States Attorney's office should not have rejected the Marshals Service's plans to negotiate surrender terms with Weaver. This action was based on a misinterpretation of the legal requirements and the Department's then existing policy relating to contacts with represented parties. The United States Attorney's office also erred in refusing the marshals' request to seek to have*

the bench warrant for the arrest of Weaver lifted and reissued under seal (at a time when there was already an indictment under seal). Together, these two decisions forced the Marshals Service to engage in extraordinary efforts to plan and execute a nonconfrontational alternative to require Weaver to respond to the warrant. It was in the reconnaissance phase of this extraordinary plan that the confrontation occurred.

2. The assumptions of federal and some state and local law enforcement personnel about Weaver—that he was a Green Beret, that he would shoot on sight anyone who attempted to arrest him, that he had collected certain types of arms, that he had "booby-trapped" and tunneled his property—exaggerated the threat he posed. Although he was dangerous, the repetition of these exaggerations to the FBI led to a higher threat assessment than otherwise might have been made. While no firm conclusion can be drawn as to whether this threat assessment affected the discussions surrounding the rules of engagement, it is certainly possible that that discussion would have been different had there been a more accurate assessment of the facts.

3. The Marshals Service adopted an unduly risky course of conduct when marshals threw rocks to see what noise would alert Weaver's dogs, and created noise when walking up the road to inspect a water shed near the house, without a plan as to what to do if Weaver responded.

4. When the FBI took over from the Marshals Service, it deployed the sniper/observers before completing a full debriefing from the marshals as to what they had found and the risks that were taken that may have contributed to the loss of Marshal Degan. The discussions on rules of engagement may well have been different had there been a more accurate and detailed description of both.

5. The FBI adopted rules of engagement for this incident that were poorly worded and highly problematic, that confused their relationship with the Bureau's standard deadly force policy, and that could be interpreted as directing FBI agents to act contrary to policy and law, although the FBI sniper's decision to shoot was guided by the deadly force policy. Legal review should have been sought to ensure clarity as to how the rules and the deadly force policy should be read together, and as to whether they comported with constitutional requirements. The FBI has recognized the importance of legal review by changing its policy to mandate General Counsel review of rules of engagement. In addition, threat advisories rather than rules of engagement will be used as a vehicle to inform agents regarding increased threat levels.

6. Although the proposed rules of engagement were submitted to FBI headquarters as part of a proposed operation plan, the deployment of sniper/observer teams proceeded before approval of the plan. While good practice may have dictated the deployment of these teams for intelligence purposes and to freeze the scene, the teams should have been operating under the clear guidance of the standard FBI deadly force policy, instead of the rules of engagement, until they were approved.

7. The FBI's internal investigation of the shootings at Ruby Ridge by the Shooting Incident Review Team was inadequate, and the resulting report should not have been approved by the Shooting Incident Review Group. The absence of outside members on either group may have contributed to these failures.

8. The U.S. Attorney's office drafted an inappropriately broad and aggressive indictment, failed to provide for internal review thereof, and engaged in misconduct before the grand jury.

9. The cooperation of the FBI with the U.S. Attorney's office in the preparation for and conduct of the trial was inadequate.

In conjunction with the April 5 letter, Deputy Attorney General Gorelick authorized the issuance of a letter of censure to acting assistant FBI director Larry Potts "as requested by Director Freeh. I have concluded that Acting Director Potts did not adequately follow through to ensure that his intent with regard to the rules of engagement was properly reflected in the final rules. He also should have acted more aggressively to ensure appropriate FBI trial support to the U.S. Attorney's office. The sanction imposed on him by Director Freeh is appropriate for these management omissions."

Gorelick also announced that the Department of Justice would release publicly the reports she had consulted as soon as possible. She included a copy of a letter from Boundary County prosecuting attorney Randall Day, dated March 28, 1995. In the letter, Day said that his office was still conducting interviews preparatory to making a decision as to whether his office would file any charges in the deaths of Sammy Weaver, Vicki Weaver, or William Degan, and that he would like to have those interviews completed before the Justice Department report was released to the public. "Of course, the information we glean from these interviews may require interviewing that is not currently anticipated, however, within those perimeters I am hopeful that we will be able to have our interviewing completed by June 1, 1995," he wrote. Consequently, the release of the various reports was delayed until at least that date.

On April 10, after a long discussion with Deputy Attorney General Gorelick, Senator Larry Craig of Idaho sent a letter to Attorney General Janet Reno regarding the promotion of Larry Potts to deputy director of the FBI, the number-two man in the bureau. "Fairly or unfairly," he wrote, "Mr. Potts has become a lightning rod for public opinion. Promoting him, after sanctioning him for his involvement in the Ruby Ridge incident, leads observers to one of two conclusions: either the agency was not sincere in its public pronouncements about the seriousness of the sanction; or it is unprincipled in overlooking the very behavior it condemned. While Mr. Potts may be extremely well qualified in every other respect, the publicity surrounding this particular incident, the unresolved contradictions to his account of the proceedings and the sanctions against him are realities that cannot be ignored. With this in mind, I hope you will give careful consideration to the signal that will be sent by your actions relating to this appointment."

One of the results of the tragic bombing of the Alfred P. Murrah Building in Oklahoma City, and the turmoil and discussion that came in its wake was heightened interest in the aftermath of Ruby

Ridge. The proposed promotion of Larry Potts—who was placed in overall charge of investigating the bombing—was already controversial within a relatively small sector of the population. Many people argued that one way to defuse the impulse to form militias would be to conduct serious and independent investigations into incidents like Ruby Ridge and Waco.

On May 2, 1995, U.S. Attorney General Janet Reno announced the appointment of Larry A. Potts to be deputy director of the FBI. As acting deputy director, he was directing the investigation into the Oklahoma City bombing. Janet Reno praised his work in that investigation, and described Potts "the very best the FBI has." In a separate statement, FBI director Louis J. Freeh praised Potts as "completely dedicated to the rule of law." Neither made mention of the fact that Potts had been formally censured on April 5. Senator Larry Craig announced that he was "very disappointed" by Ms. Reno's action. Considering the "high level of emotion" currently surrounding the interaction between citizens and law enforcement, Potts's promotion was not appropriate, said Senator Craig.

On May 10, 1995, the *New York Times* ran a story, written by David Johnston, saying that Eugene Glenn, the commander of federal operations at Ruby Ridge and the special agent-in-charge at the FBI's Salt Lake City office, had written a letter in which he "charges that the FBI's review of the operation was a cover-up intended to shield top officials, including a trusted top aide to Director Louis J. Freeh." The FBI review, as Johnston characterized it blamed Glenn for the problems "and sought to let off Mr. Freeh's top aide, Larry A. Potts, with a mild rebuke." The May 3 letter, said the *Times*, "represents a highly unusual breaking of senior ranks" in the FBI. Specifically, the letter from Eugene Glenn, addressed to Michael A. Shaheen, head of the Office of Responsibility at the Department of Justice, said the review was incomplete, inaccurate, and full of flaws that, according to Glenn's letter, "reveal a purpose to create scapegoats and false impressions."

As the *Times* story put it, "In his letter, Mr. Glenn contended that he was not asked who had written and approved the rules of engagement. He said the FBI review was biased because the agent chosen to lead it was Charles Matthews, a close associate and one-time subordinate of Danny O. Coulson, who was Mr. Potts's chief deputy during the siege on Ruby Ridge. Mr. Glenn referred to Mr. Matthews as an 'A-SAC,' a title that means assistant spackle agent-in-charge.

" 'The only logical conclusion that can be drawn to explain the deception and lack of completeness in this investigation is that A-SAC Matthews' relationship with Coulson caused him to avoid the development of the necessary facts, and caused him to cover up facts germane to the central issues,' " as the *Times* story quoted Mr. Glenn's letter. The story had more information, in paraphrases from Glenn's letter:

"Mr. Glenn also said that two unidentified witnesses at FBI headquarters who were in the agency's top secret command center during the standoff have information about the rules, suggesting that they could shed light on who approved the change. One, Mr. Glenn said, was a high-level official, and the other was a mid-level supervisor, who overheard Mr. Coulson discussing the rules with another FBI employee."

On May 11, Senator Arlen Specter of Pennsylvania, a Republican presidential candidate, offered an amendment to authorize his subcommittee on terrorism to hold hearings on the Waco and Ruby Ridge affairs on the Senate floor. Senator Orrin Hatch of Utah, chairman of the Senate Judiciary Committee, opposed having the hearings right away, arguing that the House should take the lead in holding hearings, and that now—so soon after the bombing in Oklahoma City—was not the time to be holding hearings on previous FBI or BATF actions. Senator Hatch carried the day. Hearings in the Senate on Waco and Ruby Ridge were indefinitely delayed. As of this writing, hearings in the House of Representatives were expected to take place in July 1995, with Senate hearings some time later.

What bothers and even angers many Americans about Ruby Ridge, Waco, and other incidents is that apparently innocent Americans seem to have been killed by federal agents, and nobody has taken real responsibility or been held accountable. Perhaps the

American public is not looking to have those who killed Sammy and Vicki Weaver brought up on charges and stand trial. Selective firings or other disciplinary measures might be sufficient. But many people are waiting for a frank acknowledgment that something dreadfully wrong occurred, and that some sort of compensation, some sort of accountability, some sort of effort to set matters straight is forthcoming.

The aftermath of Ruby Ridge has not been and is not likely anytime soon to be wrapped up with a neat ribbon. An internal FBI report on the incident is expected to be made public, as is the Justice Department review. Hearings will almost certainly be held in both houses of Congress. The civil rights suits brought by Randy Weaver and Kevin Harris will eventually come before a federal court. These official activities will almost certainly bring forth information that has not been known before.

The ending of the official inquiries, however, will be only the beginning of a much more complicated and subtle process during which the American people will incorporate their knowledge of Ruby Ridge and similar activities into their image of America. Was this a justified use of force or an outrageous abuse of power? If it was an abuse of power, was it an isolated incident or part of what seems to be a pattern? If it seems to have been part of a pattern of abuse, what is to be done? Will it satisfy the American peoples' sense of justice to have a few of those responsible reprimanded, or will more thoroughgoing institutional change be demanded? Different people will have different opinions about these and other questions, and attitudes could change as people learn more, and spend more time pondering implications. For better or worse, Ruby Ridge will reverberate in American society for years to come.

A Government
Out of Control?

THE TERM "RULES OF ENGAGEMENT" IS NOT TRADITIONAL LAW ENFORCEMENT jargon. It is a traditional military term. The fact that such a term was used to determine how the FBI would handle the Ruby Ridge situation suggests that the FBI—and other law enforcement agencies, especially at the federal level—think and act more like military or paramilitary units than like traditional law enforcement agencies. The fact that the Ruby Ridge rules of engagement have been at the center of subsequent disputes and concerns about the incident suggest that this paramilitary attitude has grown to an extent that a great many Americans find troubling. It could also suggest the beginning of ways to address these concerns.

A letter to President Clinton on January 10, 1994, from an unusual coalition of organizations summarized these concerns rather succinctly:

> We are writing to urge you to appoint a national commission to review the policies and practices of all federal law enforcement agencies and to make recommendations regarding steps that must be taken to ensure that such agencies comply with the law. This review is necessitated by widespread abuses of civil liberties

and human rights committed by these agencies and their failure to undertake meaningful and ameliorative reforms.

Federal police officers now comprise close to 10 percent of the nation's total law enforcement force. Today, some fifty-three separate federal agencies have the authority to carry firearms and make arrests. This represents an enormous expansion in recent years in terms of both personnel and jurisdiction. What is lacking, however, is systematic oversight and review of federal police practices. This has led to numerous cases of serious abuse—some well publicized and some relatively unknown—in which the following problems have been evident:

• improper use of deadly force
• physical and verbal abuse
• use of paramilitary and strike force units or tactics without justification
• use of "no-knock" entrances without justification
• inadequate investigation of allegations of misconduct
• use of unreliable informants without sufficient verification of their allegations
• use of "contingency payments" to informants, giving them an incentive to fabricate information since payment is usually contingent upon a conviction
• entrapment
• unnecessary inducement of criminal activities as an investigative technique
• inappropriate and disproportionate use of forfeiture proceedings to obtain financing for law enforcement equipment and activities
• use of military units and equipment in the course of domestic law enforcement
• pretextual use of immigration laws and Immigration and Naturalization Service personnel for nonimmigration law enforcement.

To illustrate its case, the letter described several examples of abuse of federal law enforcement power, including the following:

DONALD CARLSON

On August 25, 1992, at about 10:30 P.M., Donald Carlson returned to his home in Poway, California, opened his garage door with a remote control device, simultaneously illuminating the garage so that Drug Enforcement Administration agents conducting surveillance from nearby could see inside. Just after midnight, when Carlson was asleep, a group of DEA agents burst into his house. Thinking they were robbers, Carlson grabbed his pistol to defend himself. He also dialed 911 for help. The agents shot Carlson three times, twice after he was down and clearly disabled. Carlson spent seven weeks in intensive care, fighting for his life. No drugs were found on the premises.

It was later learned that the Federal Customs Service, the DEA and the U.S. Attorney's office in San Diego had relied on an informant who was known to be untrustworthy and who claimed Carlson's garage contained 2,500 kilograms of cocaine (a large amount which would have taken up most of the garage) and four armed guards. The agents conducted the raid in spite of the fact they could see the informant's information was erroneous.

As of this writing, none of the federal agents involved in the incident have been sanctioned, nor has Mr. Carlson been compensated for his injuries. [Note: in December 1994, a court awarded Mr. Carlson $2.75 million in damages and medical expenses. That payment will be paid by the taxpayers. No officials involved have yet been sanctioned.]

SINA BRUSH

Just after dawn on September 5, 1991, some sixty agents from the DEA, U.S. Forest Service, Bureau of Alcohol, Tobacco and Firearms, and National Guard, complete with painted faces and camouflage and accompanied by another twenty or more National Guard troops with a light armored vehicle, raided the homes of Sina Brush and two of her neighbors near Montainair, New Mexico. Brush and her daughter were still asleep. Hearing noises outside, Ms. Brush got up and was only halfway across the room when the door was kicked in by agents. Clad only in their underwear, Brush and her daughter were handcuffed and forced to kneel in the middle of the room while agents searched the house. No drugs were found. Just as in the Carlson case, the police had obtained a warrant using information furnished by an unreliable informant and had entered Brush's home without knocking first.

DONALD SCOTT
On October 2, 1992, DEA agents and the Los Angeles Sheriff's Department staged a raid on the Scott ranch in the Santa Monica Mountains near Malibu, California. When Scott emerged carrying a gun, a deputy sheriff shot and killed him. Although the agents claimed they were searching for marijuana plants, none were found. The Border Patrol, which had participated in the investigative work leading up to the raid, later claimed they were looking for undocumented aliens. None were found.
An independent investigation by the Ventura County District Attorney's office concluded that the Sheriff's Department was motivated, in part, by a desire to seize and forfeit Scott's ranch. The investigation also questioned the DEA's claim that marijuana was observed through aerial surveillance.

The letter noted complaints of brutality against the Bureau of Indian Affairs Police and "appalling" levels of misconduct by the Immigration and Naturalization Service, and offered a brief outline of the Randy Weaver affair. Its comments on the siege of the Branch Davidian complex near Waco, Texas, were measured but critical:

THE BRANCH DAVIDIANS
Last year's tragic confrontation between the Branch Davidians and federal agents has been reviewed by both the Treasury and Justice Departments. While these reviews find fault with the planning and execution of the government's attack on the Waco compound, they both accept the notion that armed confrontation was unavoidable. This is in spite of the fact that several independent experts who participated in the reviews seriously

questioned the assault's inevitability.

For example, Alan Stone, a Harvard professor of psychiatry and law, disagreed with "the view within the FBI and in official reports that suggests the tragedy was unavoidable." In his report, he noted that the FBI's own behavioral experts on the scene advised against the use of "all-out psycho-physiological warfare" and the abandonment of "any serious effort to reach a negotiated solution." But the FBI ignored this advice, and launched a paramilitary attack that jeopardized the lives of the very children whose health and safety it claimed it wanted to protect. In particular, Professor Stone criticized the use of toxic levels of CS gas over a period of forty-eight hours in a building occupied by so many children. As Professor Stone writes, "The question is: did a 'military' mentality overtake the FBI?"

Another independent expert, professor Nancy Ammerman of Princeton University, pointed out in her report that the FBI did not consult a "single . . . expert on the Branch Davidians or on other marginal religious movements . . ." She also noted that the psychological warfare tactics employed by the FBI, including the sounds of dying rabbits, the use of floodlights, and helicopters hovering overhead, were not favored by the Bureau's own Behavioral Sciences Services Unit. In fact, the Unit advised that the "ever increasing tactical presence . . . could eventually be counter productive and could result in loss of life."

At this time it is not clear that the reviews conducted by the Treasury and Justice Departments will lead to any meaningful changes in the way the FBI or Bureau of Alcohol, Tobacco and Firearms will handle such situations in the future.

The letter concluded with a recognition of the difficulties and hard choices faced by federal law enforcement agencies and agents, but contended that these and other cases suggested "the need for leadership and accountability to prevent future incidents of abuse." A high–level national commission, it argued "will contribute greatly to the continued improvement of federal police agencies by helping to ensure that federal police not only enforce the law in an effective, humane, and constitutional manner, but that they also serve as models for local and state law enforcement agencies."

The letter was signed by the following representatives of an ideologically diverse group of organizations:

Ira Glasser, American Civil Liberties Union, New York

John Snyder, Citizens' Committee for the Right to Keep and Bear Arms, Washington, D.C.

Eric E. Sterling, the Criminal Justice Policy Foundation, Washington, D.C.

Arnold S. Trebach, Drug Policy Foundation, Washington, D.C.

David Kopel, Independence Institute, Denver, Colorado

James Grew, International Association for Civilian Oversight of Law Enforcement, Cleveland, Ohio

John Henry Hingston III, National Association of Criminal Defense Lawyers, Washington, D.C.

Mary Broderick, National Legal Aid and Defender Association, Washington, D.C.

James J. Baker, National Rifle Association Institute for Legal Affairs, Fairfax, Virginia

Alan Gottlieb, Second Amendment Foundation, Bellevue, Washington.

The fact that such a diverse array of organizations, from those generally considered liberal to those commonly identified as conservative, from those who could be called libertarian to people not identified as especially ideological, could all agree that federal law enforcement agencies are in need of reform is remarkable. These organizations disagree on a wide variety of issues, from the meaning of the Second Amendment, to the need for drug laws, to the true sources of American disorder. But they all agree that federal law enforcement agencies have committed significant abuses of citizens' rights.

Without a systematic investigation backed by subpoena power, it is difficult to get a complete picture of just how widespread or persistent abuses are. But there is certainly enough anecdotal evidence of abuse to give one pause. The Bureau of Alcohol, Tobacco and Firearms offers many examples.

The federal government first began regulating firearms in the 1930s, by imposing taxes of two hundred dollars on weapons favored by gangsters, like sawed-off shotguns and machine guns. The collection of this tax fell under the jurisdiction of the U.S. Department of Treasury. After Prohibition, the Alcohol Tax Unit was formed, with its main purpose being to track down brewers of homemade alcohol—"moonshine"—who sold their brew without paying the requisite federal taxes. By 1952, the unit had become a division within the Treasury Department. Guns occupied little of the division's attention.

In 1968, following the assassinations of Martin Luther King, Jr. and Robert Kennedy, Congress passed the Gun Control Act of 1968. In 1968, only 214 of the division's 985 agents were concerned with enforcing firearms regulations. In 1969, the division was renamed the Alcohol, Tobacco and Firearms division. In 1972, during the Nixon administration, the division was reorganized and renamed the Bureau of Alcohol, Tobacco and Firearms, known to many as simply the BATF. By 1973, firearms enforcers outnumbered liquor enforcers in the BATF, but most of the agents were still concentrated in the rural south, a legacy of the moonshine enforcement days. Only gradually did the BATF start moving into major cities. And according to a study done in the late 1970s by Tucson lawyer David Hardy and members of the American Civil Liberties Union, the agency showed a preference for entrapment and setups of ordinary citizens rather than going after genuinely dangerous gun owners or people who illegally sold weapons to gang members or urban criminals.

In 1979, the Senate held hearings on the BATF and heard testimony that "75 to 80 percent of BATF cases brought [in a study of Virginia and Maryland] involved defendants who had no criminal intent, but were enticed by bureau agents into violating technical requirements, which the defendants did not know existed." The Carter administration had some preliminary plans to move the BATF's firearms ownership functions to the Department of Justice and keep only the firearms tax aspects under the Treasury, but the plan was never implemented. When the Reagan administration was contemplating budget cuts in the 1981–1982 budget, it had a plan to disband the BATF and place firearms regulation under the Secret Service, but it didn't follow through.

This history of threats to eliminate the agency—the Bush administration flirted with the idea of eliminating it as well—led the BATF to develop media contacts designed to burnish its image. It discovered that if it went after purported neo-Nazis or religious cults, it could usually count on favorable publicity. Kay Kubicki, a former agent who has leveled sex discrimination charges against the BATF, claims that people in the bureau were constantly talking about the Hare Krishnas during the 1980s.

A number of BATF case studies clearly suggest excess.

James Corcoran was a seventeen-year veteran of the Pennsylvania State Police in January of 1988, about to be promoted to lieutenant and admitted to the FBI Academy. But over a couple of days in January, he found himself indicted for several felonies and facing up to sixty-three years in jail. He was immediately suspended from his job without pay or benefits. Why the troubles?

Corcoran was a gun enthusiast and collector who sometimes sold guns at gun shows or got good deals for friends. Five years before, he had asked the BATF whether it was all right to make semiautomatic AR-15 rifles (the civilian version of the military M-16 rifle) from kits and sell them without a license. The BATF said that it was legal. Corcoran, as a law enforcement officer, was meticulous about requiring anybody who purchased a gun from him to fill out all the relevant federal forms, and was careful to get a specific authorization from the BATF each time he sold one of the AR-15s made from a kit. But somebody at the BATF got the idea that these kit-built weapons were rifles that could be easily converted to fully automatic weapons, despite the testimony of numerous independent experts to the contrary. So Corcoran's house was raided and he was charged with selling automatic weapons.

Since he had received an individual authorization from the BATF each time he had sold one of the guns the BATF now said was illegal, Corcoran believed he was on solid ground and refused to back down. When the case was brought to court, the judge advised the prosecution that the case was extremely weak and advised that charges be dropped. But the BATF insisted that the prosecution go forward. Corcoran was acquitted. But it cost about a year of his life and almost $35,000 to defend himself. Corcoran has since made captain in the Pennsylvania State Police, but he never did get to the FBI Academy.

In December 1991, John Lawmaster of Tulsa, Oklahoma, a construction worker who was also a gun collector, came home to find his front door ripped off and his house ransacked. Guns that he had kept carefully locked in cases to make sure thieves or children could not get to them were strewn all over the floor. Not only was his front door off its hinges, the back door was wide open. He found out from neighbors that the entire neighborhood had been cordoned off with yellow crime-scene tape while a small army of BATF agents, accompanied by some local police officers, ransacked his house. He also discovered that the BATF had called the utility companies and had his water and electricity shut off. On a table in his den, in the middle of the mess, he found a note saying: "Nothing found. BATF."

When his attorney complained and asked if some compensation would be paid for the damages caused, the BATF refused. The BATF and the local federal prosecutor also refused to release not only the affidavit on which the search warrant had been based, but even the actual search warrant itself. Lawmaster still does not know why he was targeted.

Louis Katona III is a clean-cut church and civic leader in Bucyrus, Ohio, who with his wife runs a successful real-estate business. His father is a licensed gun dealer, and Katona early on became an avid shooter, hunter, and gun collector. In 1982 he became a Bucyrus auxiliary police officer and the department's firearms instructor. He began collecting automatic weapons, each time getting a signed authorization from the police chief, Charles McDonald, until 1986, and after 1986 the new Bucyrus police chief, Joseph Beran. His collection became so extensive that he had a walk-in vault built into his home's basement, with an elaborate security and surveillance system.

Katona did have a run-in with Chief Beran. Katona's father found an old-fashioned police badge inscribed "Chief—Bucyrus Police" at a gun and antiques show, and bought it for his son. But when Katona showed it to Chief Beran, the chief "became very excited and wanted it for himself," according to Katona. Katona refused. On several occasions, Beran told Katona there were reports that the badge had been stolen—perhaps in 1947, perhaps in 1972—and that he could have Katona arrested for possession of stolen property. In 1988, the situation became so unpleasant that Katona resigned from his part-time position on the Bucyrus police force. He soon was hired as a part-time peace officer in the nearby town of New Washington.

On April 26, 1991, Katona got a call from BATF special agent Lance Kimmell. Kimmell had been contacted by BATF special agent Blair Ward, in Tulsa, Oklahoma, about a case against an Oklahoma firearms dealer. This dealer had legally sold Katona a Colt M203 grenade launcher. There was no question the sale to Katona had been legal, but Kimmell said he wanted to borrow the launcher for evidence purposes. Upon Katona's insistence Kimmell gave him a receipt for the launcher, and Katona gave Kimmell a sworn statement regarding the purchase of the weapon and copies of the paperwork and canceled check.

After three months, Katona hadn't gotten the weapon back, and he started calling Blair Ward to inquire about it. "Ward was initially polite," Katona later told journalist James Pate. But on April 22, 1993, Ward "abruptly announced that I would not be getting my launcher back and that `no one needs an M203 anyway.' I replied that the launcher was a legally registered and tax-paid firearm and that he could not just confiscate property because of his personal views." According to an affidavit later filed by Katona, Ward became angry. "How dare you speak to me that way, you little son of a bitch. You don't know who you are dealing with. I am going to have some of my boys come by and kick your ass! You screwed up this time, boy. You're going to wish you never heard of me!"

On May 8, 1992, a group of BATF agents led by Kimmell came to the Katonas' real-estate office in Bucyrus, saying they had a federal warrant to search Katona's home. When they got to his house, Katona wanted to read the search warrant, but at first Kimmell wouldn't let him do so; instead he just kept shouting, "Where's the guns?" Finally Kimmell threw the warrant down on the kitchen table. But he snatched it away before Katona had time to read the supporting affidavits.

The warrant turned out to be based on a sworn affidavit from Chief Beran that Beran had never signed any BATF authorization forms for Katona. The affidavit then alleged that Katona had forged Beran's signature to thirty-two BATF transfer and registration forms.

Katona's wife Kimberly, then several months pregnant, came downstairs. The Katonas claim that BATF agent Steven St. Pierre grabbed both of Kimberly's arms and pushed her against a wall. Kimberly began bleeding within an hour, and stayed in bed on a doctor's advice. Several days later she had a miscarriage.

Both Kimmell and St. Pierre have denied in court documents that either of them touched Kimberly.

The BATF seized thirty-two registered weapons with an assessed value of more than $100,000. More than two months passed with no word. Then on July 22, 1992, the bureau sent a letter stating its intent to make an "administrative forfeiture" of Katona's guns. Katona immediately posted the $2,500 cash bond required to protest the action. The BATF withdrew its forfeiture action. More time passed. On March 24, 1993, Katona filed a damage suit against the BATF, the city of Bucyrus, and Chief Beran.

Within days, the assistant U.S. attorney convened a grand jury and moved to delay Katona's civil suit because of a pending criminal investigation. A judge refused, saying the civil suit could be delayed only until September 1. On September 15, 1993, Katona was indicted for allegedly forging Chief Beran's name on federal paperwork. When the case went to trial in April 1994, U.S. District Judge George W. White directed a verdict of not guilty, asking, on the record, "Where's the beef?"

On April 1, 1992, Malisa Knudson was bathing her twenty-one-month-old baby daughter when she heard traffic coming up the mile-long dirt road to their house near Colville, Washington.

Her husband, Del, was at work as a carpenter. Coming to the front door, she saw several vehicles and a Ryder moving van. About thirty BATF agents piled out of the van and swarmed over her property. Although she asked that she be allowed to go back into the house to get her baby out of the bath, the agents refused and insisted she stay outside. The BATF secured the house—two other daughters, aged seven and five, were also there—and handcuffed Mrs. Knudson to a chair. A visiting neighbor was handcuffed to a chair also.

For three hours, Knudson was interrogated, mainly about her family's political and religious beliefs. Some guns were found in the house, but they were all legal. Nonetheless, they were taken. The agents kept after Mrs. Knudson. Wasn't she a white supremacist? Didn't she hate the government and want to shoot government agents? Didn't the family keep machine guns for a confrontation with the government? Knudson was baffled—and very frightened. None if it was true.

It turned out that the BATF had acted on the basis of an affidavit from a deranged relative of a friend of the family who had a history of swearing out false affidavits. The BATF agents thought to check on the reliability of their informant only after three hours of third-degree interrogation in which nothing Knudson said fit their preconceived picture. The firearms were eventually returned, but only after repeated requests.

Rich Foster, elected as a Democratic member of the Alaska legislature in 1988, had his run-in with the BATF in 1990. A Vietnam veteran and father of six, Foster ran a combination gun shop and museum. He ordered some pipes to use to make replicas of machine guns as displays for his business. The welder from whom he ordered the pipes had some honest concerns, so he called the BATF to make sure the pipes would not be illegal. The BATF told him (incorrectly) that those pipes were illegal, but ordered him to make them.

Once Foster had taken delivery, the BATF sprang its "sting," seizing the pipes, confiscating dozens of guns (none illegal) and filing charges that could have led to a $1.25 million fine and fifty years in jail. Rich Foster had the means to hire a good lawyer and put on a good defense. A jury acquitted him. One juror said, "I think Uncle Sam was loose as a goose. The man is not a criminal, never has been." Despite the acquittal, it took the BATF years to return the perfectly legal guns, some of them valuable antiques, it had seized.

On January 10, 1993, *60 Minutes* did an extensive exposé of sexual harassment of female employees and discrimination against black employees within the BATF. Several women had quit the agency to pursue their harassment cases, convinced they would never receive fair treatment within the agency. Many people believe the *60 Minutes* show had something to do with the Branch Davidian raid—that the agency top brass, suffering from the bad publicity with congressional budget hearings upcoming, felt it needed a dramatic victory over a despised, marginal group to make itself look good. If so, the miscalculation was rather dramatic—but the BATF is still around, and evidence that it is on the road to reform is scant.

On May 25, 1994, Harry and Theresa Lamplugh found their home invaded by fifteen or twenty armed men and women, many wearing black ski masks. With fully automatic machine guns shoved in their faces from time to time, the frightened couple cooperated with the intruders. They opened safes, locks, and cabinets when asked. But this didn't seem to placate the intruders, who overturned and smashed pieces of furniture and scattered papers everywhere.

The invasion had begun early in the morning, when Theresa Lamplugh was still in bed and Harry Lamplugh was sitting in the kitchen in his pajamas. The couple were not allowed to get dressed the entire day. At lunchtime, the intruders ordered pizza. They left half-empty soda cans, pizza boxes, and half-eaten slices of pizza all over the house.

Finally, after six and a half hours, the intruders left. But they took with them birth certificates, vehicle registrations, hundreds of pages of business records, school records, insurance information, family photos—and $15,000 worth of firearms.

The intruders, of course, were agents of the Bureau of Alcohol, Tobacco and Firearms. Harry Lamplugh's business is promoting gun shows. The raiders were not wearing any uniforms, and only two of the more than fifteen agents had identifying BATF vests. The agents burst into the house and stuck a machine gun in Harry's face. They did not announce who they were or why they were there, nor did they display a search warrant. When Harry asked about a search warrant, one of the agents said to him, "Shut the fuck up, motherfucker, do you want more trouble than you already have?"

Harry Lamplugh is a cancer patient and usually has about twenty bottles of prescription drugs on the top of his bureau in his bedroom. The agents opened all the bottles and scattered all the pills on the floor. Two of the Lamplughs' cats ate some of the pills and died. The agents took the names and addresses of all the Lamplughs' contacts with newspapers, a valuable part of their business operation. They took 70,000 names and addresses of exhibitors at gun shows promoted by Lamplugh.

On the way out, when the raid was over, one female agent kicked the family's Manx kitten, stomping it to death.

The Lamplughs have not been charged with any crime. Yet the BATF still refuses to return anything it seized that day. The BATF acknowledges that about $18,000 worth of property was seized.

How common is it for the Bureau of Alcohol, Tobacco and Firearms to entrap people who have previously committed no crimes or shown any inclination to do so? According to Don Stewart, who worked as an independent undercover operative for different federal agencies, including the BATF, for seventeen years, it is almost standard operating procedure. Furthermore, the BATF routinely infiltrates "fringe" groups and stirs the most volatile members to commit acts of violence to provide justification for long–term, ongoing surveillance and enforcement operations, and to provide occasions when BATF agents can look like heroes.

"It's all about job security," Stewart confided one day. "If there's no action, nobody makes any money, there's no overtime, no promotions, no awards. A lot of these guys are Vietnam veterans who miss the adrenaline rush of combat and look for ways to get it without any real danger the people they're targeting will shoot back. They like to get people under their power, to hear them beg for mercy and promise to cooperate, to create fear and terror. You can see some of them almost have orgasms when they stick guns in peoples' faces."

Among the laws recently passed that give federal (and in some cases state and local) law enforcement officers extraordinary power to prey upon innocent citizens, the most significant are probably asset forfeiture laws. In an exhaustive report, Michael Bradbury, the Ventura County district attorney, determined that the killing of Donald Scott in Malibu, California (referred to in the letter quoted at the beginning of this chapter) occurred because various government agencies wanted to take his two-hundred-acre ranch under forfeiture laws, having failed to buy it through an open and aboveboard transaction because he had no desire to sell it.

Originally passed to allow the government to seize property from convicted drug dealers whose expensive cars, airplanes, and boats were obviously the fruit of their illegal activity or had been used to carry out illegal activity, these laws have been expanded in scope in recent years so that it is not necessary for a person to be convicted or even charged with a crime to have his property taken and never returned. Far from being used against big-time racketeers or drug kingpins, these laws are often used against ordinary citizens to seize money or property just below the threshold at which it would cost more in attorneys' fees to try to reclaim it than simply to let the government keep it.

The legal concept of asset forfeiture rests on a medieval theory that property can be guilty of a crime. Since property is not a person, property accused of being involved in a crime does not enjoy the panoply of rights afforded people accused of crime under common law and the U.S. Constitution. The asset forfeiture laws are considered civil laws rather than criminal laws—the legal theory is that the government is filing a civil suit against the property for being involved in criminal activity.

Author James Bovard explains asset forfeiture quite clearly in an August 9, 1993, article in *Barron's*:

In most forfeiture court proceedings, the owner must prove that his house, car or the cash in his wallet is innocent—the government has no obligation to prove that the property is guilty. Procedural rights are so imbalanced that government agents can introduce hearsay evidence in court to justify the seizure—evidence that could not be used to support the underlying criminal accusation. But the property owner is prohibited from offering hearsay evidence to defend his ownership. There's even unheard-hearsay evidence— police routinely refuse to reveal the identity of a confidential informant who told them about the forfeiture target.

This means stories like the following are becoming increasingly commonplace in the land of the free:

Willie Jones owned a small landscaping service in Nashville, Tennessee. On February 27, 1991, he paid cash for a round trip airline ticket to Houston, something he did several times a year because he went on buying trips to nurseries in Houston. The ticket agent looked at him strangely, but sold him the ticket. Ten minutes later, drug agents stopped and searched Mr. Jones. It seems that he fit a profile for drug dealers—a black man with a large amount of cash. They found $9,600 in cash, which they took, even though Jones explained his business, and explained why he carried cash. Willie Jones was never charged with any crime. The government never gave him his money back, and his business was almost destroyed.

In 1989, police stopped forty-nine-year-old Ethel Hylton at Houston's Hobby Airport, and told her she was under arrest because a drug-sniffing dog had scratched at her luggage. They searched her bags and strip-searched her. They found no drugs, but they did find $39,110 in cash. Ethel Hylton had recently received an insurance settlement, and she had saved money from her work as a hotel housekeeper and hospital janitor. She explained this, and documented where she had gotten the money. But the drug agents seized and kept the money. She was never charged with a crime, but she didn't get her money back.

When somebody's property is taken under civil asset forfeiture laws, the only recourse is to file a notice of intention to contest the seizure along with a bond of up to $5,000. The government uses that money to prove its case, while the property owner must prove beyond a reasonable doubt that the property is "innocent." In the case of cash, this is almost impossible. Hiring an attorney to handle a forfeiture case usually costs at least $10,000, and attorneys' fees are not awarded even in the rare cases where the government is proven wrong and the money or property is returned. Originally, the proceeds of property seized under forfeiture laws went into a government's general fund, and property could not be forfeited until a criminal conviction was obtained. But under recent revisions, no criminal conviction is required for property to be forfeited, and the police agency making the seizure gets to keep most of the proceeds.

Republican U.S. Representative Henry Hyde of Illinois tells the following story in his recent book published by the Cato Institute, *Forfeiting Our Property Rights*:

> For years Billy Munnerlyn and his wife Karon owned and operated a successful air charter service out of Las Vegas, Nevada. In October 1989, Mr. Munnerlyn was hired for a routine job— flying Albert Wright, identified as a `businessman,' from Little Rock, Arkansas, to Ontario, California. When the plane landed, DEA agents seized Mr. Wright's luggage and the $2.7 million inside. The DEA confiscated the airplane, the $8,500 charter fee for the flight, and all of Mr. Munnerlyn's business records. Although drug trafficking charges against Mr. Munnerlyn were quickly dropped for lack of evidence, the government refused to release his airplane. (Similar charges against Mr. Wright—who, unbeknownst to Munnerlyn, was a convicted cocaine dealer—were eventually dropped as well.) Mr. Munnerlyn spent over $85,000 in legal fees trying to get his plane back, money raised by selling his three other planes. A Los Angeles jury decided his airplane should

be returned because they found Munnerlyn had no knowledge Wright was transporting drug money—only to have a U.S. district judge reverse the jury verdict. Munnerlyn eventually was forced to settle with the government, paying $7,000 for the return of his plane. He then discovered DEA agents had caused about $100,000 worth of damage to the aircraft. Under federal law the agency cannot be held liable for damage. Unable to raise money to restart his air charter business, Munnerlyn had to declare personal bankruptcy. He is now driving a truck for a living.

Asset forfeiture was promoted at first as a tool in the "war on drugs," but as police agencies began to understand its revenue-raising potential, it has been instituted in connection with a wider variety of cases. Automobiles have been seized from "johns" accosting undercover police officers posing as prostitutes. California passed a law authorizing the seizure of automobiles for driving without a driver's license. Seizure of property for alleged nonpayment of taxes has been common practice for a long time— although the Internal Revenue Service's own data show that it often assesses penalties without any investigation of the facts, and in the years 1989 to 1993, about 40 percent of the penalties assessed were later abated. Officials of Suffolk County, New York, have considered a local law to allow confiscation of cars, boats, and planes used in connection with any misdemeanor. The Massachusetts Attorney General tried to get an environmental forfeiture law passed that would have authorized the forfeiture of the assets of companies accused of violating environmental laws. Senator William Cohen, a Republican of Maine, wrote a bill to protect senior citizens that would have required forfeiture of property for defrauding anyone over fifty-five years of age. Several California legislators have proposed laws that would authorize forfeiture of assets for people found employing illegal aliens.

Seizing property has become standard operating procedure for dozens of federal agencies. The Food and Drug Administration has sent agents in flak jackets to raid literally dozens of holistic or alternative medicine clinics and a clinic known for dispensing vitamin B–12 shots, confiscating legal medicines, equipment, and records. During one of the raids, when an employee called the clinic's lawyer, an FDA agent came to the phone, slammed it hard, then jerked the cord out of the wall. "No one is calling anyone until we get through here," he announced. "We're in charge today!" An artist in Michigan had a collage made of bird feathers gathered from the ground confiscated because some agents of the U.S. Fish and Wildlife Service claimed it was made from the feathers of birds on the endangered species list.

In the summer of 1994, the Department of Housing and Urban Development (HUD) came under fire for undertaking a seven-month investigation of three residents of Berkeley, California, who had protested, through letters, petitions, and statements at hearings, the proposed conversion of a motel in their neighborhood into HUD housing for homeless people. HUD demanded that the three protesters turn over all files, minutes of neighborhood meetings, and everything written about the project. The agency claimed it was authorized to do so under the federal Fair Housing Act, which protects, among others, mentally ill people and drug addicts from discrimination in housing. It claimed that since many homeless people fall into such categories, opposition to federal projects for homeless people amounts to harassment and is therefore not protected by the First Amendment's guarantee of freedom of speech. After massive publicity, HUD dropped the investigation. It turned out that this wasn't an isolated example, but a concerted HUD campaign of intimidation against people who question its policies.

Then there's the Internal Revenue Service. Of all the federal government's agencies with enforcement powers, perhaps none is more familiar to more people or more feared. Since 1914, the number of pages of laws devoted to income taxes has grown from fourteen pages to more than nine thousand pages, and nobody understands them all.

Journalist and author James Bovard points out in his invaluable 1994 book, *Lost Rights*, "Since 1980, the number of levies—IRS seizures of bank accounts and paychecks—has increased fourfold, reaching 3.2 million in 1992. [The General

Accounting Office] estimated in 1990 that the IRS imposes over fifty thousand incorrect or unjustified levies on citizens and businesses every year. . . . The IRS also imposes one and a half million liens each year, an increase of over 200 percent since 1980." IRS agents make more than 100,000 direct seizures of property—homes, cars, land—every year. IRS revenue officer Shirley Garcia told a Senate Finance Committee hearing in 1987 that IRS managers regularly pressure employees to make seizures, in part so that IRS managers can earn bonuses based on them.

From James Bovard's book: "Two old ladies who run a credit union for a Catholic church in Coopersville, Michigan, sent a letter to the IRS in 1985 requesting a waiver because they didn't have a computer and had only fifty-nine forms to file. The IRS never responded, and the credit union filed its tax return on paper. A year later, the IRS slapped a $2,950 penalty on the two women; when they refused to pay the bill, the IRS imposed a lien on their checking account."

In 1985, armed IRS agents seized a day care center in Allen Park, Michigan. The agency claimed the center's operators owed more than $14,000 in back taxes. The raid was carried out while children were there. Sue Stoia, one of the parents, went to pick up her seven-year-old daughter. But the agents told her that before she could leave with her child, she would have to sign a form pledging to pay to the government whatever she owed the day care center. "They indicated you could not take your child out of the building until you had settled your debt with the school, and you did that by signing a form to pay the IRS," said Stoia. "What we were facing was a hostage-type situation. They were using the children as collateral. . . . It was like something out of a police state."

In the summer of 1993, the IRS disclosed that 368 IRS agents in the Atlanta region had been discovered illegally snooping through the returns of thousands of citizens, mostly neighbors, friends, or celebrities. In July 1994, John Glenn, a Democrat from Ohio and Senate Government Affairs Committee chairman, reported that 1,300 cases nationwide had been reported of IRS employees browsing through supposedly confidential tax returns. Only five IRS employees were fired. And the General Accounting Office (GAO) in

1993 discovered that safeguards against such abuses are virtually nonexistent. "Though heavily dependent on automated systems to process and safeguard taxpayer data," the GAO reported, "IRS did not adequately control access authority to this information. Further, controls did not provide reasonable assurance that only approved versions of computer programs were implemented."

In addition to all the law enforcement activities now being carried out by federal agencies, sometimes in inappropriate ways, there is growing sentiment to use U.S. military forces for civilian law enforcement. The "anti-terrorism" bill proposed by the Clinton administration before the Oklahoma City bombing, and beefed up and pushed harder afterward, includes provisions for the use of military forces in certain areas deemed related to terrorism by the executive branch of the government. In fact, U.S. military forces have already been used for civilian law enforcement, beyond the use of military aircraft to try to interdict shipments of illegal drugs into the United States. The Associated Press reported in October 1993, that the National Guard, along with regular police, had virtually taken over twenty-three public housing projects in Puerto Rico. In certain neighborhoods, soldiers in camouflage outfits, carrying M-16 automatic rifles were checking every passing car, standing guard in schools, and putting up barbed wire fortifications. And in Alaska, National Guard anti-drug units with military vehicles have been used for no-warrant "knock-and-talk" operations conducted against people suspected of growing marijuana on the basis of anonymous tips.

A good deal of evidence, then, suggests that the federal government has expanded the realm of laws it enforces beyond sensible (let alone constitutional) limits, and has become fascinated to an unhealthy degree with the use of military and paramilitary force as a law enforcement tool. Both houses of Congress have promised to investigate Ruby Ridge and Waco. But those investigations should not be limited to those two incidents. Congressional committees might consider investigating skeptically the increasing use of military and paramilitary weapons and tactics by agencies most Americans think of as innocuous regulatory agencies. Does the Food and Drug Administration really need a

SWAT team? Does the Bureau of Land Management or the Environmental Protection Agency? Do they have legitimate authority for such invasive enforcement techniques? They should try to determine if a genuine pattern of pervasive abuse exists, as suggested by the letter quoted earlier. If it does, remedies beyond merely punishing a few agents who have overstepped their authority should be considered. It could be that institutional reforms—including the abolition of a number of federal law enforcement agencies—will be more appropriate.

A thorough reassessment, in Congress and in society at large, of recent actions of federal law enforcement agencies will almost surely lead to consideration of whether the federal government has grown beyond a size that is healthy in a free society. Since the New Deal in the 1930s, most of America's political and journalistic elites have looked to government—and especially to the federal government—for solutions to society's real and imagined problems. The election of 1994 seems to have demonstrated a widespread belief that many government solutions are not solutions at all, but the seeds of new problems. An increasing number of people view government in many instances as not just ineffective but as downright harmful. The question of the proper size of government is edging its way onto the national agenda, propelled by credible stories of abuse of power.

As noted earlier, Tony Cooper, a law enforcement consultant and teacher at the University of Texas, talked about "a curious crusading mentality among certain law enforcement agencies"—an exaggerated concern about an imminent conspiracy against the government that will soon veer out of control if it isn't stamped out. Almost certainly—it is impossible to get inside his mind but possible to draw reasonable inferences from his actions and statements—Ron Howen shared this mentality. Howen wasn't content with a charge of killing a federal officer or aiding and abetting that killing. He insisted on getting an elaborate conspiracy charge, as if he badly wanted the Weaver family to be the Order 3, a violent, determined band of vicious racists intent on murder and pillage, whether the actual defendants really fit into this preconceived mold or not. This insistence led to friction between Howen's office and FBI headquarters, to ridicule from Judge Lodge (who previously had a reputation as a prosecution-sympathetic "hanging judge"), and ultimately contributed to the prosecution's failure to make any serious charges stick.

A reassessment of government's proper role should include a fresh look a federal asset forfeiture laws. It is outrageous that property can be taken from people when no criminal activity has been proven or even formally charged. The desire to see to it that people cannot enjoy the fruits of criminal activity is understandable, but these laws have evolved into revenue-raising tools. At the very least, they should be changed so that no property can be taken until a crime is proven in a court of law. And the proceeds of seizures should not go to the enforcement agency doing the seizing, but to a general fund. Otherwise, a clear conflict of interest exists.

Consideration of law enforcement abuses should lead honest people to consider whether there are some laws that simply cannot be enforced—even ineffectively—without abuse. Most people want government to try to protect them from those of their fellow citizens who seek to do them harm. But when the very possession of certain items, like guns or drugs, is made illegal, without the necessity of any harm having been done to innocent people thereby, law enforcement agencies are forced to use increasingly intrusive means to try to enforce such laws.

Such laws create "victimless crimes" in the special legalistic sense that there is no complaining victim to go to the police, offer to cooperate, and demand that the perpetrators be brought to justice, as is usually the case with a robbery or a mugging. Instead, enforcement agencies must penetrate private places to gather evidence of law breaking or use undercover agents to set up provable crimes by people they suspect of being inclined toward law breaking. Whether or not one believes such tactics are inherently abusive, there is little question that they hold more potential for abuse than more straightforward tactics against crimes with a clearly identifiable victim.

A great deal has been written about the siege of the Branch Davidians at Waco. One of the best analyses, from the standpoint of religious liberty, was done by Dean M. Kelley, counselor on religious liberty to the National Council of Churches for the April 1994 newsletter of the American Conference on Religious Movements:

> *A careful analysis, using a broad understanding of the significance of religion and the right of its free exercise under the religion clauses in the United States Constitution, suggests that* the most central and important element in the right to religious freedom and autonomy was grossly and specifically annihilated by government action at Waco in 1993: the right to be let alone. *That right has fallen into some neglect in an age of ever-more-intrusive government, but perhaps the tragic events of Waco can help to give it new meaning.* [Emphasis in original.]

Kelley points out that the first Supreme Court decision on the constitution's religion clauses quoted from commentaries on Virginia's religious liberty statutes: "To suffer the civil magistrate to intrude his powers into the field of opinion, and to restrain the profession or propagation of principles on the supposition of their ill tendency, is a dangerous fallacy which at once destroys all religious liberty," and "It is time enough for the rightful purposes of civil government for its officers to interfere when principles break out into overt acts against peace and good order." Thus government shouldn't decide what religious beliefs are "dangerous," and should wait until believers do something to disturb the peace before acting against them. Kelley also notes that for most religious believers (as distinguished from intellectuals like Thomas Jefferson, who wrote the commentaries quoted above), actions are more important than words, but "both are to be protected from state interference." When in doubt, a generous understanding of liberty demands that "the benefit of the doubt should always be given to the religious group. . . ."

Dean Kelley then discusses the question of whether this view places religious groups "above the law":

All citizens (and noncitizens within the jurisdiction) are bound by the law. But not all laws are equally enforced; in fact, few laws are fully enforced. Police and prosecutors (rightly) enjoy considerable discretion in selecting the targets for enforcement because they could not possibly enforce all laws fully all the time. So if the laws are underenforced or differentially enforced (as they are), the decisions of enforcement are necessarily related to questions of priorities. Which of the many threats to peace and good order should be the targets of limited law enforcement energies and the burdens of an overburdened criminal justice system and overcrowded prisons? Presumably a rational law enforcement decision would be to go after the most serious threats to peace and good order first, and leave the lesser for later (or not at all). On this scale, most religious groups would normally not be in the top range of priorities for any sensible agency of law enforcement. . . .

On any sensible ranking of law enforcement priorities, the Branch Davidians should fall very low on the scale. Yet the governments of Texas and the United States expended millions of dollars to quell them. When one considers the investigations beginning a year prior to the assault, then innumerable high-level planning meetings in Washington and Texas, the assembling of a strike force, the assault itself, the fifty-one-day siege, during which there were never fewer than 719 law enforcement personnel committed on-site round the clock—and, presumably, often more—the post mortem investigations, autopsies, analyses, the imprisonment and prosecution of survivors, etc., how much have the taxpayers had to pay for this huge and arguably unnecessary debacle? Surely more than enough to send every one of the Branch Davidians around the world (separately) on a first class tour plus a year at Harvard, which might have dispersed the supposed threat more cheaply (if they would have accepted the bait!). On the other hand, it was precisely the immense expense that served as a heavy incentive for the law enforcement agencies not to let the siege go on indefinitely. . . .

These federal agencies bear a preponderant responsibility for the outcome rather than Koresh and his followers, although they in

*turn contributed substantially as well. Each seemed fated, despite
their sporadic efforts to the contrary, to bring out the worst in each
other, which is of the nature of true tragedy.*

This commentary sheds light on the general issue of threat
assessment, which was a factor in the Ruby Ridge ambush as well.
When the U.S. Marshals Service did a threat assessment on Randy
Weaver, knowing he had Green Beret training, it came up with an
outlandishly exaggerated caricature. The cabin was heavily fortified,
the property had land mines and sophisticated booby traps that
could be detonated by remote control, and Randy Weaver and his
vicious dogs patrolled the "perimeter" regularly looking for federal
agents to shoot. None of it was true.

But if the marshals came up with an exaggerated threat
assessment on Randy Weaver, think of the threat assessment that
evolved over the years in the minds of the Weavers about the federal
government. The feds weren't just misguided people with a tendency
to abuse their power. They were sworn agents of the Zionist
Occupational Government or servants of the Queen of Babylon—that
is to say, they were evil incarnate. That's a threat assessment of sorts,
and one that doesn't leave much room for compromise or negotiation.

James A. Aho, the Idaho State University sociologist who has
studied Idaho Christian Patriotism as fair-mindedly as anybody,
recently wrote a book called *This Thing of Darkness: A Sociology of the
Enemy*, in which he studies just how enemies are created through
societal mechanisms. The value in understanding this, he writes, is
that "by grasping the detail of how we construct an enemy, we are
positioned to see that many of our battles are gigantic jousts with
our own illusions. This can be a painful realization, particularly
when the costs in treasure and human lives are counted. But the
pain may be seen as a necessary injection to inoculate us against a
particularly virulent plague, political anthrax, carried by hate
mongers—a plague that respects no nation, race, or religion."

In a sense, all politics and a good deal of life outside the
political realm consists of choosing up sides and trying to take the
spoils of political action away from the other side. In the process,

we often convert adversaries, even honorable adversaries, into enemies—and not just enemies, but creatures of unspeakable evil and degradation. Such "threat assessments" are usually unrealistic and exaggerated. Yet most people (if they're honest with themselves) participate in them quite often, and sometimes rather enjoy them. It can be exhilarating to believe—or to act as if we believe—that people with whom we disagree could not possibly have any redeeming qualities or characteristics whatsoever.

As the United States has become increasingly diverse, what might be called "identity politics"—political actions or beliefs built around the group with which we choose to identify—has become increasingly prominent. Such identity politics haven't led this country into the kind of terror and hostility we see in Bosnia or in other parts of what used to be Yugoslavia. But that is the direction in which identity politics leads.

In such a diverse society, we might do better to recapture and cultivate something that is a deeper part of the American tradition—what the late Nobel Prize-winning economist and philosopher Friederich Hayek called, in his book, *The Road to Serfdom*, "The individualist virtues of tolerance and respect for other individuals and their opinions, of independence of mind and that uprightness of character and readiness to defend one's own convictions against a superior . . . of consideration for the weak and infirm, and of that healthy contempt and dislike of power which only an old tradition of personal liberty creates." Hayek also commends "those little yet so important qualities which facilitate the intercourse between men in a free society: kindliness and a sense of humor, personal modesty, and respect for the privacy and belief in the good intentions of one's neighbor."

Hayek points out that "these individualist virtues are at the same time eminently social virtues—virtues which smooth social contact and make control from above less necessary and at the same time more difficult. They are virtues which flourish wherever the individualist or commercial type of society has prevailed and which are missing according as the collectivist or military type of society predominates."

Embracing such sturdy virtues, however, will mean more than simply asking the government to reform itself. The asset forfeiture, income tax, and other laws are sometimes abused because people demand that they be abused. Somebody with a vendetta might call a federal agency—or a local agency like a zoning or code-enforcement board—drop a hint that something illegal is going on, and watch in self-satisfaction as the government settles the person's real or imagined score. Government agencies (as institutional entities; there are many honorable exceptions among government employees) are only too happy to settle such scores, because when they bust people their power increases. Until the number of people willing to ask the government to do the work of settling scores declines, it seems only natural to assume the government will continue to abuse power in this way.

Government efforts to demonize various groups, from gun owners to gun-grabbers, from militia members to illegal immigrants, also depend on the cooperation of people willing to believe the worst about people on the other side of an issue. "Divide and rule"—setting groups against one another and controlling them both in the process—is the oldest political maxim because it works.

People who want to live in a free society, who recognize that the United States is a diverse society in many ways that's likely to become more diverse, will be inclined to view most efforts to stir up hostility with skepticism rather than enthusiasm. It can be tempting to think the worst of the tribe on the other side of the hill, especially since, being human, they are bound to have some genuine weaknesses. But if we want to keep our freedom, it behooves us to work at adopting an attitude of tolerance, perhaps even understanding, of those whose ideas or beliefs differ dramatically from our own.

For more than two centuries, America has been the land of promise, a haven and refuge for those oppressed by tyranny or devastated by economic crisis or grinding poverty. It was the place where people could make a new start, where the government left you alone and respected your rights, where people judged you by what you did and how you acted, not by who your ancestors were or what you believed in. And while the promise was broken more often than those who love this country might like to acknowledge, it was kept—genuinely kept, in sometimes astounding and inspiring ways—for millions of people who really did find freedom, opportunity, and the chance to make sure that their childrens' lives would be immeasurably better than they could have hoped for in the old country.

Has the land of freedom and opportunity finally become pretty much like most other countries in the world and worse than some—a land of strict hierarchies and corrupt officials, where favors and political privilege have more to do with success than ability and hard work, a land where minions of the rulers can swoop down unexpectedly on decent citizens and unravel or even destroy their lives in bizarre acts of terror, vengeance, or arbitrary violence? Or are the people of the United States still strong enough, decent enough, and jealous enough of their freedom to overcome what seems to be a government out of control, and peacefully reestablish a land of liberty, comity, and decency?

O NE OF THE STORIES OF THE AFTERMATH OF RUBY RIDGE SEEMED MORE appropriate here than in a chronological narrative, because it speaks to the larger issue of what Ruby Ridge tells us about what our country is becoming, or is in danger of becoming.

The Deep Creek Inn is a modest resort on the paved highway, Old Highway 95, that runs between Naples and Bonners Ferry. Located about a half-mile north of the junction where Ruby Creek Road meets the highway, it consists of a rustic, European-style family restaurant, a few dozen comfortable motel rooms, and a park with hookups for recreational vehicles. In mid-July, 1992, Lorenz Caduff, along with his wife, Wasiliki, and their three children, moved into the Deep Creek Inn. Along with a partner and his family, Lorenz Caduff had just purchased the resort. It seemed like an ideal, quiet business for this recent immigrant from Switzerland and his family to run.

Just a bit more than a month after the Caduff family moved into their new business, however, came August 21, 1992, and the siege of Ruby Ridge. The Deep Creek Inn quickly became a beehive of activity. Many of the federal agents took rooms at the inn, as did a few of those keeping vigil at the roadblock and some members of the media. The inn's dining room became a center for planning and meetings, as well as meals—Lorenz Caduff was a chef of some accomplishment. But while the siege might have been, at a superficial level, good for business, Lorenz Caduff became increasingly troubled. He was astounded at the use of such overwhelming military force against one family. He told several reporters that this was exactly the kind of thing he had hoped to get away from by moving his family from Europe to the United States.

Early in the siege, Lorenz sent his wife, Wasiliki, and his three children, Larry, sixteen, Sarah, ten, and Manuela, two, away from Naples. While he was unfailingly courteous to the federal agents who took rooms and meals at his resort, he began quietly helping those keeping vigil at the bridge. He made his phone, copy machine, and fax machine available to those who wanted to get firsthand accounts to friends and compatriots in other parts of the country. He made his own residence quarters, upstairs from the restaurant, available to Bo Gritz and Jack McLamb after they arrived to try to help negotiate an end to the standoff.

After the siege ended, the effects lingered on Lorenz Caduff. He received a few anonymous telephone calls berating and sometimes threatening him for "siding" with the Weavers. He feared that because he had taken such overt actions as establishing a trust fund for the surviving members of the Weaver family, that immigration authorities might cause problems for his family, who were not yet naturalized citizens, though they planned to become citizens. According to his wife, Lorenz began to black out and have "fits of terror" in which he feared that armored vehicles were in the area again, coming to get him and his family.

In November, he checked into hospitals in Spokane and Coeur d'Alene to try to get help for his ongoing fears. He checked out of the Coeur d'Alene hospital the weekend of November 14 and decided to take a trip to Calgary, Alberta, with a friend. He reportedly had an anxiety attack while near Alberta, but refused hospital treatment. Then, while on the way back to Idaho, when his friend's van had stopped by the side of the road for some reason, Lorenz Caduff grabbed his Bible, stepped out of the van, and stepped in front of a speeding cattle truck. He was killed instantly.

His wife, Wasiliki, blamed the Weaver incident. "It was the ruin of our family," she told the *Spokesman-Review.* "There's one more victim of this whole thing. He was the most gentle man and he couldn't understand any of this." A few months thereafter, Wasiliki Caduff took her children back to Europe, to Greece, where her parents live. They had come to what they had long thought was the land of the free and the home of the brave, the land of opportunity. They had found instead a place where the government sent massive numbers of heavily armed troops to confront an obscure fugitive and his family, where the government's agents— not all of them, but some of them—acted like arrogant thugs when they patronized a local restaurant. The Caduffs had believed in the promise of America, but found themselves deeply disillusioned by the reality they discovered within a few weeks of opening a new business and beginning what they hoped would be a peaceful and modestly prosperous new life.

To be sure, the reality Lorenz Caduff discovered at Ruby Ridge is not typical in America today. Ruby Ridge has become a symbol in part because it was so unusually excessive. Lorenz Caduff saw the "business end of government" applied against a lone family in a way that very few Americans have witnessed personally. Most Americans still find it difficult to believe that their government could act in such a way. Yet it happened. And something very precious was lost in the process.

BIBLIOGRAPHY

Aho, James A., *The Politics of Righteousness: Idaho Christian Patriotism*, Seattle: University of Washington Press, 1990.

Aho, James A., *This Thing of Darkness: A Sociology of the Enemy*, Seattle: University of Washington Press, 1994.

Barkun, Michael, *Religion and the Racist Right: Origins of the Christian Identity Movement*, Chapel Hill, NC: University of North Carolina Press, 1994.

Bovard, James, *Lost Rights: The Destruction of American Liberty*, New York: St. Martin's Press, 1994.

Boyer, Paul, *When Time Shall Be No More: Prophecy Belief in Modern American Culture*, Cambridge: The Belknap Press (Harvard University Press), 1992.

Ferris, Kirby, *A Mountain of Lies*, Stinton Beach, CA: Rapid Lightning Press, 1993.

Fulbright, William J., *The Arrogance of Power*, New York: Random House, 1967.

Hayek, Friedrich A., *The Road to Serfdom*, Chicago: Phoenix Books (University of Chicago Press), 1944, 1961.

Hyde, Henry, J., *Forfeiting Our Property Rights*, Washington, D.C.: Cato Institute, 1995.

Kagan, Donald, *On the Origins of War and the Preservation of Peace*, New York: Doubleday, 1995.

Massacre at Ruby Creek: The Randy Weaver Story, Hayden Lake, ID: Concerned Citizens of Idaho, 1993.

Richardson, Craig E., and Geoff C. Ziebart, *Red Tape in America: Stories from the Front Line*, Washington, D.C.: The Heritage Foundation, 1995.

Spence, Gerry, *From Freedom to Slavery*, New York: St. Martin's Press, 1993.

INDEX

ABOUT THE AUTHOR

ALAN W. BOCK IS SENIOR COLUMNIST FOR THE EDITORIAL PAGE OF THE *Orange County Register*. A California native, he attended UCLA and has been a book editor, magazine editor, advertising writer, lobbyist, and radio commentator. His columns are syndicated, and he has written for *Reason, National Review, Harvard Business Review,* and other magazines. A former director of the Free Press Association and a judge for the Institute of Humane Studies' Felix Morley writing competition, he has received journalism awards from the Orange County Press Club, Freedom Newspapers, the Baltic-American Freedom and the Information Council of the Americas. He is married and lives in Lake Elsinore, California.

Other Books from Dickens Press